Praise for

COMMUNITY LED HOUSING

"The world needs this book! *Community Led Housing* delivers essential tools for those who dream of building a community where neighbours know, trust, and support one another. Ronaye Matthew helped bring my own community's cohousing dream to life. In this powerful book, she and co-author Margaret Critchlow offer the wisdom to help others do the same."

CHARLES MONTGOMERY, author of *Happy City: Transforming Our Lives through Urban Design*

"Ronaye Matthew is a cohousing professional who has successfully managed eleven cohousing projects. This achievement is astounding because many others have tried and not succeeded. I believe she is the leading expert in Canada. What's even more important is that this book holds the secrets on how she has achieved that success. This book is essential for groups considering cohousing, and more importantly, this is a great guide in helping other professionals work on cohousing developments. I am grateful that she is willing to pass along all that she has learned over the years so that others may benefit."

ALAN CARPENTER, director and founder of the Canadian Cohousing Network

"Ronaye Matthew and Margaret Critchlow have crafted a much-needed how-to book for creating community-based housing. As people around the globe search for new ways of living to reduce our carbon footprint and enhance social relationships, documenting successful community-building is more important than ever."

SETHA M. LOW, former president of the American Anthropological Association, professor of environmental psychology, and the director of the Public Space Research Group at the City University of New York

"*Community Led Housing* is a beacon of inspiration for those eager to embrace a more harmonious and sustainable lifestyle. The profound wisdom of Ronaye Matthew and Margaret Critchlow offers a road map to community-led living, where friendships thrive and shared values flourish. Their leadership in the realm of Canadian cohousing is unparalleled, making this book an essential resource for anyone looking to embark on a journey of meaningful connection and purposeful living."

NEIL PLANCHON, Swan's Market Cohousing co-founder, CohoUS ambassador, Cohousing Research Network director, and Sociocracy for All circle member

"In a world that struggles mightily with inequality and power-over dynamics, Ronaye Matthew and Margaret Critchlow offer a blueprint for how to live more cooperatively—advice grounded in eleven successful communities. This book is important for anyone looking to craft viable alternatives to the squabbling and isolation that too often characterize traditional neighbourhoods."

LAIRD SCHAUB, experienced communitarian and group process consultant

"*Community Led Housing* provides an excellent overview of the cohousing development process, passing on the authors' deep experience creating these communities. As someone who has done similar work in the US, working as a development consultant with cohousing groups across North America, it's great to see how much we agree on ... especially the strength of combining a dedicated group of homebuyers with strong, experienced professionals. The practical approach of this book makes the whole process of community-led housing more accessible to both the people who want to live in such a community and the professionals who want to develop more community-oriented housing. The eleven communities that Cohousing Development Consulting has worked with also speak to the value of involving professionals who take the lessons learned forward to new communities. This book should inspire more professionals to do this work. I will be recommending *Community Led Housing* to all of my clients, both cohousing groups and the professionals that work with them."

KATHRYN MCCAMANT, president of Cohousing Solutions and co-founder of cohousing in North America

Praise for
COHOUSING COMMUNITIES

"As mayor, I'm glad to have supported the development of not one but two cohousing communities in our small town—Harbourside and West Wind Harbour. The ongoing actions of these engaged citizens have enriched the larger community. Cohousing projects offer great prototypes for sustainable, multi-family development. I was proud to hold my golden shovel!"

MAJA TAIT, mayor of Sooke, BC

"We are so grateful to be living here at West Wind Harbour (most of the time...) and we're constantly reminded, as we look at the physical property and the positive community processes that we learned about, of all the work that Ronaye Matthew and Margaret Critchlow put in to make our dream come true. I'm convinced it wouldn't have happened without them. Covid-19 certainly added a few bumps along the way, especially for us after move-in, and as they say, life in cohousing 'has its moments.' But the foundation we were given is proving to be solid enough to help keep us focused on our values and willing to come to acceptable solutions."

IRENE TODD, founding member, West Wind Harbour Cohousing

Community Led Housing

A Cohousing Development Approach

RONAYE MATTHEW

MARGARET CRITCHLOW

Cataloguing in publication information is available from Library and Archives Canada.
ISBN 978-1-77458-454-5 (paperback)
ISBN 978-1-77458-455-2 (ebook)

Page Two
pagetwo.com

Copyedited by Rachel Ironstone
Proofread by Crissy Boylan
Cover and interior design by Jennifer Lum
Cover illustration by Michelle Clement
Indexed by Donald Howes

communityledhousing.ca

In loving memory of Bradley Albert Cassidy
(March 29, 1955–April 10, 2023)

We dedicate this book to the memory of Brad Cassidy, Ronaye's beloved husband and a dear friend to us both. Brad supported us in so many ways while writing his own (forthcoming) book on the new alchemy and evolution of our future. He nourished our minds, bodies, and souls with stimulating conversations, delicious meals, and his irrepressible sense of humour. Brad was crucial to our creative process, from the first moments of our book's creation with yellow sticky notes poolside in Loreto, Mexico, to the completion of the working draft which, although he was unwell, he read thoroughly before giving us invaluable feedback. Brad lives on in this book, in our lives, and in the lives of the many others who loved him, learned from him, and laughed with him.

Contents

Appendices

Creating Community Led Housing Is a Journey…

THE FIRST, or "zero," card in the tarot deck is the Fool: a simple soul with the innocent faith to undertake the journey of life. At the start of the trip, the Fool is a newborn—fresh, open, and spontaneous, arms flung wide, head held high. The Fool is ready to embrace whatever comes their way but is oblivious to the cliff's edge, unaware of the hardships to be faced in venturing out to learn the lessons of the world.

Just like the Fool in the tarot, when we begin the community led housing journey we are taking a leap into the unknown.

The second card, which is number one in the Major Arcana, is the Magician, "the bridge between the world of the spirit and the world of humanity," according to Brigit Eselmont's *Ultimate Guide to Tarot Card Meanings*. "The right hand holds a staff raised toward the sky and the left hand points to the earth. The Magician takes the power of the Universe and, channeling it through the body, directs it to the physical plane."

The Magician represents the ability to manifest dreams, but we can't get to the magic without first taking the Fool's leap. And in order to manifest on this plane, we need to be grounded in what is possible in the current reality...

1

Introduction

"It is a pleasure and a privilege to work with people who are willing to take a risk, to pioneer new ways of doing things, in order to create a better world for themselves and for those who will follow."
RONAYE MATTHEW of Cohousing Development Consulting at Harbourside Cohousing's ground-breaking ceremony, September 19, 2014

O F THE ELEVEN COMMUNITIES for whom Cohousing Development Consulting (CDC) has provided project management, all
are examples of community led housing, every one of which
exemplifies what a group of people of goodwill with a shared
intention can accomplish when working together with skilled professionals to create housing that is responsive to their needs. In
attendance at the ground-breaking ceremony for the seventh such
project, Harbourside Cohousing, wielding golden shovels, were the
local Indigenous spiritual leader, construction project manager, civil
engineer, development consultant, two founding members (one of
whom provided the site), and the acting mayor of Sooke, BC. Can you
imagine yourself in this crew? If so, this book is for you.

The term *community led housing* is relatively new, but the idea
is an old one. Existing or potential neighbours get together in some
form of "building group" to create housing with and for each other.
From traditional villages to contemporary cohousing, community
led housing offers practical, inclusive approaches that grassroots
groups can use to create housing for themselves in which they
control the leadership, ownership, and/or management of their
housing. Cohousing is widely recognized as a major form of community led housing, along with cooperative housing, community
land trusts, and various kinds of self-help housing.[1] This book's focus
is on cohousing because that is where CDC's experience lies, but we
believe that the information we provide can support any kind of community led housing group.[2]

Much has been written about cohousing, most notably by Califor-
nian architects Charles Durrett and Kathryn McCamant who brought
it to North America from Denmark in the late 1980s. Their focus is

on the many communities they have developed in the US, and they emphasize the design of cohousing communities as much as the specific steps for creating them. Much like our book does, Chris and Kelly ScottHanson's *Cohousing Handbook* includes Canadian examples and is a how-to guide, but it was first published in 1996 and last updated almost twenty years ago. American author Diana Leafe Christian writes about ecovillages and other intentional communities, not specifically about cohousing. We admire the structure of her book *Creating a Life Together* and have adopted a similar organization for ours.[3]

Our intention in writing this book is to support more people to achieve the goal of developing their own community led housing. We provide information that professionals can use as a guide to assist the member group to manifest that goal. By following the experience-based path we outline, founding members and their professionals will potentially dodge many of the obstacles that can trip up a project and will learn how to be effective in a development context where collaboration is key and time is money.

It is important to note that the CDC experience is based mainly in the Lower Mainland of British Columbia and on Vancouver Island. Land costs in these localities are high. Negotiating changes in municipal land use is extremely complex and requires a high level of sophistication. It is from this context that the recommendations in this book arise. British Columbia is a highly regulated jurisdiction, so some of these recommendations may not be applicable where the local jurisdiction is less regulated, land costs are low, and the municipal process is less complex. We acknowledge that our context is not strictly applicable to all situations—every context is unique and every group needs to research and discover what that means for their project. However, because our experience has included particularly complex and challenging projects, readers may enjoy discovering that their dream is simpler to manifest.

Furthermore, it is important to remember that legislation related to land development is constantly changing. So some of the details that were applicable in 2023, when this book was written, may no longer be applicable when it is read. However, the lessons in this book are what matter, and they will help any group, in any location, to succeed in developing a community led housing project. Appendix A provides an overview of the completed projects that CDC has managed to date and includes images, project statistics, information about how the site was secured, and the number of founding members. It also includes information about how long it took to build a group, find and acquire a site, get development approvals, complete construction, and sell all the homes.

National, regional, and local contexts make a difference for each project, but much of what we share is globally applicable. We provide information that can be used to prepare a development proforma. Readers will find practical steps to follow in their local contexts, including: the organizational structure for the member group during development; the importance of creating a collaborative culture and how the underlying collaborative process works; how to work with conventional legal structures in a particular region; a membership-building process that can be adapted to a project's needs; a flexible and effective consensus decision-making process; the underlying values of collaborative living, adaptable to anywhere. Readers of this book will also learn how to look at the economic context of a project and identify what they need more information about to make their project work.

The organization of the book is based on the order in which each aspect of the development process needs to be considered. Many things occur concurrently, but, for example, it is risky to secure a site before the financial structure has been determined and potential financing identified for the land purchase, construction, and eventual home ownership. As the project progresses, the need for detailed information increases. At the beginning of the chapters about the more complex aspects, we have summarized what needs to be in place at each stage of the development process.

On completion in 2016, Harbourside celebrated with a colourful paper banner proclaiming "WE'VE MADE IT!" that also featured the names of every member and professional who worked on the project. Our hope is that this book will result in more completed member-led communities, proud of making it happen together.

What Is Cohousing?

Many people hyphenate the term *cohousing*, but we follow the spelling used by the Canadian Cohousing Network, the Cohousing Association of America, the UK Cohousing Network, and Cohousing Australia. We contributed to the collaborative process that resulted in this definition that the Canadian Cohousing Network adopted in 2022:[4]

Cohousing is the name of a type of collaborative housing that attempts to overcome the alienation of modern housing, where few people know their neighbours and there is little sense of community. The future residents are integral to the design and development of the community. Cohousing combines the autonomy of compact self contained private dwellings with the benefits of shared, spacious community amenities that typically include a large dining room, kitchen, recreation spaces, meeting rooms, children's play spaces, guest rooms, workshops and gardens. Cohousing neighbourhoods tend to offer environmentally sensitive design with a pedestrian orientation and have documented lower vehicle use than conventional neighbourhoods.

Although many multi-family developments include some amenity spaces, in cohousing the extensive common spaces not only make it possible to live in a smaller home, they also function as the heart of the community and offer many opportunities for social interaction. Although each home has its own private kitchen, shared meals are one of the many regular events that support relationships among neighbours.

The physical design provides opportunities for spontaneous connection as well as maintaining the option for privacy. This can be achieved with a variety of building forms. Completed communities vary in size, but typically range from 20 to 30 homes. Some have a special focus (e.g., for seniors) but most are intergenerational with a mix of family types and ages. Building forms mirror the range found in the larger society: single-family, townhouses, duplexes and apartments.

Cohousing is not a particular legal form or means of holding interest in real property. The legal ownership form generally chosen for the completed community is the strata/condominium, however some communities have chosen to use the co-op/share structure. Although community decision-making is non-hierarchical and usually by consensus, this does not impact the ownership form. Regardless of the legal structure chosen, the community is ultimately bound by the rules and laws set out by the provincial acts governing stratas/condominiums or co-ops/share structures.

"A year or two after moving in, I looked at things and thought to myself, Well if I had sat down and written down all the things I would like... in a place to live... it wouldn't have been nearly as good as this is!"
QUAYSIDE VILLAGE COHOUSING MEMBER

The development process does not of itself generate below market priced homes. Although that process does not include profit if the resident group is the developer, the homes are often of higher quality with more green-built features than conventional housing. This makes them less costly to maintain and operate, but does contribute to higher construction costs.

An aspect not often considered when looking at affordability is the cost of living. Because of the social structure and easy access to shared resources, cohousing homes provide opportunities for reducing living costs that are not available in conventional neighbourhoods. The homes can be smaller without negatively impacting lifestyle, and the sharing reduces consumption. As a result cohousing contributes to the affordable housing continuum.

Our Journeys

Ronaye Matthew: After completing a degree in Environmental Studies (Faculty of Architecture, University of Manitoba) in 1977, I worked with various residential developers in Alberta and British Columbia. In 1994, a life-altering experience led me to shift my focus, and I spent the next two years doing workshops at the Haven Institute, a transformational learning centre on Gabriola Island, where I had the opportunity to experience the healing power of community first-hand.

I was introduced to cohousing in 1996. After being invited to help with Quayside Village in North Vancouver, BC, I became aware that the skills I'd learned working in conventional development could support people to create cohousing communities. What I found most inspiring was the reduced environmental footprint; the social aspects were of much less interest, personally, although I could see how important they were to others.

"Cranberry Commons is grateful for the role Ronaye played in developing our community, but even more, we are deeply appreciative of the leadership skills she continues to share with us as a valued community member and neighbour."

FOUNDING MEMBER, CRANBERRY COMMONS COHOUSING

In 1998, I decided to join a project that I had been providing consulting services for, Cranberry Commons in Burnaby, BC. This decision was made based on the desire to live in a more sustainable way; I found the idea of the social commitments frightening. However, having lived at Cranberry Commons for more than twenty years now, and seeing the impact it has had not only on me but also on others who have chosen this lifestyle, it is evident that my initial fears were unfounded and that this housing model contributes to a better world. I have experienced the richness of living in a connected community where people know and care about each other, and I have learned how to work with differences without creating separation, how to share more and work co-creatively with others—skills we humans need if we are to be good stewards of this beautiful planet.

———————

Margaret Critchlow: Before I ever heard the term *cohousing*, I learned the importance of neighbourly mutual support and collaborative decision-making from villagers in Vanuatu (SW Pacific) where I lived and worked as an anthropologist; people's relationships with each other and their environment intrigued me. Back in Canada, I co-authored a book on cooperative housing and was attracted to this way of sharing resources and having more connection with neighbours. In a course I taught on the anthropology of place and space, along with cross-cultural case studies, I began to include an innovative European neighbourhood design called "cohousing" that had recently been introduced to North America. In theory, I thought, cohousing looked appealing.

In 2010, a convergence of changes in my personal and professional life led me to retire and relocate to Sooke, BC. The idea of living more sustainably and harmoniously with nature, with less stuff and more community connection, greatly appealed— but how could I do that *and* age in place? The housing options available to my aging mother were institutional, expensive, and depressing. In my search for a better way, I found Charles Durrett's *Senior Cohousing Handbook*, shared it with friends, and was moved to put into practice what I had been teaching. I wanted to co-create a senior-focused community that would affordably support flourishing as members aged, with neighbourly mutual support to enable aging in place. The member group met with Ronaye Matthew who agreed to provide development services for the project that became Harbourside Cohousing. Ronaye and I discovered that we shared similar visions of a better world. We became friends and were drawn to working together to develop a second cohousing project in Sooke and still another on the nearby Saanich Peninsula.

> "Thank you both for all the work and facilitation and people management and project management and all the other roles you have played for so many years that has culminated in Ravens Crossing... It feels so good to be home despite the chaos of moving!"
>
> **FOUNDING MEMBER, RAVENS CROSSING COHOUSING**

I live and breathe cohousing, and I love it; I hope never to live any other way!

What Is CDC?

Cohousing Development Consulting, Inc. (CDC) is a small, full-service, incorporated consulting company that has been providing cohousing development management services since 1996. We understand what

> "We were fortunate to have the talent and experience of CDC to lead our project to completion... It was critical, essential, and indispensable that they were at the helm. It really is the reason we exist."
>
> **FOUNDING MEMBER, RAVENS CROSSING COHOUSING**

> "I hope it is clear to you what a far-reaching and impactful legacy you have crafted in so many communities across Canada. Those of us who live in the communities you helped create see it every day... I hope you never lose sight of it."
>
> **FOUNDING MEMBER, LITTLE MOUNTAIN COHOUSING**

it takes to support a group to generate the membership and financial resources required to build a project in a timely and cost-efficient manner. By the end of 2021, CDC had provided start-up, project management, marketing administration, and community-building services for eleven of the twenty cohousing communities completed in Canada, working with them from the initial forming stage to move-in.

Why Have We Written This Book?

In response to the increasing desire from member groups wanting to create communities, CDC ended up managing four simultaneous projects between 2016 and 2021: two in the Vancouver area—Little Mountain and Driftwood Village—and two on Vancouver Island—West Wind Harbour and Ravens Crossing. All were successful, but the pace was not sustainable. Moreover, we had to turn down many requests from new groups eager to start communities.

At the completion of CDC's eleventh cohousing project, Ravens Crossing, in fall 2021, we had a visceral sense of having "made it to the bell" like a bull rider in a rodeo. There is more demand for community led housing in Canada than CDC can meet.

We believe professional services are essential for developing every community led project, and there are too few knowledgeable professionals to meet the demand. Often, groups don't know what they don't know so few succeed. We offer this book as another way of promoting groups and professionals to develop successful projects, openly sharing information about what has worked so well so far and in a way that makes it clear how the information is applicable to readers' local context, lest it do more harm than good.

Self-Responsibility and Self-Development

The book has a lot to say about how to be self-responsible and be your own developer. This does not mean going it alone! It does mean that the founding members of a group take initiative. In the self-development model, the group is actively involved in decision-making and is generally legally and financially responsible for the results. In a developer-initiated project, the developer takes on the legal and financial responsibility, but future residents have, at best, limited input in the decision-making. Although this book is a resource for developers who want to create community led housing for groups, the focus is to support groups to know what it takes to self-develop. The self-development model requires a deeper level of commitment and provides a medium for people to connect more genuinely in a collaborative process.

As of January 2023, British Columbia is home to 80 percent of the completed cohousing communities in Canada. Of BC's fifteen completed communities, CDC has provided project management for ten, as well as for Wolf Willow in Saskatoon, Saskatchewan. California-based Charles Durrett and Kathryn McCamant provided services through completion to three BC cohousing communities. Chris ScottHanson (also from the US) was the project manager for WindSong in BC. Only one community, Pacific Gardens in Nanaimo, BC, succeeded in getting their project built without the services of a cohousing development consultant.

So far, only three of the completed communities in all of Canada have succeeded without a cohousing development consultant. We support the development of more community led housing, including cohousing, but even in only our home country CDC can't make it happen alone. There is a lack of knowledgeable consultants. So, we decided to write this book to encourage more member groups *and* more professionals to venture into creating cohousing and other community led housing.

Groups that follow the guidance offered here can be their own developers. Our hope is that the professionals, housing developers, and people with real estate experience who read our book can use its lessons to support the success of more community led housing; member groups or professionals that want more help can turn to CDC for advice.

This book marks CDC's transition from a proprietary approach towards being open source. The book is designed to be publicly accessible. Readers should expect to adjust the method that has worked for us to adapt to changing times and places. Groups have to work with "what is." That might include everything from a challenging local official to a global pandemic. Such adjustments, of course, bring risk along with opportunity. Being open, thorough, and transparent about the method that has worked so well is CDC's gift to future communities and to the people who will make them happen. We hope that among the professionals and groups who find this book useful collaboration will continue, improving our method through experience.

Collaboration

We are careful to use the term *collaboration* in this book instead of *cooperation*. Canada has a well-developed cooperative movement, including co-op housing, that started in the mid-nineteenth century. Housing cooperatives share many principles and practices with cohousing, and both value cooperation. So why do we avoid the word *cooperation*? Quite simply because cohousing is not widely understood and is often confused with a co-op. In our experience, the public tends to use the words *cohousing* and *co-op* interchangeably. This has consequences. Financial institutions unwilling to finance cooperatives often mistakenly believe that cohousing is the same thing. As noted in the definition, cohousing is not a particular legal structure. Appendix B provides a chart that attempts to illustrate the different legal structures and how cohousing fits. We need to minimize confusion. Re-educating financial institutions, and everyone else, is important.

Collaboration, too, has connotations that can negatively impact any form of community led housing—it can mean traitorous cooperation with an enemy—but it is more often used, as we do here, to mean *working together to produce something*. We define collaboration as working together to identify what needs to happen and how, in that process, everyone will take responsibility together to find appropriate solutions to challenges.

A robust process of collaboration can only be built on a solid foundation. Collaboration in a housing context depends on good legal, financial, and organizational structures for success. Without a strong structural foundation, collaboration can give an illusion of productivity but be on the brink of disaster. As we will elaborate in Chapter 2, a well-structured collaborative housing project is "grounded." It is in contact with the present moment with its metaphorical feet on the ground and eyes wide open. As pleasant as dreamland can be, real estate development is not a good time for members to allow their dreams to cloud their vision! We don't want to see more articles proclaiming "They Took a Chance on Collaborative Living. They Lost Everything."[5]

Collaboration characterizes CDC's approach to the entire housing development process, including the work with professionals described in Chapter 3. Collaboration also sets the parameters for how people live together once a project is complete. We believe that this, in its own small way, is revolutionary. One relationship at a time, our approach to collaboration is a step towards creating a culture that values hearing each other and working together to solve problems more than it values power and control.

> "At the conclusion of this very successful project, I would like to repeat that it was a pleasure to work with you and the Creekside group. If all clients and project managers attained the same standard of cooperation, professionalism, and vision, the world would be a better place."
> **PROJECT ARCHITECT, CREEKSIDE COMMONS COHOUSING**

Consensus Decision-Making

Consensus decision-making is a particular form of collaboration that supports groups to arrive at good decisions everyone can support. Chapter 5 explores consensus decision-making in more detail, but here we want to point out that it begins with being open to all perspectives. In cohousing, the admonition to approach an agenda item with an open mind instead of a firm opinion is a reminder of how different these communities can be from the public discourse addressed in a book memorably titled *I'm Right and You're an Idiot*.[6] Encouraging open minds supports people to change their own minds. The goal is for the group to arrive at a decision everyone can support, even those who like it the least. The old maxim still applies: *Those convinced against their will are of the same opinion still.*[7] So groups invite minds to meet and to be agreement-oriented.

Shared responsibility is integral to both collaboration and the consensus process. In the process of working together to identify what needs to happen and how to do it, all decision-makers share responsibility. Because the group ultimately makes every important decision in the recommended development process, as well as after move-in, the members take ownership of the result and are more likely to look for solutions collaboratively when things do not turn out exactly as planned rather than looking to cast blame.

In our experience, consensus decision-making is the thread that stitches collaboration and shared responsibility into a strong fabric of community connection. From the beginning of each project, members learn that their opinions matter. But having your say doesn't mean getting your way. As Chapter 6 explains, new members sign a document acknowledging that they accept all prior decisions the founding group has made. They also agree to accept decisions made in their absence if an alternative way to participate cannot be found. In other words, each member accepts and contributes to the wisdom and responsibility of the group. Of course, levels of acceptance and contribution vary.

Although we recommend that decisions be made by consensus as much as possible, there are moments in any development process when consensus is elusive and a decision is required. Only if consensus is not possible *and* the decision is necessary at that time does it make sense to use the provision for a majority vote in an alternative process that we describe in Chapter 5. In those situations, having such a fallback voting process can be critical to a project's success.

Community Led Housing Development Is a Business

Having a voting alternative process is important because each project needs to be run like a business in order to succeed. Timely decisions to stay on schedule and on budget are as important in community led housing as in any other development. Balancing the business of development with collaborative community relations can be challenging, but as we discuss in Chapter 2, that balance is essential.

Running a community led housing project like a business means solving problems together, being transparent, practising clear and inclusive communication, keeping good records, and adhering to or appropriately adjusting schedules. Good business discipline and a collaborative orientation support all phases of a project's development, whether responding to an unexpected underground spring or to a delay in a municipal permitting process. In contrast, a lack of business discipline can be fatal. Sometimes groups are unsuccessful in adhering to good business practices. Occasionally some choose to travel "off road" in hopes of producing housing more cost-effectively, faster, or better. If business discipline is jettisoned in the process, success is jeopardized.

What You Can Learn from This Book

In summary, our hope is that this book will support better understanding and communication between group members and the professionals they hire to create their community. We want people who come together with a dream of creating a community led housing project to understand *why* they need professionals and *what* they need from them. We want professionals to better understand the collaborative process needed to work successfully with member-developers. CDC can provide additional training and support as needed; examples of the type of documents that can be provided to groups and individuals who engage us for consulting and participate in our workshops and training can be found on CDC's website, CohousingConsulting.ca.

There are rich opportunities for learning in our project development process, as there are in other collaborative approaches to community development. Participating in a community led housing development supports people to learn to:

- integrate theory and practice
- become more aware of themselves and their impact on others
- better manage stress and risk
- better understand teamwork and collaboration
- develop skills in managing conflict
- present their project to the world and to potential community members
- develop their personal and collective potential

What you can learn from this book may depend on where you saw yourself in the ground-breaking group we described to begin this introduction. Those wielding golden shovels could include the following.

- Mayors and anyone else who holds elected office will see the benefits of community led housing for their constituency and how they can support it. If there is a political will, there is likely a way to make this approach to housing work for your community.

- We would love to see a municipal staff person in the picture. They can learn about how to work more effectively with groups throughout the site selection, feasibility, rezoning, and development permitting processes.

- Founding group members, individuals with a dream of creating housing that nurtures community connection, will find in this book the tools they need to achieve their goals with the support of professionals, and the help to know which ones are needed and when.

- Landowners and developers with property suitable for a community led housing project, or realtors with clients interested in socially connected neighbourhoods: This book can help such individuals navigate that landscape. They may even see the benefit of selling land to a member group that they can join!

- A developer or a project manager may see how they can learn from this book and become more central to the process and team.

- Engineers and a wide range of professionals, from accountants to traffic consultants, will find pieces of wisdom within what we hope is a comprehensive description of the development process that worked for us.

- Construction project managers and others in that field who are curious about what it's like to work with a community led housing project will find Chapter 11 especially helpful.

Finally, a critical participant in Harbourside's ground-breaking ceremony, was the local Indigenous spiritual leader who was called in to bless the new community. It is our hope that others will be glad to see their non-Indigenous neighbours finally begin to understand what your communities have known all along: that we are all related, that we belong to each other, and that, as author Richard Wagamese notes in his book *Embers*, "we shine most brightly in community, the whole bedraggled, worn, frayed and tattered lot of us, bound together forever by a shared courage, a family forged in the heat of earnest struggle."[8]

Our goal with this book, as with all our community led housing efforts, is to maximize collaborative inter-relations and minimize the bedraggling and fraying. We want your project's journey to be much smoother than riding a bull! And we encourage everyone involved to grin at the end and say together, "We made it!"

2

What It Takes to Develop a Community Led Housing Project

"Don't be afraid to take a big step if one is indicated. You can't cross a chasm in two small jumps."

ANONYMOUS

THE COMPLEX PRODUCT that is a community led housing project consists of two elements forged into a whole. This is often referred to as the two wings of a bird. One wing can be described as the tasks associated with creating the physical structure (legal, financial, design, construction). The other is the process associated with creating a connected community (communication, conflict resolution, effective boundaries, decision-making protocol). Both must be in balance for a successful project to take flight.

The amount of time it takes varies from project to project and is dependent on when the group is able to secure a site, the length of time that it takes to build a group with the financial capacity to develop the project, and the rezoning and development process. The development timeline can range from as few as two years to many more depending on the situation. Every group's process will be unique because there are many different variables.

The Main Ingredients

The following is an overview of the elements that need to be in place to develop a project.

Vision or project objective: A clear and concrete vision with a practical objective provides an anchor for the project.

Members: A core group of members with the ability to participate in a collaborative process and accept responsibility for the project.

Time: The core group of members must be willing to spend the time that it takes to bring the project to completion.

Land: A site that meets the members' criteria for cost and location that either has the zoning in place or the potential to rezone based on the desired objective.

Professionals: A team of people with the knowledge and ability to provide legal, financial, development, design, marketing, community process, and construction expertise.

Finances: Members who are willing and able to take some financial risk in the early stages to get the process moving forward and who have the ability to invest enough equity into the project to become a developer if the intention is to self-develop. Financial institutions expect to see 25 to 30 percent of the total project value as cash equity before they are willing to finance the development.

Where the Money Comes From

A minimum of 25 percent of the project value equity is required from members, and the balance is supplied in the form of a construction loan from a financial institution.

Directors of the company have one share per household,	and shareholder loans during development ...	... get converted towards the purchase price at completion.

All members must have the ability to purchase a home in the completed community unless there are rental units. If rental units are desired, then a financial plan that is economically viable is required. Generally, financial institutions will not provide construction financing unless at least 70 percent of the units are sold to qualified purchasers. If rental units are being included, financial institutions will need to know who is paying for them and how the cost is being covered.

Risk equals control, so the more equity members can invest the more control they will have over the decisions regarding the development. If the group does not have the financial capacity to provide the equity for the project, then a developer partner will need to be brought in. But a developer partner will expect a profit, so if the members can come up with all the equity themselves, the project will save money. For all the CDC-managed projects, the members financed 100 percent of the equity required to make the project happen. As a result, CDC does not have any experience working with a developer partner and cannot discuss that aspect in this book and instead focuses on the self-development process.

Typical Steps for Development

This is not an exhaustive list but is meant to give a summary overview of the typical steps taken in developing a community led housing project. All of these topics are discussed in more detail in the applicable chapters. The development process is not strictly linear; some activities may occur in a different sequence, and many things need to occur concurrently. It is also an iterative process that evolves as the project proceeds, with lessons learned at each step. Chapter 3 describes why some groups never go beyond the stage of talking about a project and what it takes to succeed.

Get Started
Build a strong foundation!

Set Up the Development Corporation
Get help from knowledgeable professionals!

Determine the Community Organizational Structure and Build Membership
Become efficient, effective, and connected!

Find and Secure the Site
Take the leap!

Undertake the Design and Development
Make it real!

Construct the Project
Get it built!

Completion
Move in and celebrate!

Get Started

There are things a group can do to get their project started. Taking these initial steps will help build a strong foundation for the project. The items listed below give an overview of what is required to seed a community led housing project. "You" in this instance refers to the founding members. It would be a different process if it was developer initiated.

Educate Yourself about the Concept

Start by making sure you understand what community led housing is and what it is not! There are lots of resources available (books, videos, interviews), and many are listed on the websites of Canadian Cohousing Network, the Cohousing Association of the United States (CohoUS), and the Foundation for Intentional Communities (FIC). Make a point of visiting completed communities listed on the national cohousing websites or in the FIC directory in person and talk to founding members of completed communities to find out what they did to create success.

Reach Out to Your Networks

Contact friends and associates. Use free or very low cost advertising (community group newsletters, for example) and hold a few information meetings. Marketing a project that is focused on creating community is about inviting people to find out more, gauging if they are interested in the concept, and encouraging them to participate. Providing information and helping potential members feel welcome are the most important ingredients. If you have the ability to create a simple website, that will help make the project feel more real.

Name the Project

You can always change the name later on, but you need to be able to call it something, particularly when you set up a bank account. If you are creating a cohousing community, you will need to decide whether you want to use the term in your name; the word *cohousing* is often misunderstood. There are currently a number of financial institutions, including many Canadian credit unions, that are not willing to finance cohousing homeowner mortgages. They don't understand the concept and believe higher risks are associated with making a loan on a cohousing home. If it is difficult to get a homeowner mortgage, then it becomes more challenging to develop a cohousing project or resell homes in the future. It may be in the best interest of the project's success to avoid using the word in the project's name in order to reduce the challenge of dealing with inaccurate assumptions.

Identify a Core Group

Identify who is willing to take the time, spend the money, and expend the energy to bring the project to completion—or at least get it started.

Open a Bank Account

At this stage it makes sense to open an account as a community organization. Once a site has been identified and secured, it will be important to set up a corporate account. But for the interim, the recommendation is to keep it simple. Collect a small fee to help cover costs of room rental, food, babysitting, and so on to facilitate members' ability to meet and work together. Funds will also be needed to pay for the professional services required to get the project started. Money invested at this stage will not be recoverable if the project does not proceed; however, it is essential that members be willing to take some financial risk to move the project forward. The financial phases of development are discussed in more detail in Chapter 9.

Establish Communication and Preliminary
Document Management Systems

Once it's clear who the people are in your core group, work with them to determine your meeting and communication strategy: When and where will the core group meet? Will you hold regular outreach or information meetings? How will people be informed? Will there be formal agendas and minutes? Set up a system for effectively communicating between meetings. You will also need to keep track of the decisions you make and be able to easily access that information as the project proceeds.

Establish Preliminary Decision-Making Protocols and Practices

Learning the skills and establishing protocols and practices for how you will make decisions together will support you to have a joyful and successful process. There are many resources available online describing collaborative decision-making processes, and we have included a list of some of these resources on the CDC website, CohousingConsulting.ca. We recommend using consensus decision-| making for many reasons and discuss this in Chapter 5. At this stage, the decision-making process does not need to be very structured, and in our opinion it would be best not to get too attached to any one model. The development consultant you engage may have deci- sion-making protocols and practices that they want to use to support an effective and efficient development process.

Develop a Statement of Shared Intention or Project Objective

A clear and concrete statement of shared intention or project objec- tive will help clarify your purpose, inform others what you are about, and provide a foundation to build on. Things you need to talk about include:

- What is the main purpose or intention for wanting to do this?

- What is the desired form and character of the community (town- houses, apartments, single-family homes, number and size of units) and what are the desired attributes?

- Who do you want to attract (singles, couples, families, seniors)?

- When do you want this to happen (desired timeline)?

The following is an example of a statement of shared intention for a successfully completed project:

> Our mandate is to build an intentional neighbourhood of twenty to twenty-five strata-titled single-family homes with common

amenities for seniors that is affordable, environmentally friendly, and socially/culturally supportive, allowing people to flourish through mutual support as they age in place and in community.

Our mission is to be a sustainable senior cohousing home-owner community that promotes healthy aging in place. The physical structures as well as the social fabric of our community will nurture an innovative elder culture with lively connections to the larger society. While respecting personal privacy, we will foster cooperation, social connection, and affordability through design and through the sharing of elder care as well as physical and social resources.

The statement of shared intention may evolve and change as more information becomes available, but it is important to have something solid as a starting point. For example, the group who created the project objective in this example changed their focus after investigating possible sites and ended up developing a project with thirty-one homes in a combination of apartments and duplexes. However, having the clear project objective to start with helped focus the site search.

Determine Site Criteria

As a group, you need to determine:

- what general area you want to be located in
- what services or amenities you want to have close by
- what the likely costs are for a home in the neighbourhood of your choice

Attending open houses at new developments in the neighbourhoods of your choice will help identify the likely costs and may help to give you ideas about the building form you want. Determining the average cost per square foot for new homes in the area will give you an idea of the likely cost per square foot for a newly completed home nearby. If prices are higher than what you were expecting, you may want to consider another neighbourhood. Also consider how small a space you could live in or perhaps the idea of sharing a home with one or more other individuals or families. Communal living arrangements within the cohousing context are quite common. As well, renting out a bedroom can reduce housing costs and increase diversity.

Keep in mind that cohousing homes are typically smaller than conventional homes, so even though the cost per square foot may be somewhat higher than for conventional developments, the total cost may be moderate for the area. And common amenities function as an extension to the private dwelling. Including such extensive common spaces as a guest room, workshop, children's play space, meeting room, and other amenities that the group may choose makes it easier to live in smaller or shared homes.

Research Potential Site Locations

Talk with a planner in your local municipal area to identify what locations might be possible from a zoning and land use perspective to achieve the kind of development you want. Chapter 10 includes more information about how to find and secure an appropriate site once a group has taken the steps to get started.

Collect Preliminary Financial Information

It takes money to develop a housing project. You need to know where that money will come from before purchasing land. The following questions need to be answered:

- What are the likely costs to develop the type of homes and amenities in the location the group has chosen?

- Do members have the financial capacity to achieve the vision? If not, then what?

- What will it take for members to feel comfortable contributing equity to the development?

- What are the requirements for bank financing?

If many of the members already own homes (with minimal mortgage financing in place), then it is likely the group will have the financial capacity to develop a project using their own resources. If many of the members are first-time purchasers, then you may not have the resources within the group that are needed. One group with whom CDC worked wanted to focus on creating a community for young families; however, the preliminary feasibility study indicated that they did not have the financial resources that would be required. Once they opened their membership more broadly to include older households, they were successful at attracting the membership needed to finance their development and ended up with a very balanced intergenerational community as a result.

Putting together a preliminary budget based on likely costs and developing a financial plan is an essential early step. You will need to engage someone who is knowledgeable about financing housing developments to help you with this step if you do not have the expertise within your core group. Chapter 9 includes more information about the financial requirements of a housing development.

Determine a Strategy for the Selection of the Professional Team

If after following the steps noted above you think it might be feasible to develop a community in the neighbourhood of your choice, then CDC recommends your next step would be to engage a consultant to prepare a feasibility study. We believe this step to be essential to grounding the project in reality.

Chapter 3 includes a list of the professionals, and the qualifications, typically required for housing development. That information can be used to establish the criteria for the selection of professionals. Hiring from within the group creates unique opportunities as well as challenges, so clear guidelines and boundaries are essential if the decision is made to do so.

Set Up the Development Corporation

Once the group has accomplished the above steps to get started, we recommend working with experienced professionals for the balance of the items, identified below. The development process is risky and complex. Working with experienced professionals has been shown to save members money in the long run, reduce risks associated with all aspects of a community led housing process, and increase the likelihood that the project will be successful. Chapter 10 provides more detailed information about what is required to establish project feasibility, which is an essential step in the initiation stage.

The legal and financial structure are the backbone of the development process. Clear and transparent financial management and decision-making processes as well as legally binding agreements contribute to the project's viability and support the outreach endeavours.

Establish Criteria, Select and Engage Professionals

The first professional that we recommend selecting is the development consultant, or project manager. We use the term *development consultant* throughout to describe the person or company who is responsible for seeing the project from inception to completion and acts in a lead management role. Once the development consultant has been selected, they can provide recommendations on the other professionals that would be most appropriate and prepare the preliminary scope of work to secure proposals for services. The design professionals will have a big impact on how well you are able to stay within budget. Choosing professionals who have the right kind of experience is essential. Good development also requires collaboration, so selecting the professionals involves assembling a team that will work well together.

Establish Feasibility, Determine Financial Development Strategy

The financial capacity of the members will have an impact on project feasibility. Each member household will need to complete a statement of personal net worth so that the financial viability of the project can be determined. You must also determine the amount that members will be willing to invest, assuming that the site secured is one they are satisfied with. A preliminary financial analysis of equity potential will be required to establish feasibility and prepare a financial development strategy. Funds will be required in increasing amounts as the project proceeds, and periodic cash flow projections should be prepared to help identify how much will be needed and when. This information is essential to ground the project in reality.

Determine Member Commitment Procedure and Equity Requirements

How are new members included and what is the financial commitment? Are there stages to member commitment? What are the member responsibilities and obligations? How are the financial investments secured? Chapter 6 includes more information about membership structure during development, and Chapters 8 and 9 include more information about legal agreements and how to attract and manage member investments.

Establish an Accounting and Document Management System

In the early phases this can be very simple; however, as the project progresses it is essential to have a system in place that will make it possible to track a multitude of expenses and manage a large and complex budget. Another essential ingredient of an effective collaborative process is easy access to information. There is a lot of information produced in the process of developing a community. Internet-based systems that are easy to use have proven to be highly effective ways to facilitate information access during a development process and can continue to function as effective tools even after move-in.

Determine Formal Decision-Making Procedure

Although this is related to community organizational structure and building community (see more below), it is also something that needs to be incorporated into the legal agreements. The more clearly defined the protocols and guidelines are for decision-making, the easier it is for members to participate effectively in the process. As well, a transparent decision-making process reduces the likelihood of conflict. Having a way to assess the level of participation required for any decision, for determining whether a decision is important enough to be made by the group as a whole or whether it can be made by individuals or committees, is an important aspect for effective decision-making. Chapter 5 includes recommended protocols and processes for decision-making during development.

Create a Legal Entity and Legal Agreements for Membership

Eventually, a legal entity is required to buy land and enter into contracts. Also, legal agreements need to be in place to secure member investments and other financial commitments. Chapter 8 includes more information about the legal structure and legal agreements required for a community led self-development process.

Agree to a Method for Establishing Home Prices

The recommended approach is to price the homes based on a "market model." In this method, the desirability of a home is assessed in relation to the other homes (square footage, location, lot size, exposure, etc.) by a qualified appraiser. Home prices are then established as a percentage of the total development costs. This way, if any of the costs associated with the development (professional fees, financing, construction) increase or decrease, the home prices will increase or decrease proportionally. There is no cap on costs in a community led housing process where the group is the developer. The only control the group has over the costs is in the decisions they make about the development.

Establish Bookkeeping and Open a Corporate Account

The project's financial information needs to be transparent and reconciled monthly with bank statements, and an accounting system for the development phase will be needed. It is useful to have two accounts: one for day-to-day casual group expenses (the account that was set up during the getting started phase) and a separate development account for project expenses. This allows for a general petty cash fund, which can be managed by members throughout the process. The corporate account should be managed professionally once the project is past the feasibility phase.

Collect Members' Equity Money

Members' contributions can be staged, with smaller amounts required earlier on; these will be gradually increased as larger amounts are needed and the project becomes more concrete. The cash flow projections (noted above) will provide information about the amount of investment that is required at each stage.

Secure Commercial Loans

Identify at least one financial institution willing to lend on the land purchase and/or project construction. Confirm requirements and make applications as needed. In some cases there may be enough equity in the group to finance the land purchase, but generally a commercial loan is required to finance construction.

Determine the Community Organizational Structure and Build Membership

One of the challenges in a community led housing development is in having an organizational structure that allows for participation by all members yet has a communication and decision-making process that will support an efficient and effective development process. (Time is money!) The project's success depends on having a robust outreach program and a community of individuals who feel connected. Chapter 4 includes more information about organizational structure for development, and Chapter 6 addresses building membership and community.

Determine the Committee Structure and Tasks

Organize members into committees to perform tasks that are essential to building community. A recommended committee structure and list of tasks is discussed in more detail in Chapter 4.

Establish Community-Building and Recruitment Strategies

A group with effective communication skills is better able to build a connected community as well as work productively through the development process. This is only one of the important aspects that is discussed in the section on building membership and community. To reach the right people, you'll need to devise a solid strategy for membership recruitment and outreach. Confirm the content of the message, who to reach out to and how. A good website is an important element. As well, new member education and integration will need to be considered.

Establish Priority Sequencing for Unit Selection

As members join and commit to being part of the development, it is important to be clear about who gets to choose their home first. A recommended approach is to establish a priority sequence based on the timing of financial commitment.

Achieve Membership Threshold for Site Control

The financial plan will identify how many members and how much money needs to be in place to progress into each phase. At each phase of the development, the risk should be reviewed: Does it make sense to proceed? What is the potential loss? Are there enough members to proceed?

Find and Secure the Site

Finding an appropriate site can be very challenging—particularly in an urban context. Chapter 10 provides information about how to go about securing a site. Many groups fail because they don't take the right steps. Just because a site appears to be one that could work does not mean that the site is viable. There are many steps that need to be taken to determine viability. What follows is a brief overview of the essential steps in the process.

Confirm Site Criteria

This should be part of the getting started process, but it is important to revisit the site criteria that was set then in more detail once the financial strategy has been identified. Are the criteria realistic? Finding a site within the group's budget often requires a certain amount of compromise.

Determine a Strategy for Identifying and Securing a Site

Depending on the context, whether rural or urban, the strategy for identifying and securing a site may be different.

Determine Land Use and Development Strategy

Investigate official community plan and zoning regulations in the local jurisdiction to determine what land use designation will be required for the type of development that is desired. A professional land use planner is an important member of the team at this stage of the process.

Program Architectural Design Requirements

The architect will need to know the design requirements in order to prepare initial concept plans for potential sites. This is discussed in more detail in Chapter 7. An architect that has experience working with groups will be able to guide this process.

A note on design and cost control: The more standardization in the home design, the lower the cost; customization of all kinds will add to the cost. In conventional developments there is generally a maximum of three to four unit types, and there is a good reason for this—the more unit types there are, the more complex the project is, and complexity increases costs. Cohousing groups typically attempt to meet the needs of a diverse group of people—singles, families, youth, and elders—which can make it more difficult to come up with a set of standard plans. However, the more successful a group is at achieving a high level of standardization, the better it will be at controlling costs.

Prepare a Preliminary Analysis of Possible Sites

The design professional or architect will prepare a preliminary concept plan to determine a site's development potential. The development consultant uses this information to prepare a development proforma (preliminary budget) to estimate the potential cost for a completed home in the project.

Meet with Local Land Use Officials

Evaluate the challenges and opportunities for developing a potential site. Educate the officials about the concept and benefits of having a community led housing development in their jurisdiction.

Select Preferred Site and Obtain Site Control

Enter into a contract to purchase or option on the preferred site, subject to a feasibility study.

Complete a Feasibility Study

Before finalizing the purchase of the site, the opportunities and challenges for development will need to be determined to assess the risk of proceeding. Chapter 10 includes information about what should be included in a feasibility study.

Prepare Initial Development Budget and Financial Plan

The preliminary budget needs to be updated based on the results of the feasibility study, and financing for land purchase needs to be formalized, whether by member equity or a commercial loan.

Determine Construction Delivery Method and Select a Manager or General Contractor

Even though the construction section is the last phase in the development process, it is important to select a construction method and manager or general contractor once the site has been secured to ensure the project is in a position to begin construction as soon as permits have been issued. As well, the construction manager can provide preliminary costing information to support the design development and help keep the project on budget. Information is included in Chapter 11 about construction methods and how to find and select a construction manager or general contractor.

Undertake the Design and Development

Once the site has been secured, the work on design can commence. This is an intense period that requires diligence and skills to support a collaborative design process that is as efficient as possible. The longer it takes, the more it will cost because land carrying costs begin to accumulate from the moment the site has been secured.

Meet the Neighbours

Regulatory authorities often require you to familiarize neighbours with the project as a formal part of the rezoning process (separate from the public hearing), but it is important to do regardless. There may be impacts on neighbours that can be mitigated during the construction process, and these should be considered in the planning. It is in the project's best interest to do what can be done to keep the neighbours happy.

Prepare and Approve the Design

This is a multi-phased process that results in the creation of a final detailed design for the buildings, landscape, and site works. The land use approval requirements will impact the process and timing.

Revise Development Budget

Getting preliminary costing information from a contractor at different phases of the design helps to keep the project on budget. Can members still afford the decisions that have been made? Are some design revisions required to meet budget constraints?

Obtain Land Use Approvals

In some locations it can take several years to get the required land use approvals. This is very costly when land prices are high, so it is essential to have a knowledgeable professional to manage and support a process that is as efficient as possible.

Home Selection

When the land use approvals have been obtained and the budget has been updated based on the design drawings, preliminary home pricing can be prepared. CDC recommends engaging a professional appraiser at this stage to ensure home pricing is fair and equitable. Once the members have agreed to a pricing structure, they can select their homes according to the established priority sequence.

Prepare the Disclosure Statement, Strata Bylaws, and Operating Budget

In BC there are many elements that need to be in place before individual contracts can be entered into for home purchase. Under the Real Estate Development Marketing Act, the province of BC requires property developers to make disclosure statements—on the financing details as well as the nature of the development—prior to purchasers entering into agreements to buy a home in a new development. This may not be required in other provinces or states, so a legal professional in the jurisdiction in question would need to be consulted. But it is a useful document for fully informing a purchaser regardless of whether it is required. Groups in BC need to be very careful how they promote themselves prior to filing a disclosure statement. Prior to filing, outreach cannot legally advertise homes for sale. Chapter 8 includes information about what a disclosure statement includes and how to prepare and file one.

Construct the Project

Once the land use permits are in place, an application can be made to permit construction of the development. Chapter 11 includes detailed information about how to prepare for construction.

Prepare the Construction Documents and Permit Application

Detailed construction documents as well as a lot of other documentation are required prior to making the construction permit application. In BC, all developers, including groups that are self-developing, must be licensed under the Homeowner Protection Act and show proof of new home warranty coverage prior to making the application.

Finalize the Construction Budget

Once construction bids are received, there will be a more accurate picture of costs—up to this stage, everything has been estimated. If a knowledgeable contractor has been involved, there shouldn't be any big surprises. At the start of construction, a 5 percent contingency is typically required by financial institutions if the delivery method is some form of fixed price contract, and at least 10 percent is recommended if it is a construction management contract.

Establish Home Prices, Enter Into Purchase and Sale Agreements

Now that the construction budget has been finalized, the home prices can be determined more accurately and the members can enter into purchase agreements for the homes they have selected. Financial institutions typically require at least 70 percent of the homes to be sold (with purchase and sale agreements in place) before they are willing to lend construction financing. It is also important for the group's risk management to have at least this many of the homes sold and confidence that the remainder can be sold prior to construction completion. Members of the group will be required to cover the cost to carry unsold homes at completion, so this needs to be considered in the risk management strategy.

Secure a Construction Loan and Obtain Construction Permits

Chapter 9 includes information on what an application for construction financing should include. Financial institutions will need to see a copy of the construction permit before they are willing to fund the first draw on the construction loan.

Establish the Construction Protocol

It should be clear from the start of construction what is expected from members at this stage. How will decisions of an immediate nature be dealt with? How and when will members be allowed on site? Making changes during construction is very costly and should be avoided, even though it can be tempting when members see something that could be "better." Chapter 11 includes detailed information on construction communication and protocols.

Completion

Preparing for completion is the final stage of the development phase. After this, the members will be in the living in community phase!

Set Up Homeowner Financing

Once the purchase and sale agreements have been completed, members who need mortgages can apply for the homeowner financing that has to be in place at home completion. CDC recommends working with a mortgage broker who fully understands the legal and financial aspects so they can provide clear and accurate information to financial institutions.

Address Any Contingency Excess or Shortfall

Until the project is complete and all costs have been confirmed, the exact amount of any remaining contingency cannot be determined, but at this stage a likely range can be identified. If a shortfall is anticipated, this has to be calculated and collected from the purchasers on closing. If there will be an excess, then this can be used to reduce home costs or left in the development account to cover unbudgeted development costs. Any decision to accept a discount in home purchase prices needs to be made prior to members closing on their homes.

Prepare the Living in Community Agreements

How will the use of common spaces be managed after move-in? There are many topics worth considering, and the more agreements that are in place prior to move-in, the smoother the community will function. Chapter 13 discusses how to prepare for living in community and provides examples of the topics that groups often discuss.

Deficiency and Warranty Management

At the completion of construction, information for homeowner maintenance manuals and warranties needs to be collected and organized to support the community to properly manage and maintain the building over time. Protocols need to be in place for managing any deficiencies or warranty items.

Move-In Management and Coordination

Building forms vary, but in a multi-level multi-family building, move-in is not a simple process. Creation and distribution of a schedule for equitable elevator and/or parking access, coordination of key delivery, transfer of utilities, setting up mailboxes for postal delivery, and installing an entry phone system are just a few of the things to be done. Every project will be somewhat different, but consideration should be given to making this process as easy and stress free as possible!

Obtain Occupancy Permit

The occupancy permit needs to be in place before anyone can legally move in. What is required is discussed in more detail in Chapter 12.

Complete Legal Closing and Changeover to Individual Ownership

Once the occupancy permit has been issued, the members can close on the purchase of their homes and the construction loan can be paid off. Any contingency remaining can be managed by the members.

And the final stage of the development process: Members move in and start enjoying the fruits of their labours! Professionals celebrate the project's success!

Success Rates

Creating community led housing is not for the faint of heart. Diana Leafe Christian says that new intentional communities and eco-villages in the US and other parts of the world have only a 10 percent success rate.[1] Canadian cohousing results are more encouraging according to data collected by the Canadian Cohousing Network (CCN). This national cohousing association maintains a website listing cohousing groups in the forming, development, and construction stages, as well as those that have completed.

The CCN kindly allowed us to analyze its membership data from 2001 through 2021. To be a member, a community must pay an annual fee, which, in 2021, ranged from fifty dollars for a new group to twenty dollars per household (capped at five hundred dollars for a completed community). Since 2001, eighty-five communities have belonged to CCN. Of these, half no longer belonged in 2021: two were completed communities (Cohabitat Quebec and Middle Road in Nelson, BC), and the rest—about forty—had not completed as cohousing communities and apparently had ceased to exist.

Of CCN's forty-three listed cohousing projects, twenty had completed by the end of 2021. Four were under construction by then. Five were listed as "in development," and fourteen were in the "forming" stage. In 2021, almost 50 percent of the groups belonging to the CCN had completed, much better than the 10 percent reported for the US. Considered over two decades, however, only 25 percent of projects that got as far as joining the CCN succeeded, if success is measured by completion—i.e., members move in.

As noted in the introduction, only one in five of the completed communities in Canada has succeeded without a development consultant. Real estate development has become increasingly complex over the years with more stringent requirements on every level (legal, financial, design, and construction). Land and construction costs have escalated. Regulatory authorities are taking longer to address development applications, which increases costs and adds to the risk. It is becoming increasingly difficult for professionals to manage a successful development. Although it is possible for a group to achieve success without the support of a knowledgeable development consultant, the risk of financial loss is extreme.

In addition, the members need to have a realistic perspective on what is possible. Groups often start the process believing they can create environmentally sustainable, universally accessible, aesthetically beautiful buildings with extensive common facilities at a more affordable price than what is available in a conventional development. However, all of these attributes contribute to higher costs. And while it may be possible to secure some government subsidies to help reduce costs, public funds come with obligations, and generally subsidies are only provided to those with the greatest need. So it is important for groups to have a practical understanding early in the process about what the likely costs will be to manifest their vision.

Impediments to Success

The following provides an overview of some of the many risks associated with a community led housing development process and identifies ways to mitigate them.

Ineffective management: Poor management contributes to a longer timeline, higher costs, and increases the risk of failure. A skilled and experienced development consultant addresses not only the challenges that are a part of every real estate development but also the unique challenges of a community led housing development. Check references closely; do not make assumptions based on appearance.

Impractical expectation of what it will cost: A financial analysis should be completed at each step of the process to review the budget and identify the risks associated with moving forward. A qualified development consultant should be able to provide a realistic estimate of costs based on the local market conditions at project inception. Working with a qualified general contractor throughout the design process to provide estimates will show the impact of decisions on costs and will help to keep the project on budget.

Not knowing what is required to support a collaborative process: A successful collaborative process requires an effective, transparent organizational structure and communication system; knowledgeable leadership; and skilled facilitation. There needs to be a system for ensuring that everyone has the opportunity to access the information they need to participate effectively in decision-making.

Ineffective group dynamics or decision-making processes: Ensure there are legal agreements in place that have been proven to be successful in supporting harmonious relationships and effective decision-making to balance the interests of individuals with the needs of the group. This reduces the potential for conflict and misunderstandings that can stymie progress.

Conflict: Conflict within the group or with people outside the group is sometimes unavoidable, but it can arise when collaborative processes are unclear. Unresolved conflict makes it difficult to work together effectively. It is important to find a way to address conflict directly, and that may involve engaging a conflict management specialist for support. Learning how to effectively work with conflict is one of the important skills required for a collaborative process to succeed.

Inability to achieve the desired land use designation or having set unrealistic goals: It is important to start building a collaborative relationship with the local jurisdictional agencies from the project's inception to find out what kind of development would be supported in the location being contemplated. Having good relationships can be very helpful when dealing with the issues that come up in any development process. Select a site with a high likelihood of achieving the desired land use designation based on municipal bylaws, official community plans, and what other development is happening in the neighbourhood.

Mismanagement or unpredictable construction costs: A construction management or cost-plus contract is riskier than a fixed-price contract and does not necessarily result in the lowest cost even if the management fee is lower; with a fixed-price contract, the final cost is much more predictable. Regardless of the nature of the construction contract, the relationship between client and general contractor benefits from collaboration. Working with a collaborative attitude creates a team relationship where all parties are working towards the same goal of achieving the highest quality product for the best price.

Inability to attract members: It is important to assess the risk at each milestone and determine whether there are enough members in place to move to the next step. Experience has shown that if the project is managed well, with effective legal, financial, communication, and organizational structures, people with the financial capacity to purchase will be attracted to the project if the concept is attractive to them. The success of the outreach, and ultimately the financial success of the project, is directly impacted by the effectiveness and transparency of the project organization.

General market and world conditions: As we know, it is impossible to predict or control general market or world conditions. Real estate development in itself is risky, and the value of the finished product can end up being lower than the cost to produce it if market conditions change. Housing that owners design and develop for themselves, where their relationship with each other is important, is much more stable and secure than a conventional development because of the level of commitment of the purchasers. The more connected members are to each other, the greater their capacity will be to make decisions that are in the best interest of the collective and ensure resilience if there are challenges.

Innovation: Even though a project that is developed by the future residents is not as dependent as conventional housing on the need to be attractive to the general market, it is still important to keep the general market in mind, particularly where it relates to the cost of comparable developments in the area. For example, cohousing groups tend to include a higher level of green building than a conventional developer would be willing to risk. The lowest risk is to follow a path that has been proven to be successful. Any innovation increases risk and the potential of higher costs—and in the worst case can result in failure.

Changes to life circumstances: It is important during the development phase to maintain stability, so the legal agreements should make it difficult for members to leave the project. However, life circumstances can sometimes make it impossible for someone to continue, so the agreements need to be structured to allow for these potential situations while still protecting the interests of the larger group.

Unsuitable community candidates: During the development phase, the recommended approach is to set up as a private company whereby the directors and shareholders determine who else is accepted as a director and shareholder. However, a robust education and integration process is what ensures that the project attracts potential purchasers who are suited to the lifestyle. After completion, if the legal structure is strata title, under the Strata Property Act in BC, the owners cannot control who purchases a unit. This may be different in other jurisdictions—legal counsel would be required to confirm the regulations. The recommended approach for managing resales is to maintain a process that educates potential purchasers and gives first opportunity to purchase to people who are familiar with and are attracted to participating in the community lifestyle. Experience in completed communities has shown that this is sufficient to attract suitable purchasers.

Why Success Is Important

Groups that fail can negatively impact the chance of success for others. Financial institutions that supported failed projects will no longer lend money for other community led developments. Some people have lost their life savings because of mismanagement, resulting in legal disputes that have lasted for years. If this trend continues, it is likely the government will step in to protect the interests of the public, which will add even more regulations to an already difficult and challenging process. CDC is writing this book in an attempt to contribute to the success of cohousing and other community led housing, to equip people who have the knowledge and capacity to develop a successful conventional real estate development with the information they need to support a successful community led housing group.

On February 11, 2022, the *New York Times* published an article titled "They Took a Chance on Collaborative Living. They Lost Everything." From reading the article, it is obvious that the failed group did not have the support of experienced professionals. In March 2022, Charles Durrett made the following statements in the Cohousing Company newsletter in response to that article:

> Katie and I perhaps overemphasized in our first book, which brought cohousing to North America, how grassroots cohousing development was in Denmark. We were young and idealistic and enamored with "the people just doing it" and that was what we emphasized. But it wasn't until my fifth trip back to Denmark when Jan Gudmand-Høyer finally got it into my head all of the various clearly extraordinary skilled players that it really took to make a successful cohousing community happen.

And he was right—good cohousing is just as complicated as flying a commercial airplane if not more. The emphasis on community is critical to the ultimate success no doubt, but navigation on the business side is just as critical [...]

While we extensively cover the design principles that contribute to what make a cohousing project successful in our latest book *Community-Enhanced Design: Cohousing and Other High-Functioning Neighborhoods*—from having thorough sets of programs & design criteria to common house designs that maximize people-hours, we also emphasize the importance of group process and project management in the success of cohousing.[2]

3

Finding
and Hiring
Professionals

THE ROLE OF THE PROFESSIONAL is to define the container in which the creative process can occur. As noted in Chapter 2, good development requires successful teamwork, so selecting the right professionals also involves building a team that will work well together. We use the term *professional team* here to refer to all the professionals that are engaged to provide services for the project. Furthermore, in land development there are all kinds of regulatory bodies with very precise protocols that need to be adhered to; therefore, it is essential to work with professionals who understand the requirements.

From "They Took a Chance on Collaborative Living. They Lost Everything," in the February 11, 2022, *New York Times*:

> A group that sought to create Connecticut's first experiment in collaborative living fell short. Some of the investors lost their life savings [...]
>
> "People were involved in so many circles and so many meetings a day, I don't think they could step back and get a fresh perspective because of the time commitment... They did the best they could, but these were not professional developers. There was a kind of fantastical thinking."

The Importance of Member Involvement

One of the defining characteristics of cohousing, and all community led housing, is the involvement of the future residents in the planning and design of the community. For the project to be successful, the professional team must be able to guide the process in a way that will keep the project on time and on budget, while also including the members in the decision-making. The members need to play an active role and take risks in order to fully form as a community. They need to be "in the dance," making important decisions that will impact the design and development but not interfere with progress and efficiency.

Members need to be onside with the professional team and realize that the recommendations coming from the professionals are based on knowledge and experience and are intended to serve the best interest of the project. The professional team needs to support the members to know what they don't know and help them clearly see the risks associated with some choices. The whole point of engaging professionals is to benefit from their expertise, but there are times when the members may not like the direction that is being recommended. This can be especially challenging in early days when relationships are forming, but it can remain a problem throughout the project. Education is an essential part of the process, and information needs to be easily and readily accessible. In the end, if the group is self-developing, they are the ones who will suffer if they chose the wrong path, but it is in the professionals' best interest to find a way to support success.

When a group doesn't like the professional recommendation, allowing some latitude for the group to "go rogue" or "go into the weeds" can motivate them to come together and see the value of the professional support. Chaos can result in a new order. The trick is to find a way to support this without jeopardizing the ultimate success of the project.

The Organizational Structure for the Professional Team

The organizational structure for the group and how they interface with professionals is discussed in Chapter 4. The following diagram shows one option for the relationships of responsibility among the professional team in a development process. This is typically how the CDC-managed projects were organized. An arrow with a solid line indicates a primary relationship of responsibility and communication. A dashed arrow indicates a secondary relationship. For example, the architect should be in regular, direct communication with the other design professionals to coordinate the design of the project. The development consultant does not need to be involved in these day-to-day communications except when issues arise that impact the design or cost.

Example Organizational Structure for the Professional Team

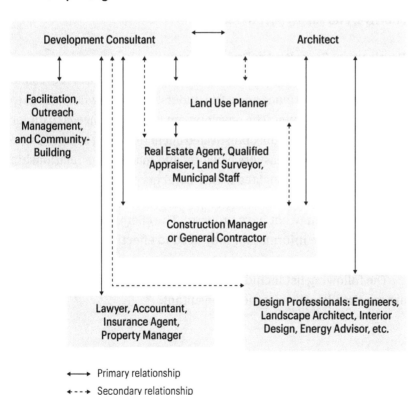

Professional Roles and Capabilities

What follows is a list of the professionals that are typically required in a community led housing development. The list is roughly in the order in which professionals are engaged (some need to be brought in concurrently) and is based on the assumption that a site needs to be identified and secured. The development consultant or project manager can help define and select the professional team and determine when each professional needs to be involved.

As noted in the introduction, collaboration characterizes CDC's approach to the entire development process, and we believe it is just as important in the work of the professional team as it is with the members. Working collaboratively supports everyone to work towards the common goal of serving the best interests of the project. When there are problems, and there inevitably are, we work together to find solutions. People who are working joyfully tend to put their hearts into the work, which results in a higher quality, more cost effective, and satisfying product.

Development Consultant or Project Manager

The person or persons who take on this role need to have real estate development experience and a full understanding of what it takes to make a project happen. The development consultant needs to understand how to guide an unsophisticated client (meaning someone who has not done this at least once before) and manage the relationship between the professional team and members. This would be similar to a developer working with a property-rich church group, except that the group may not have property. The client must be educated so they have the information they need to effectively participate in decision-making.

The following list includes some of the basics of what we believe are required in a development consultant:

- the knowledge and experience to manage a development of the size and scope that the group is contemplating

- an understanding of the municipal process for any land use changes to construction and occupancy permits

- an understanding of how to coordinate the work of the professional team, including identifying the scope of services and managing the service contracts

- knowledge about how to create and manage budgets and an understanding of all the elements that are included in a development proforma

- the capacity to manage the investment from members, apply for commercial financing, and manage the flow of money throughout the project

- an understanding of the legal structure required for development and how to transition that for home ownership once the project is completed

- the capacity to support the group with decision-making and planning, setting up an organizational structure that supports member participation, and helping to facilitate timely and appropriate decisions throughout the process

- good communication and organizational skills and the capacity to act as liaison between the group and the regulatory authorities, professionals, financial institution, and general contractor

Facilitation, Decision-Making, Conflict Resolution

To support an effective development process, it is essential to have someone on the team who has the skills and knowledge to facilitate and manage a collaborative decision-making process and to support the group to deal with conflict if it arises. (This may be the development consultant or a separate professional.) To support harmonious community life after move-in, it is important for group members to get some training in these areas. A common pitfall with community led housing groups is the belief that everyone already has these skills.

Outreach Management and Coordination

In a development process that is focused on creating community, it makes sense for the group to take on a large role in building membership. However, someone knowledgeable about what works and what doesn't is needed to help coordinate the group's marketing and outreach efforts.

Website Developer

Experience has shown that one of the most effective tools for generating interest in membership is having an attractive and informative website. As well, ongoing education of members throughout the process requires having an effective system for communicating and managing information. Internet-based systems that are easy to use have proven to be highly effective ways to facilitate information management and dissemination during a development process and can continue to function as an effective tool after move-in.

Land Use Planner

A land use planner can support the group (and the real estate agent) to identify appropriate sites that will meet the group's defined objective. They can also act as liaison with local officials to determine development potential and regulatory requirements. Once a site has been secured, depending on the nature and scope of any land use changes required, a planner may be needed to facilitate the approval process and provide support with meeting the regulatory requirements to secure the building permit.

Market Analysis, Site Search, and Negotiations

One of the elements of a feasibility study involves determining whether the estimated cost of the completed units will be marketable, so someone with knowledge about the local market values for similar properties will be needed to provide that information—usually a real estate agent suits this role. If the members have done a thorough job of researching costs (as described in the getting started section in Chapter 2), then a real estate agent may not be required for the feasibility study. However, a local real estate agent, with access to information about potential development sites, is typically required for the site search. Good development sites are often not listed through the MLS (multiple listing service) system. Sometimes the group will find a site without an agent, but an agent still may be needed to help negotiate the purchase.

Appraisal

There are typically three stages where an appraisal from a qualified professional is required: the purchase of the land (if bank financing is required), negotiating the development financing, and for securing homeowner financing for the completed units. There is more information about the appraisal requirements and how the appraisal impacts the development included in Chapter 9.

Legal

A lawyer familiar with real estate and corporate law will be required to set up the development corporation, act as legal counsel for site purchase, work with the development consultant to set up the member or shareholder agreements to ensure compliance with the government legislation, prepare disclosure statements (if required in the province or state where the project is being contemplated), provide legal advice and services as required during the development process, and coordinate legal transfer of ownership on completion. For many reasons, it is very helpful if the law firm has experience with community led development. This is discussed in more detail in the section about selecting a lawyer in Chapter 8.

Accounting and Financial Management

This role involves contract negotiation and management, managing the bank account, coordinating member investments, coordinating payment of invoices, providing monthly financial statements, filing goods and services tax and corporate tax returns, managing communication with the Canada Revenue Agency or Internal Revenue

Service, making applications for construction financing, managing all communication with the financial institution, and preparing the monthly loan progress draws during construction. Many of these services can be included as part of the development management contract, but having a chartered professional accountant on the team is typically required at least to prepare the corporate tax returns.

Architect

The architect is one of the lead professionals and coordinates the activities of all the other design professionals. For the CDC-managed projects, the architect worked with the development consultant to plan and prepare the design workshops that facilitated group decisions about site design, and the common house and individual unit designs. On completion of design, the architect prepared the construction documents, coordinated building permits with the jurisdictional authority, managed the tender process, and provided construction administration. For a successful development process, it is important for the lead architect to have the following characteristics:

- experience with the design and contract administration for the size and type of project being contemplated

- be a "developer's architect"—someone who knows how to design with a minimum of unique floor plans and who can support an unsophisticated client to make cost-effective decisions

- be knowledgeable about green building techniques and ecologically sensitive design

- possesses an aesthetic that is appealing to the group

- experience designing "medium-priced" housing and well-informed about construction costs and constructability

- an interest in and a willingness to learn about community led housing (if no previous experience)

- experience working with groups in the design programming phase

Other Professionals

A landscape architect, geotechnical engineer, mechanical engineer, building enclosure consultant, electrical engineer, structural engineer, and interior design consultant are generally needed. The architect usually coordinates the activities of these professionals and typically has relationships with professionals in whom they have confidence to provide the quality of work that will serve the project well. Therefore, it is normally in the best interest of the project for the architect to select these professionals.

Depending on circumstances and the nature of the project, there may be a need for studies requiring the services of such specialized professionals as a traffic engineer, habitat or environmental consultant, arborist, specialized utility consultant, etc. The need for these additional professionals is generally determined as part of the land use approval process.

Because of the desire to include as many environmentally sustainable features as is economically viable, groups benefit from having a professional on the team who has the knowledge and skills to provide cost benefit analysis for green building options as well as energy modelling.

Depending on the site selected, a civil engineer may be a required member of the team.

A land surveyor may be required during the design phase, depending on the property and whether the lots need to be consolidated, but will definitely be required on completion of construction to prepare a legal survey of the completed development.

Liability and property insurance are required for site purchase, throughout the course of construction, and upon completion.

Property Manager

A professional strata, or condominium property manager, can help create the operating expenses budget for after move-in and can also help establish effective systems and protocols for managing and maintaining the completed development. It is important to understand and adhere to the requirements of the applicable provincial or state acts concerning strata property or condominiums that govern the use and management of multi-family developments. A property manager can help the group manage the development after completion. Some groups will choose to do this themselves if there are knowledgeable members with the time and capacity; however, many groups choose to engage a professional property manager to provide legal and financial management and give recommendations for appropriate service contractors.

Construction

A construction manager or general contractor is a business or person who contracts for and takes responsibility for completing a construction project. For any given project, there are a number of construction delivery methods available, primarily design-build, design-bid-build, construction management, and construction management at risk. The pros and cons of these delivery methods, as well as the approach that CDC has taken, which has proven to be successful, are discussed in more detail in Chapter 11.

How to Find the Right Professionals

CDC has developed a collaborative relationship with the professionals we have worked with over the years that supports success and contributes to an enjoyable experience for consultants and members. Therefore, in many instances, the group did not need to search out the professional team because they were willing to engage the ones that CDC had worked with previously and had recommended based on past experience. Hiring known professionals who work well together saves time and reduces risk.

Identifying Potential Candidates

If there are no recommended professionals for a particular role or location, the first step is to define the criteria for selection. Depending on the nature of the services, some specific criteria may be required, but the following provides a list of general criteria that would typically apply:

- knowledgeable and experienced with projects of the size and complexity contemplated

- proven track record, has good references

- has understanding of cohousing (or whatever type of community led housing that is being contemplated) or has interest in learning about it

- good communicator

- good team player, collaborative, adaptable

- honest, trustworthy

- organized, structured

- available in the time frame desired

- fee for services is in line with the market

Once the criteria have been defined, the next step is to prepare a preliminary scope of work. The scope of work does not need to be detailed, but should provide an overview that includes the following:

- information about the project, the members, the site, and any professionals engaged to date

- proposed building form

- proposed timeline

- project budget assumptions

- required services

If you are not sure what services will be required, ask the professional to list the services they would normally provide based on the project description.

The next step is to identify potential candidates and send out a call for an expression of interest with a time frame for making a response. After reviewing the responses, a decision can be made about whom to ask to respond to a request for proposal. Once the proposals have been received, the recommended next step is to select three candidates to attend an interview.

As noted in Chapter 2, having group members perform the professional roles has unique opportunities as well as challenges. When considering engaging a group member to provide some of the professional services, first carefully consider the pros and cons of doing so.

Example Interview and Assessment Process

The architect, for example, is an extremely important member of the professional team and can have a big impact on the project's success. It is important to get enough information to make an informed decision. The following provides an overview of how an interview could be structured for architect selection:

- arrival / set-up: ten minutes
- presentation: thirty minutes
- free question period: twenty-five minutes
- wrap-up and completion: ten minutes

In advance of the interview, the professional will be provided with an overview of the expectations for the presentation. For no more than thirty minutes after arrival and set-up, the professional will present information about themselves. This is their opportunity to show how they meet the group's criteria and to respond to the questions that were provided ahead of time.

Questions to be addressed in their presentation should include the following:

- Describe at least one recently completed project of a similar size and scope to the proposed development.

- Provide a recent example of a situation where you did not immediately achieve the results that you had hoped for; how did you solve the problem?

- We are interested in sustainable development but will need to balance the need or desire for this with the economic realities of cost constraints. What approach would you use to facilitate decisions that would give us the best value for our dollar while meeting the municipal requirements?

- What ideas do you have about how to maximize the usable outdoor space and incorporate activities such as children's play spaces; outdoor gathering or eating space; vegetable gardens, other gardens, and green space; outdoor laundry drying; some at-grade bike storage for guests and residents; rainwater collection; and composting?

- Describe a successful project that you designed that fosters community. What design elements contributed to building community and supporting opportunities for spontaneous connection and socializing?

- Our current budget assumes a [whatever is the current estimate] square foot (SF) common amenity area (common house) that will include a kitchen, dining room, children's play area, guest rooms, etc. We have not yet established priorities for our common house and would like to hear any ideas you may have that would support us to maximize the usable area and create flexibility in the use of the spaces.

- Our current development proforma estimates construction costs of [whatever the current construction cost is], including parking. Please comment on whether you think this estimate is feasible for a building of this size and what expertise you would bring to help keep the construction costs on budget.

- What experience do you have working with user groups, and what did you find contributed positively to the process?

- What is your knowledge and/or interest in cohousing (or whatever type of community led housing is being contemplated)?

- What most interests you about this project?

- Describe how you would propose working with the group and management team to facilitate a smooth and effective process.

- If you have other ideas about the project that you'd like to present, we welcome you to do so.

Afterwards, each member household is allowed to ask one question during the free question period (of approximately twenty-five minutes). If time allows, more and follow-up questions may be permitted.

During the interview process, each member is asked to write down comments to keep track of their thoughts about the different candidates, identifying the ways in which the professionals fit the agreed to criteria and, as we suggest, ranking each firm from 1 to 10 within each of the indicated categories:

  1–3 indicates little to no knowledge or experience
  4–7 indicates a moderate knowledge or experience
  8–10 indicates an exceptional understanding or experience

The final stage is to make a selection based on members' rankings, ideally using the consensus decision-making process.

Organizational Structure

"I see consistency in ease of navigation, friendliness and engagement of people, clarity and firmness of agreements and communication, boundary setting and adherence ... in the website ... the documentation, the welcoming of new members, the construction process—everything."

NEW MEMBER OF HARBOURSIDE COHOUSING, email to CDC, September 9, 2014

Why Organizational Structure Matters

New households, such as the one quoted above, often remark on how the professionals and the members consistently practised respectful, orderly communication in person and online. They comment on how many hours of meetings it took to create the community, but also on the quality of those meetings: their inclusivity, respectfulness, and efficiency. In other words, new households appreciate the organizational structure that CDC presented and which members accepted in the early days of the project.

Organizational structure delineates the paths and relationships through which communication flows and work gets done. This is one aspect of governance, the other being decision-making. Good organizational structure is what creates what we call "the container" that supports the creative process of collaborative decision-making and helps make it effective.

The following is our recommendation on when to give each section in this chapter greater consideration:

- **Organizational Structure and Meeting Types:** These should be considered in the getting started phase; however, our recommendation is to not get attached to whatever has been decided at that time. Once the development consultant has been engaged, the organizational and meeting structure, as well as decision-making, may have to be adjusted in order to support an efficient development process.

- **Typical Roles and Responsibilities of Members:** In the early stages when the group is small, this is not as important because everyone can be, and often is, involved in everything. However, once the group has more than ten core members and the project complexity has increased, it becomes crucial to identify key roles and their respective responsibilities.

- **Communication Systems:** This needs to be considered early in the process, but it becomes particularly important as the group grows in number. It is absolutely essential to have an efficient communication system in place during the development and construction phases.

- **Information Management:** Decisions need to be documented, and it is important that there be a way for current members, and new ones, to easily access that information. Once the project has entered the development phase, having a well-organized and easily accessible system for managing information is crucial to ensure members are as informed as possible for the decisions they will need to make.

- **Meeting Management:** Good meetings make for a happy process. When the group is small, it is possible to have good meetings that are informal and somewhat "on the fly." However, when there are ten people or more, care needs to be paid to the agendas and facilitation to ensure the meetings are effective and contribute to community connection.

CDC-Recommended Organizational Structure

As mentioned in Chapter 2, one of the challenges during development is to design an organizational structure that allows for participation by all members yet has communication and decision-making protocols that support efficient and effective development. The CDC-recommended decision-making process is consensus with a voting fallback and is presented in detail in Chapter 5.

In this chapter we focus on describing the organizational structure used in developing the projects that CDC managed. The structure supports members to participate and to connect with each other, while also encouraging clear communication and boundaries and supporting the development process to proceed in a time-efficient manner. In past CDC-managed developments, there were generally only four or five formal meetings a month (workshops, committee meetings, and general meetings). Members would often meet outside of these settings, but the business of the development all happened during those formal meetings.

As soon as a group begins to hold regular meetings, we recommend adopting a clear and transparent organizational structure that describes how members can participate and how decisions are made. To do so, the group needs to have agreed upon their decision-making process so a mechanism is in place to accept and implement the proposed organizational structure.

The flow chart below provides an illustration of the organizational structure that has successfully worked for development for CDC. The lines and arrows in the chart represent how communication flows among relationships during development. CDC organized member groups into three main committees to perform tasks: legal finance, design, and community-building. Each committee could develop sub-committees when there was a need. Members serving as focus people came together periodically to coordinate agendas. This simple structure worked effectively during the development phase. It allows for participation by all members, yet has a communication process that supports efficient and effective development. Over the course of a project, the design committee evolved into a construction progress committee.

Organizational Structure for Cohousing during Development

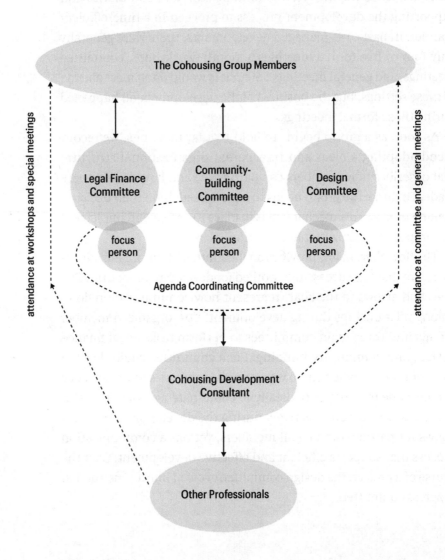

Sociocracy offers an alternate governance system to the one CDC has used so far, and we want readers to be aware of it as an easily accessed resource. Sociocracy includes a complete toolkit for organizing collaborative groups, planning and facilitating meetings, making decisions, selecting people for roles, and evaluating how well everything is working. Extensive resources and support are available through the Sociocracy for All website.

Obviously, CDC's recommended organizational structure has worked well for us, and we think it will work well for new groups in development too. We are aware that some groups have successfully used sociocracy during the development phase; however, we are unsure how to use it in the early forming stages when a group seems too new for the trust in each other that sociocracy requires. When the financial commitment is high, all members typically want to be involved in all the important decisions rather than designating decision-making authority to others. As well, based on the research that we have done, it seems that the time commitment to use sociocracy is much greater than for the organizational and decision-making structure that CDC has managed. One group told us they had held more than 365 meetings in the year before construction start, whereas the average for the CDC-managed projects would be less than a hundred. However, this was with a lot of facilitation and agenda-planning support from the CDC team, which may have accounted for the greater efficiency. CDC has never facilitated a development process using the sociocratic structure, so it is not possible to truly compare.

Meeting Types

For efficient use of members' and professionals' time, CDC's goal was to have as few meetings as possible. The four types of meetings described below are what we recommend for groups developing community led housing.

Committee meetings: Each committee generally gathers once a month in a meeting open to all members of the group. In preparing for and holding the committee meetings, members perform tasks, do research, and prepare information to better facilitate group decisions.

General meetings: The general meetings receive recommendations from each of the committee meetings. They are usually held monthly and are also open to all members. High impact, long-term decisions are made in these meetings and recorded in their minutes.

Workshops and special meetings: Workshops and special meetings are held when it is important to give information to, or gather information from, the whole group. These include a series of design workshops with the architect and other professionals, which are open to all members.

Information meetings: Information meetings can be held as needed to build membership. Their goal is to raise awareness of the project and to provide information to potential new members. Historically, in CDC-managed projects, members played key roles in information meetings, but CDC attended if needed. Some projects also required new members to take a weekend informational workshop such as "Is Cohousing for You?" or "Aging Well in Community." These information meetings and workshops have proven very important parts of outreach and are discussed in Chapter 6.

Typical Roles and Responsibilities of Members

There are many tasks associated with development, and it takes all kinds of skills and talents to build a community. Tasks that have a financial consequence if not completed in a professional or timely manner are best performed by paid professionals. Costs increase when there are delays or problems, and this has an impact on everyone. We recommend creating a clear task structure that focuses on the community-building aspects while giving the group "big picture" control over the project, with professionals performing the majority of the day-to-day activities of managing development.

In CDC's projects, all professionals communicated through the development consultant team, which in turn communicated with the member group at committee and general meetings. Between monthly meetings, communication among professionals and members flowed through the development consultant to the focus members of the committees. Special meetings facilitated direct communication between consultants and the member group for such things as design workshops, information reports, etc. The primary decision-making body was the group as a whole at the general meetings. Some decisions were delegated to the individual and committee levels to facilitate an efficient process. Protocols for delegating decision-making authority are discussed in Chapter 5.

CDC recommends that each committee have at least one "focus person"; often, in past projects, members wanted more and this role was shared by two or three members. Sometimes these positions were filled by volunteers, but because members need to have a high level of trust in the focus members' skills and availability, CDC supported groups to use other selection processes when desired. The tools for decision-making section in Chapter 5 provides examples of processes that can be used to select members for roles.

Together, the focus members make up the agenda-coordinating committee. This committee is responsible for working with the development consultant as needed to prepare agendas for committee and general meetings. We say more about agenda coordinating later in this chapter.

Communication Systems

The communication systems we have used in past projects included a public website for the outreach process discussed in Chapter 6. Each project's public website included a password-protected link to what we called the "private website" or "wiki" that the development consultant team created and maintained during development. We discuss the wiki more in the sections below on information management.

Communication Protocol

As part of accepting the organizational structure we've outlined, groups agree to a communication protocol and email guidelines. The protocol describes how members should address all their questions and concerns to the appropriate focus members. New members can also raise questions with their assigned "buddies." Focus members may turn to the development consultant team to request guidance, if needed, and together decide how to respond to the concern. Most of the time, the focus member responded to the individual one-on-one. However, a member's concern could become an agenda topic for information or discussion in a general meeting if it was considered to be of importance to the whole group.

All communication with the development consultant was required to flow only through the focus members of the three committees. This was important for supporting self-reliance in the member group. The focus members needed to be able to respond to member questions, so this required them to access and understand the information, such as the issued for construction drawings, which would serve them after project completion. CDC was available as a back-up and to explain what they did not understand, but the intention was to support the members to find the information for themselves and to integrate it so they could use it in future when CDC was no longer involved in the project.

As stated in the protocol, the members also agreed "not to communicate directly with the architect, engineers, planner, general contractor, site superintendent, sub-trades, suppliers, governing bodies, or anyone related to the project unless an individual has taken on a specific role for a specific purpose and the communication protocol has been agreed upon ahead of time." The purpose of this part of the protocol was to ensure that communication with all parties associated with the project remained clear and consistent, thus reducing the potential for misunderstanding and conflict. There were, of course, slip-ups. However, with a clear agreement in place, and a general understanding of why it was important, it was simple enough to remind members to use the agreed-upon communication channels.

Some members of past projects complained that the communication system was too rigid and restrictive. We believe, to the contrary, that it supported communication to flow through the channels that best served the project. General meeting decisions reflected the will of the group as a whole, not a particular member's opinion that a professional might have heard if bolder group members could contact them directly. We strongly recommend having boundaries around communication to minimize distracting and unduly influencing the professionals while ensuring that every member has a voice in the development process.

Email Protocol

On the same web hosting platform used for the wiki, the development consultant team created a mailing list that supported mass emails among everyone on the list and "forwarders" for mailing to smaller internal groups such as focus members, committees, or sub-committees.

New members were given access to the private website, and their names and contact information were added to the contact list on the home page. Their email addresses were also added to a members distribution list—for internal electronic communication set up under one address—members@projectname.ca, easily allowing members to send and receive mass emails, and to receive messages from the development consultant team. Other professionals did not have mass email access and communicated instead through the development consultant as shown in the diagram at the beginning of this chapter.

During development, some of the reasons to communicate with everyone between regular meetings include:

- distribution of minutes
- making announcements
- logistics and planning
- providing factual information or clarification
- providing background information and documentation

- distribution of agendas
- distribution of proposals
- invitations to social events
- community-building (borrowing items, ridesharing, etc.)

The email distribution list system supported all members to communicate easily with each other on topics relevant to the group as a whole. Using a single email address, anyone on the distribution list could send a message to the entire group.

Email Communication Guidelines

What could possibly go wrong? Community led housing can generate a great deal of mass email. Without clear communication guidelines, these emails can become overwhelming and divisive. CDC would only work with groups that adopted clear guidelines for use of the distribution list. Such communication guidelines encouraged members to ask, "Does a message *need* to go to everyone on the members email list, or could it be sent to fewer recipients?" The guidelines also pointed out that while email can be a wonderful communication tool, misunderstandings can easily arise if email is used for more than simple, factual information. Therefore, members agreed that email would not be used:

- for resolving interpersonal tensions or providing feedback about behaviour
- for discussions with emotional content (e.g., when someone has strong feelings about an issue)
- for recommending revisions to proposals
- to make decisions
- to discuss complex topics

Not surprisingly, breaches of this agreement did occur, but once the group had committed to the email guidelines, they could see the benefits, and the members generally reminded each other to follow them. Developing the members' skills in communication and conflict resolution went hand in glove with the email guidelines.

Email has played a very important role in every project's development, but it is no substitute for face-to-face meetings. Even video conferencing or an old-fashioned telephone call can be more effective than communication by email. Members were expected to do a *lot* of reading just to keep up with the development process. The volume of information and its technicalities could feel overwhelming to members unless there were other opportunities to highlight in person what was most important, to ask questions, and to receive answers where everyone can hear them.

Information Management

Information that is easy for all members to access is critical to community cohesion and effective decision-making. As well, new members need to be informed about all past decisions before committing to equity membership during development or purchasing a resale home after completion. To meet legal and financial requirements, it is important to keep a paper archive and maintain it after project completion for seven years to meet the requirements of the Canada Revenue Agency. However, we recognize that paper systems are unwieldy and challenging to keep up to date and organized, so we recommend that groups also develop and maintain electronic records.

Tools for Information Management

To help facilitate effective communication during the development phase, CDC provided technical support to set up a private members' website including the following elements, all of which remained available after completion if members wanted to continue to use them:

- **Calendar:** to provide information about upcoming meetings and other events

- **Contact list:** to provide easily accessible contact information for all the members

- **Document storage:** to provide a way to organize information, agendas, minutes of meetings, past decisions, agreements, etc., accessible for all the members

CDC managed a simple wiki calendar, for the various meeting types including workshops. In some projects, a separate calendar was created to which members could post social events. In other projects, members preferred to manage and use other software, such as Slack or Google Calendar, to create and manage activities outside the regular meetings. Harbourside Cohousing continued to use the wiki calendar, adapting it after completion to include guest room bookings and social events as well as meetings.

The wiki contact list included the household members' names, phone numbers, mailing addresses, and email addresses. The lists grew organically, providing an informal record of the order in which households joined a project. The development consultants managed the calendar and contact lists throughout the development process, but also trained members of a "wiki team" to take over as the project completed.

Document Storage

For the projects that were completed after 2005, the development consultant team used PmWiki to create and maintain a private website. There are other document storage systems, but PmWiki has some advantageous features which made it ideal for the development phase.[1]

Starting with a carefully structured table of contents, the private website could grow along with the project to contain all the information that members needed. As new members joined, they were given access to the private website and instructed in its use. Clicking on the linked text below the headings—for example, clicking "Appliances" under "Design and Development"—gave access to detailed information. After move-in, members could choose to adapt the same structure to support their completed community or simply use the wiki as a development archive. Collaborative decision-making relies on participants being well-informed, and the wiki made that possible.

It was easy to direct members to read particular files by linking them in email messages to the whole group or a subgroup, and files in the wiki could be linked directly to meeting agendas.

CDC kept the private website as up to date and clear as possible. The wiki also served as an archive, but this did not mean keeping every document ever posted! Information could be posted to support discussions and decision-making, then replaced with the decision. Earlier information was often edited or removed to make way for final versions of designs, decisions, and agreements. This minimized confusion and supported easy navigation. Updating the wiki also made it clearer what choices or options were still available to members.

The private website allowed easy access to very large files, including architectural drawings and design workshop presentations that would have been challenging to send as email attachments. Through the wiki, members could watch videos external to or posted on the site, including drone images used to determine unit desirability or videos of construction progress.[2] They could link to suppliers' websites or PDFs to compare, for example, kitchen appliance packages.

The wiki also made it easy to include textual information with basic formatting. The text on the appliance sample wiki page, for example, was edited many times as the project responded to global supply chain delays for the refrigerators due to the Covid-19 pandemic.

The benefits of a wiki:

* The sharing and storing of large files are more possible in a wiki.

* The wiki has the ability to include text in the document management system—if you think of such a system like a digital filing cabinet, the wiki is what allows you to add sticky notes to different files or folders.

Special care was taken with financial information. None of a project's monthly financial statements, bank statements, and invoices were ever posted to the wiki. Instead, a soft copy was emailed directly to the members who had asked to receive them and a hard copy provided for the company records. Financial statements were presented at the monthly legal finance meetings with the development consultant, which were open to all members.

Information Management Protocols

As will be obvious by now, document storage for project development requires making many decisions about how to manage information—what information is shared with whom, by what medium, in what format, when, and for how long? Someone must expertly manage flows of information to develop housing in a way that meets both members' needs and those of the professionals while keeping the project moving forward and staying on budget. The expertise, time, and effort required for this is substantial—typically more than what could reasonably be expected of a volunteer.

A key to success, in our experience, is giving information to members that clearly presents their options and supports them to make well-informed decisions. Managing information can encourage members to look at choice points in terms of what is best for the group (rather than for individuals). Organizing information in a particular way can support a smoother process in a member meeting. For example, in past projects, when supporting the members to create a task group, only the most relevant background was included, along with a clear mandate identifying who was in the task group and what they were expected to do, a reminder of specific design constraints, and a timeline. When the project was close to completion, CDC prepared task timelines, which are discussed in more detail in Chapter 13.

A monthly project update was another way that CDC managed information with each group under development. This was circulated with the meeting agendas and then presented in the general meeting. Each project update consolidated information received by the project professionals during the month between meetings and presented it concisely, emphasizing anything that required a decision from the group.

Clarity and concision should also be prioritized when giving information to the project professionals. Most of the time, the only contact professionals have with the member group is through the direction that the development consultant relays to the architect, who then communicates with the other design professionals as required, so this information must be crystal clear.

Meeting Management

Initially, the CDC team provided leadership and did most of the agenda coordination. Over time, members gradually took on more responsibility and did more of the work. Monthly meetings during the development process provided members with lots of experience! The focus members from all three committees—community-building, design, and legal finance—worked closely with the development consultant team to plan the monthly committee meeting agendas and identify the items needing discussion or decisions at the general meetings.

CDC offered mini-workshops to support interested members to develop their skills in agenda planning, facilitation, and communication. CDC also encouraged the members to engage professionals to provide workshops that would enhance their skills in these areas. In some groups, skilled members themselves can offer this kind of training. As the project nears completion, the goal is for the members to be fully planning agendas, conducting and facilitating meetings, and keeping accurate minutes without outside support.

Agendas

What follows is the agenda-planning process that supported CDC to organize the formal meetings each month for as many as four projects at a time.

Members who were not focus members but who wanted to include items on the agenda for a committee meeting needed to email the applicable committee focus member a minimum of ten days before a scheduled meeting to request that an item be included. Some groups created a Google Doc or Word template that members could use to submit agenda requests. This typically would include the name of the person making the request, date, topic, background information, who will be presenting, suggested length of time, and purpose (announcement, report, discussion, or decision).

The agenda coordinator (CDC until near project completion) emailed draft agendas to the focus members one week before scheduled meetings to get their feedback. Focus members were responsible for responding within two days of the draft agendas being sent to them. If they did not respond, the agenda coordinator would assume the agenda was approved as presented. The agendas were then distributed to the general membership a minimum of three days before a meeting was scheduled to take place.

The agenda coordinator attempted to estimate the amount of time that each agenda item would take. If there were too many items to be appropriately discussed at the meeting, the agenda coordinator might recommend postponing lower priority items to a future meeting and/or changing the amount of time allotted for each item.

The following information was typically included on each agenda:

- date and time of the meeting

- meeting location and/or link to the virtual meeting platform

- names of the members acting as facilitator and minute-taker

- check-in

- role selection for the next meeting (facilitator and minute-taker)

- approval of minutes from the previous meeting (if applicable)

- item number, topic, number of minutes allocated to the topic, start and end time for each topic, some minimal background information about the topic with a link to other information posted on the private website if applicable, and the purpose of the topic (whether it was an announcement, report, an item for discussion, or proposal for decision)

- the draft wording of a motion, if the topic was intended for decision

- a break if the meeting would be longer than two hours

- meeting evaluation

- check-out

Proposals coming to the general meeting for decision would have been discussed in the applicable committee meetings beforehand. If the topic were considered to be high impact and/or long term, then the initial discussion would be brought to the community at a general meeting to gather input before proceeding to proposal development. The process is discussed in more detail in Chapter 5 on decision-making.

The agendas for the groups under development included as much supporting material as the development consultant team and focus members thought made sense. Some information appeared as notes below the agenda while other information was hyperlinked. Information was carefully organized in the agendas to flow from community-building, legal finance, and design committees to the general meeting where the decisions were made.

The following is a member's comments after an agenda-planning workshop on July 28, 2014:

> We had fun, and learned a lot with [expert trainer of collaborative groups] Kavana Tree Bressen's agenda planning exercise. Some of the learning for me is that:

- Sometimes big picture items, like revising the community's vision statement, do belong on an agenda for a meeting that the whole community attends if the goal is to draw out the range of opinion on what's important to include.

- Decisions about aesthetics generally need a vote by household—e.g., floor tile choice, can we agree to have a base set of appliances from a single supplier?

- Focus on the goal of each agenda item. Clarify with presenter? Send it back to committee? Get a decision.

Facilitation

The meeting facilitator is responsible for guiding the meeting through the agenda in the allotted time. Their job is to help keep the discussion on topic, monitor the time, ensure participants have equal opportunity to speak, provide appropriate focus when necessary, attempt to summarize and organize the ideas expressed, and lead the group to the decision mode when required. When a decision is expected, the facilitator supports it to happen by the agreed-upon process. A more detailed description of what is involved in facilitation is included on Kavana Tree Bressen's website Effective Collective; we also recommend facilitation materials available from Laird Schaub's blog, *Community and Consensus*.[3] Facilitation training can be very beneficial for groups during and after development. And because more than one person may share this role, there is ample opportunity to exercise the skills learned!

Facilitators do not "chair" the meetings. It is crucial that facilitators and groups understand the facilitator is a "servant of the group" who sets aside personal opinions to provide neutral leadership of the meeting. The facilitator deserves the group's cooperation and respect. In turn, the facilitator needs to listen well, summarize effectively, and be agreement-oriented. A facilitator may delegate some of the pieces associated with this role to others if desired. For example, time-keeping responsibilities could easily be delegated to another member, as could those of room set-up and "keeper of the stack" of people wanting to speak.

During development, the number and length of meetings can be tiring for everyone—members *and* professionals. Varying meeting formats can lighten the mood, deepen the connections, or simply change the pace a bit to help keep participants engaged. CDC encourages members to try out a variety of meeting formats.

Kinesthetic mapping is one example of a method groups can use in meetings to reduce the amount of time it takes to gauge the interest of members for issues that have a natural continuum of opinion. What the facilitator, and the group, do with the information gleaned from such mapping varies, but the process uses steps similar to the following example:

> Lay out a spectrum in the room, e.g., "Everyone who thinks our work requirement should be one hour stand at this end of the room, ten hours stand at the other end, and arrange yourselves accordingly in the middle." Once everyone is standing in place, a variation is to then fold the line at the halfway point, pairing up the two people at the extreme ends and so on down the line (until the middle people are paired with each other) and then ask the partners to have a short conversation about why they feel the way they do.

Deciding what formats to use was part of meeting preparation, as CDC worked with the agenda committee and facilitators to decide "how to have the conversations." This included being very clear about the purpose of the item: Was it for discussion or a decision? Was it to gather the broad range of views on a topic or to narrow differences and move towards consensus about an outcome? Did the facilitator need to follow up with a presenter to clarify the item?

If the meeting was in person, attention needed to be paid to setting up the room, preparing flip charts, etc. If it was online, the facilitators prepared any polls and set up breakout rooms ahead of time. The wording for any prepared motions was put on a flip chart or made ready to paste into the chat and sent to the minute-taker before the meeting started.

Facilitators learned that a good meeting is orderly but not quiet. A wide range of members speak. All can be heard, but not everyone will get their way. The facilitator works with the group to keep the meeting agreement-oriented—in other words, attendees and the facilitators try to work together towards decisions everyone can support.

We discuss this process more in Chapter 5 on decision-making, but for now the point is this: Facilitators play key roles in how a meeting runs, but they are only part of the dance. Each member is responsible for ensuring that they are adequately prepared and familiar with the information to be discussed at the meeting. All members share the responsibility for the facilitator's duties outlined above and should remain aware of their own parts.

Minutes

Minutes are a record of a group's important decisions and are essential for conveying information to new members. However, it is often difficult to find volunteers to take minutes because it can be a stressful and time-consuming task. Therefore, CDC set up a format and process for minute-taking that would be as efficient and effective as possible, taking minutes for only two monthly meetings and recording only essential information.

Members filled the roles of minute-takers for the community-building and general meetings in the groups with whom CDC worked. No minutes were taken for design or legal finance committee meetings; items from those meetings that required a decision always came to the general meeting for decision by the membership as a whole. Members who took on tasks for these committees were expected to keep track of the information themselves. The general meeting minutes were especially important as they became the corporate records of the group's development company.

A key difference with some other ways of taking minutes was that the minute-taking protocol asked for no attribution of comments to individuals. Minute-takers were to record only an overview of any discussion in order to capture what was essential for understanding the meeting outcomes. They were not to write down in the minutes "who said what to whom" in a discussion. Nor were they to try to transcribe exactly what was said.

This minimalism was not part of CDC's early minute-taking protocols, but we believe that in community led housing development, as in life, it is beneficial to be flexible and stay curious about learning from others, including group members. The Wolf Willow

Cohousing group had agreed to "no attribution" in their minutes before contracting with CDC. One member had found it worked well in a previous organization. She advocated successfully for it at Wolf Willow where members agreed it was very valuable for smoothing the minute approval process. With no names attached, members were less inclined to reframe, justify, or correct anything recorded in the minutes regarding a discussion. CDC saw how well this worked and incorporated it into the minute-taking protocol for all subsequent projects.

Some members who were experienced in taking more detailed minutes found "no attribution" challenging. Although the reason CDC adopted "no attribution" was to streamline acceptance of minutes, the effect of this requirement supported groups in other ways. No attribution supported members to let go of interpersonal disagreements and memories of stormy meetings. It also kept the focus on the group and its consensus decisions rather than drawing attention to individuals, while also encouraging succinct minutes.

Early in each community-building and general meeting, the facilitator would call for volunteers to facilitate and take minutes at the next month's meetings. Some groups identified a back-up minute-taker to apprentice with or to assist the main minute-taker. A member of the CDC team shadowed the minute-takers in the early days because accurate minutes were an extremely important record of the group's decisions.

The member volunteer's job during development was to prepare a clear and accurate account of the business transacted at the meeting. They sent their draft meeting minutes to CDC for review. The edited version was sent back to the minute-taker for approval. CDC then posted the minutes to the wiki and notified the members by group email. At the beginning of the next month's meetings, any corrections or additions were noted before the minutes were approved. The original minutes were not changed and remained as posted. New members reading minutes from past meetings were reminded to check the subsequent month's minutes for any corrections. Decisions were extracted and added each month to a wiki file called "Decisions to Date."

Organizational Structure and Change

The organizational structure we have described has served groups well during the development process. It was designed to be dynamic, responding to the needs of each group and each project over time, while following the three-committee structure and communication process we have outlined in this chapter. For example, at construction start in each project, the design committee would cease to meet as the series of design workshops wrapped up and the design process completed. Instead, monthly construction progress meetings would begin. Construction focus members were selected to attend these meetings, which were ideally on site and in person (though they sometimes were, by necessity, virtual). Construction focus members were authorized to liaise with the site superintendent and construction manager to coordinate any site tours.

In preparation for the end of the development process, when the legal structure shifted to strata (condominium) title, CDC worked with members to create the organizational structure that would serve the community after move-in. We will talk about preparing for living in the community in Chapter 13.

5

Decision-Making

"Ironically, many cohousing groups wishing to promote community and the common good choose unanimous voting (wrongly called 'consensus') for most of their membership decisions and inflict upon themselves many of the worst aspects of individualism... True consensus is the most inclusive form of decision-making. Unlike unanimity, it is the group that decides whether to honour an individual dissenter."

TOM MOENCH, quoted in *The Cohousing Handbook*

How CDC Approaches Collaborative Decision-Making

To set the tone for this chapter, we chose five "Group Works" cards: "Good Faith Assumptions," "Embrace Dissonance and Difference," "Common Ground," "Trust the Wisdom of the Group," and "Letting Go." They come from a deck that Kavana Tree Bressen and others developed to express the shared wisdom underlying successful approaches to group process.[1] We chose these particular cards because, for collaborative decision-making in a development that has a goal of creating community, good intentions on the part of all group members is assumed. We expect them to embody the same good intentions with each other and with the professionals. We teach groups a consensus process that embraces dissonance and difference to gather the full range of views in the room; convergence then becomes possible as people find common ground. This process encourages trusting the wisdom of the group as it manifests in decisions everyone can live with. Finally, perhaps most important is for people to let go of their own positions in favour of what seems best for the group, and to accept the outcome.

Non-hierarchical decision-making is often cited as a feature of community led housing. This fits well with other features, particularly an emphasis on non-hierarchical member participation and self-management. In CDC's approach, all members can participate equally in a group's process of finding solutions that generate as much agreement as possible while also supporting the efficiency that is crucial during the development phase. The "normal decision-making process" for the groups with whom we worked is the structured form of consensus decision-making we will describe in this chapter along with an alternative decision-making rule for specific circumstances.

Any consensus process requires commitment and a willingness to dance to a tune unfamiliar to most of us. The cooperative culture of using a consensus approach runs counter to the winner takes all, majority rule decision-making structure of mainstream Western culture, and so it can be hard to learn. The gradual development of each group over a period of years gives members time and a supportive environment in which to learn how to facilitate and participate in well-grounded, clearly structured consensus processes (much different to the loose, undefined process that many suppose consensus to be). Support from the professionals involved in the project creates a cadre of members with enough facilitation experience to support a clear consensus decision-making process after move-in. *Clear*, however, does not mean *rigid*. During a project's development, members often adapt the consensus process and make it their own. After move-in, their governance structure may continue to evolve. Expert consensus facilitation trainers C.T. Butler and Amy Rothstein emphasize that formal consensus "must be defined by the group using it."

Above all, formal consensus must be taught. It is unreasonable to expect people to be familiar with this process already. In general, cooperative non-violent conflict resolution does not exist in modern North American society. These skills must be developed in what is primarily a competitive environment. Only time will tell if, in fact, this model will flourish and prove itself effective and worthwhile.

We are now convinced more than ever that the model presented in this book is profoundly significant for the future of our species. We must learn to live together cooperatively, resolving our conflicts non-violently and making our decisions consensually. We must learn to value diversity and respect all life, not just on a physical level but emotionally, intellectually, and spiritually. We are all in this together.[2]

One of the first steps that a collaborative group needs to take is to decide how to make decisions. This should be considered in the getting started phase. As noted in Chapter 4, our recommendation is to not get attached at that stage since there may be a need to adjust the process to accommodate the requirements of the professionals that are engaged to support an efficient development process. However, it will still be important to have had these discussions and a rationale for why a particular decision-making method is preferred. This chapter gives an overview of consensus decision-making because that is the method that CDC used with the groups with whom we worked.

Deciding How to Decide

In our experience, the main reason for using consensus decision-making in community led housing development is to build community connection. Paradoxically, a certain amount of community connection, or at least trust, is also a prerequisite for consensus. The founding members need to build enough trust and shared vision to take the first step of agreeing how they will make decisions. Alternatively, the founding group needs to trust the professionals and the decision-making method that they recommend to facilitate an efficient development process. Either way, a new group must agree how it will make decisions before it can accomplish anything else. A list of resources for collaborative decision-making can be found at CohousingConsulting.ca.

Why Not Conventional Meetings?

How people feel about the decisions they are making is impacted by the type of decision-making process they choose. Since 1870, Robert's Rules of Order have supported well-organized meetings on levels ranging from parliaments to hobby clubs. Like a consensus process, Robert's Rules were intended to restrain individuals in order to hear everyone's opinions and identify the will of the group efficiently. In recent years the US Congress may not seem a paragon of efficient or effective decision-making, but faced with leading a church meeting in 1863, Henry Robert saw in Congress a model from which to borrow. He wanted a standard parliamentary procedure his group could follow to reach decisions efficiently by majority rule without having to resolve disagreements. He ended up writing a manual that has sold millions of copies, predominates in the US, and is widely used in the English-speaking world.

Why don't we recommend using Robert's Rules in these meetings? First, as many video clips of the US Congress and Canada's parliament illustrate, Robert's Rules are often not an effective way to handle disagreements if you want to have good working relationships among the members; they often appear to foster adversarial rather than collaborative approaches. Second, the preference for simple majority voting encourages moving on from challenging issues rather than resolving and moving through them together. In the voting alternative process we recommend, which is discussed later in this chapter, majority voting is effective when the group agrees that just making a decision is preferable to spending more time or money on a topic. But as a decision process regularly employed, majority rule supports polarization, lobbying, and oversimplification; it can produce a disaffected minority looking for ways to win the next vote or the next election. Within this matrix of politics as usual, we believe it is important to educate members about another way to run meetings: a way that combines clear agendas, skilled facilitation, and consensus decision-making.

Finally, although Robert's Rules are widely used, they are not widely understood. The devil is in the details, and the details are many! Ironically, a set of rules designed to level the playing field of meetings and standardize process ends up favouring insider knowledge about the rules of the complicated parliamentary procedure game. Members often suggest their group should adopt Robert's Rules because they want a more efficient, orderly decision-making process, but we don't favour this. Even some lawyers advise against using Robert's Rules for non-profits, because misuse of these rules can create the very chaos that they were intended to avoid:

> Adherence to Robert's Rules can also lead to an uneven balance of power if certain members are more informed of the rules than others. A self-proclaimed parliamentarian may use their procedural prowess to steer decision-making in one way or another.[3]

While we recommend against wholesale adoption of Robert's Rules, we do recommend that groups use some features of them, and the groups we have worked with sometimes appear to be following Robert's Rules: They have formal agendas, but without many of the standard items—e.g., old business, new business—of parliamentary procedure such as tabled or amended motions. Attendance is recorded but not "regrets" because the consensus process assumes people will attend or find another way to participate if they care about the issues on the agenda. If they are unable to attend, they will trust the group wisdom. Minutes are as important in this structure as they are under Robert's Rules. But, as described in the previous chapter, we recommend handling changes to the minutes differently. Groups often do adopt clear proposals that are moved, seconded, and minuted so they conform to the expectations of the development company, strata/condominium, or whatever legal structure the group has adopted.

A professional consultant can support the group to clearly understand, define, and commit to its decision-making agreements early in the development process. Ultimately, we believe that the decision-making process chosen matters less than how well the group functions as a decision-making body and how new members are included in that process.

Why Use a Consensus Approach?

Although groups in their earliest days often commit to using consensus, what that means is seldom clearly spelled out or understood, partly because it is normal for new groups to operate informally. The following two definitions of consensus are ones that we find useful:

> "Consensus decision-making is a cooperative process in which a group of members develop and agree to support a decision that is in the best interest of the whole." —Kavana Tree Bressen[4]

> "Consensus is a group decision—that some members may not feel is the best decision but which they can all live with, support and commit themselves to not undermine—arrived at without voting,

through a process whereby the issues are fully aired, all members feel that they have been adequately heard, in which everyone has equal power and responsibility, where different degrees of influence by virtue of individual stubbornness or charisma are avoided, so that all are satisfied with the process. [It] requires the members to be emotionally present and engaged; frank in a loving, mutually respectful manner; sensitive to each other; to be selfless, dispassionate and capable of emptying themselves; and possessing a paradoxical awareness of both people and time, including knowing when the solution is satisfactory, and that it is time to stop and not re-open the discussion until such time that the group determines a need for revision."—M. Scott Peck[5]

A consensus is general agreement about an issue within a group. People working together to reach as much agreement as possible is a collaborative, agreement-oriented process. They may use consensus, a vote, or some other means to make the actual decision. As Tim Hartnett writes, "A consensus-oriented process can be used in conjunction with any type of final decision rule."[6] CDC supported new groups to make full use of a consensus process but not to rely entirely on consensus for all decision-making.

Shared Principles

There are many different opinions about what makes a good consensus process and what the "true" definition of consensus is, but one shared belief is this: A good consensus process ensures that everyone who wants to participate can contribute their ideas. Kavana Tree Bressen has many useful handouts about consensus on her website, Effective Collective.

Here are some basic principles that were important in our process work with groups:

- Consensus gathers experience from everyone in the belief that the wisdom and creativity of the group will yield better proposals for the group as a whole than those developed by a few individuals. For this to work, participants must educate themselves and be well prepared.

- The process is agreement-oriented—wanting to work together towards decisions everyone can support. Being open minded, and holding a position lightly, supports achieving consensus.

- Because everyone has the chance to develop the solution, in relationship with each other, the resulting decision will need less enforcement. "Buy in" happens before the decision is made.

- The relationships themselves back the agreement. In turn, such agreements strengthen the relationships. Communication of ideas and feelings and empathetic listening build communication skills among members.

- Documenting all decisions (e.g., in minutes) provides a cumulative record of a group's agreements.

Relationship-building *is* community-building. Members of a new group learn and grow through the consensus processes that are routinely followed yet always unique. People are encouraged to speak what is on their minds and in their hearts, to be authentic. Members learn how to communicate more effectively so they can articulate their wishes, be heard, and also listen. Group leadership often becomes more shared. In M. Scott Peck's sense, there is often a "flow of leadership" and a community may become "a group of all leaders," each with a piece of the collective wisdom and a task to do.[7]

Differences

Ironically, there is no consensus on what consensus means. Confusion arises when people to whom consensus means different things try to have a conversation. Experienced consensus facilitator Tim Hartnett has written about different ideological camps and the difference between *consensus* and *unanimity* and *consent*. We have created the following table to summarize the three camps as described in his article.[8]

	Camp One: Unanimity	Camp Two: Consent	Camp Three: Process, Not Outcome
Uses a consensus-building process before presenting for decision	Yes	Yes	Yes
Every individual's concerns need to be addressed before a decision is approved	Yes	No	No
The good of the group is primary; it's not as important for an individual's concerns to have been addressed, but everyone must consent to it before a decision is approved	No	Yes	No
As long as a consensus-building process has been used, everyone does not have to agree to the decision for it to be approved	No	No	Yes

For the development phase, the groups with whom CDC worked agreed to use a consensus-building process (Camp Three), not outcome, with a voting alternative for some situations. Detailed definitions for decision-making during development were included as a schedule in the shareholder agreements for each group's development company.

Phases of Consensus Decision-Making

Consensus-Building Process

Consensus building followed by consensus decision-making was the normal process in CDC's project development. An inclusive, collaborative process was "business as usual." CDC's goal was to ensure that everyone could participate in such consensus-building processes if they wanted to and if they could do so within the time available. "Everyone" included the earliest founding members, the latest members to join, and everyone in between. Why? The logic of this inclusivity is that in a well-facilitated meeting each person can add to the group wisdom in making a consensus decision, and that doing so builds community.

Of course, the road to achieving consensus can be bumpy, but conflict is a chance to be authentic with each other, learn, and grow. A common lament (often accompanied by an expletive!) in a development process that uses consensus is "Great, another 'opportunity for growth'!" C.T. Butler and Amy Rothstein put this more positively:

> Conflict is usually viewed as an impediment to reaching agreements and disruptive to peaceful relationships. However... non-violent conflict is necessary and desirable. It provides the *motivations* for improvement... Do not avoid or repress conflict. Create an environment in which disagreement can be expressed without fear. Objections and criticisms can be heard not as attacks, not as attempts to defeat a proposal, but as a concern which, when resolved, will make the proposal stronger.[9]

How does the inclusive process work during development? Three features of the process encourage its success: facilitation, organizational structure, and the use of coloured cards.

Facilitation: First, the facilitation process described in the previous chapter supports members to express and hear divergent opinions. Guidelines for behaviour in community meetings encourage civility. Mutual respect grows as people spend more time together, even virtually. For example, during the Covid-19 lockdowns and earlier in groups with many distant members, Google Docs and Zoom were helpful tools. One group held regular "explorer sessions" where members could freely discuss the gamut of concerns and desires without CDC or other professionals in attendance. Results from such sessions might be brought to a committee meeting for further discussion.

Organizational structure: A second support for the consensus-building process comes from the organizational structure recommended in Chapter 4 for each project. This structure channels needs and ideas through focus members to the committee meetings where they are discussed and, as appropriate, proposals are developed for decision at a general meeting. Decisions made at general meetings are recorded and the information is passed on to the professionals when appropriate. Communication from the professionals is delivered through a point person to the focus members, who in turn communicate with the group as a whole. The process is orderly, transparent, and easy to understand. In projects CDC has helped facilitate, CDC has been the "point person" or main conduit for communication between professionals and the group, but this could be a member or small group of members. The important thing is to manage communication with the professional team so that it is streamlined, consistent, represents the will of the group, and keeps everyone informed. This is what contributes to a cost- and time-effective development process.

Coloured cards: Finally, the use of coloured cards also supports the consensus-building process during the development phase. Cards are used to encourage broad and effective participation in discussions while supporting speakers to stay on topic and allowing the group to express its needs and wishes (e.g., for a break) as they are raised (as in a silent auction) by members during the course of discussion or presentation. An example of a definition for the use of the cards is included in Appendix C. In CDC-facilitated projects, we encouraged each group to make its own cards—an excellent community-building opportunity! Members might gather in a someone's house to cut out coloured paper and print instructions, laminate them, then assemble the cards on key rings. Each group's homemade cards were similar but unique, and some card sets evolved both in design and content.

COLOURED CARD VARIATIONS

Design changes to the cards included varying the size and how they were made. One version of the cards slid onto a conventional key ring. Another group used hinged key rings which were easier to load but sometimes failed mid-meeting, spilling cards on the floor. During the pandemic, five years after move-in at Harbourside, the group adopted one member's innovation, which reduced the cards' bulk by placing all the information and colours on a single five-by-seven-inch laminated card. These cards were far easier to sanitize and store, but some users missed the fun of fidgeting with the cards on a ring!

Some changes were more substantive. For example, Harbourside removed the red cards entirely. Instead, they used the blue card for decision-making, believing that it was less likely to result in an inappropriate block. They found that worked for them. Harbourside's neighbour, West Wind Harbour, adopted the same card system during their development, as did Ravens Crossing Cohousing.

While group members invested a lot of care in their versions of the consensus cards, from CDC's perspective the choice of method was less important than ensuring the method was a clear, well-understood decision-making process that supported community connection. Some groups prefer to use a method of raising hands, or showing a certain number of fingers, believing this is friendlier for dissenting voices. Dot voting may be preferred for some kinds of choices, such as decisions about interior finishes. Dot voting, also known as *dotmocracy*, is a simple way to identify preferences with sticky dots or markers by placing them next to the preferred option in a list or on a ballot. When groups had to learn to make consensus decisions remotely, polls proved to be good enough. Our point is simple: Whether decisions are made using cards, fingers, or dots, all that really matters is that there is a clear and agreed-upon mechanism.

In the groups with whom we worked, members were expected to learn how to use the cards. An overview of the use of the cards was provided at the beginning of meetings that new members attended. Each topic could find its own rhythm, with facilitated use of the cards and good preparation. The topics deemed most urgent and/or simplest tend to move most quickly from the information-gathering step to preparing a concrete proposal for decision. Sometimes a potential, nonessential topic would attract little or no interest and never became a proposal. Sometimes there was no way to meet the need within the current budget, or the members did not think it was a high enough priority, or perhaps there was insufficient energy at the time to address it. For whatever reason, in any development process while some needs are rejected by consensus, others are simply set aside, often with the members' intention of revisiting them sometime in the future.

The following diagram provides a brief overview of CDC's recommended process of consensus building, elaborated on in more detail below. It is simpler than what other consensus experts recommend, including some we have cited in this chapter. In practice, we sometimes added more steps, and groups may want to expand this process after completion when decisions are not typically as financially impactful and therefore not as time sensitive.

We tried to keep the process inclusive yet simple because efficiency is crucial to successful project development. Time is, of course, money.

The committees are central to the consensus-building process during the development phase. In the projects we've been a part of, members facilitated monthly committee meetings with support from CDC and used the toolbox of meeting formats to gather members' opinions and preferences. We encouraged members who cared about any agenda topics to attend the committee meeting where the item would be discussed. That was where discussions took place that influenced the direction of the decisions made in each month's general meeting. Members sometimes volunteered, or were asked, to gather more information and take on tasks between monthly meetings.

Consensus-Building Process

Step 1: Forming the Proposal Process / Gathering Ideas
Once a need has been identified, work together to
identify the criteria for a policy and solicit ideas from the members.

Step 2: Preparing the Proposal / Distillation
Attempt to find a solution that includes as much of the ideas that have
been gathered as possible, recognizing that perfection is not achievable!

Step 3: Testing for Consensus / Making the Decision
Bring the proposal to a first meeting to "test for consensus,"
and respond to questions. A decision may or may not be
possible after this first test for consensus.

Step 1: Forming the Proposal Process / Gathering Ideas

The first step in our recommended consensus-building process is to seek a broad range of views on the identified need or issue. This is a divergent, creative phase seeking input from as many participants as possible. Many "needs" are routine steps that CDC identifies in any development process, for example, drafting a pet policy or narrowing the range of unit interior paint colours or agreeing that receipt of the occupancy permit would trigger closing requirements. Some needs are identified by professionals—design changes required for cost-effective constructability, for example. Many needs are anticipated, but there are always surprises, things that could not have been foreseen during the design process. In our experience, although a decision in a general meeting was not always possible in a fast-paced development process, finding solutions always involved collaboration.

The following provides more detail about how the process typically works:

- The person or committee bringing forward the item identifies a problem that needs to be solved or an issue that may need to be addressed and includes that item on the agenda. Example: We have agreed that we are going to allow pets in our community, and in order to ensure as much harmony as possible when living together, we want to identify clear guidelines and expectations.

- The purpose of the meeting is to identify what factors need to be addressed and the next steps required to facilitate a decision.

- The next steps should identify the working group and main contact, whether additional meetings will be scheduled to solicit ideas for solutions, and when the proposal is expected to come forward for initial testing of consensus. The purpose of the working group is to create a proposal that *best* addresses the factors that have been identified, knowing that *perfection is not possible*!

Step 2: Preparing the Proposal / Distillation

Once the proposal is broadly formed, a distillation process begins, undertaken by members who volunteer (or are selected) to prepare a proposal that they believe is likely to gain everyone's support. Not all ideas can be included and some may be mutually exclusive—I want a gas barbeque on my deck versus I don't want any gas on the property, for example. The goal is to craft a proposal that is likely to achieve consensus as an idea that is, to borrow language from sociocracy, "good enough for now" or "safe enough to try" when it comes to a general meeting for a decision.

Step 3: Testing for Consensus / Making the Decision

The committee meeting can test to see if a proposal is ready to come for a decision to a general meeting. The test can be as simple as a show of hands, but to get more of a sense of where members stand, facilitators will often use a technique such as kinesthetic mapping or dot voting. Testing for consensus can highlight how to modify the proposal to build more agreement. This can sometimes happen on the spot, or the task group may be asked to revise and bring it back to a future meeting. If all goes well, this testing process can feel like a decision, so unless the committee has been given authority to make the decision, it will be important to remind everyone in the committee that the primary decision-making body remains the group as a whole at the general meetings.

Normal Decision Process

In the CDC-managed development process, general meetings tend to have the biggest turnout, and this is where everyone expects decisions to be made. Members know that they need to show up for their views to count. There are no proxies, and members agree to accept all decisions the group makes, including those made in their absence or those that were made before they joined.

Consensus is the "Normal Decision Process" recommended during development. Everyone can participate in it, including the newest members and each member of a household. Typically, a proposal comes for a decision at a general meeting only after the discussion process at the committee level is complete. This typically will have included a test to see if the proposal is ready to come to a general meeting for a decision.

The following is the Normal Decision Process definition from the Shareholder Agreement:

> The Normal Decision Process is the agreed to method used for decision-making. A decision is reached when all Shareholders present at a meeting with quorum agree that a motion (either written or verbal), with modifications as required, is either acceptable to them or they stand aside and agree not to impede implementation. If agreement cannot be reached, the Voting Alternative Process applies.

At a general meeting if there is support for the decision when the call for consensus is made, the proposal passes. If concerns are raised, then the group works together to find a way to address them, which may mean coming back to another meeting with a revised proposal.

How does this work in practice? The facilitator of a decision in the general meeting usually calls first for any concerns. This is a reprise of the discussion stage at the committee meeting to see if the agreement reached in the "test" stage still holds. To identify serious opposition to the proposal, a facilitator would first ask, "Does anyone want to stand in the way?" As noted in the definition for the use of the cards included in Appendix C, a member may choose to stand in the way and raise a red (or blue) card if they believe the proposal violates the group's principles and stated objective in some way. If there are one or more members who have this level of concern, the facilitator will start by ensuring that all concerns are clearly understood before attempting to facilitate potential solutions.

If there are no members who want to stand in the way, or if a solution has been arrived at that is supported by the members who had showed red (or blue) cards, the facilitator calls next for yellow cards to see if there are any unaddressed concerns. Most will have been heard and addressed earlier. *Addressed* does not mean a concern becomes part of the final proposal but rather that expression of the concern contributes to the consensus-building process. A few new points may be raised as yellow cards in the general meeting. Some may be tweaks to improve the proposal, perhaps attending to an overlooked detail. Yellow card concerns are recorded. Then the facilitator calls for attendees to show their approval by raising green cards. There is no need to count green cards, but the affirmation they give is important for community-building. If there are no red (or blue) cards shown, the decision is approved.

Yellow cards in a general meeting may simply reflect someone's desire to have their concerns recorded in the minutes, perhaps anticipating a future moment when they can say, "I told you so! I didn't think this was the best decision because..." Furthermore, having concerns recorded can support members to let go, a crucial skill in a consensus process. During development, CDC encourages members to let go of their positions once a decision is made. Letting go, as is indicated on the Group Works card noted at the start of this chapter, supports people to release their preconceived notions, their ego, and their fears. For example, a group member who stood aside on a decision to have all windows be triple glazed said after the project was completed how happy he was that the group made that decision. Though the triple glazed windows were a greater investment at the outset, they not only saved energy, they also greatly reduced the street noise in his home.

How many yellow cards are too many for a proposal to pass by consensus? Groups often ask this question, forgetting that a yellow card signifies *only a concern, not opposition* to the proposal. Those who show yellow cards stand aside, they don't stand in the way, so there can be no magic number signifying "too many." In theory, there could be consensus amidst a sea of yellow cards; in practice, a lot of yellow cards in a general meeting suggests that the proposal still needs some refinement. If the decision is not time sensitive, it may be worthwhile to continue discussions to address the concerns and bring it back for decision at a second meeting.

If consensus is not reached in a second meeting, a decision is required at the third one. There, the voting alternative process described below is used if consensus still proves elusive.

Decision Process

Decision—First Meeting

Coloured cards are used to facilitate the decision-making process. A decision is considered passed by consensus if there are no red (or blue) cards shown. If the proposal or motion is a required decision, and if it does not pass by consensus, then it immediately goes to a voting fallback as described in the definitions for decision-making during development in the shareholder agreement. If the proposal is not a required decision, and if it does not pass by consensus, it will come back to a second meeting.

Decision—Second Meeting

If the proposal does not pass by consensus, it will come back to a third meeting.

Decision—Third Meeting

If the proposal does not pass by consensus for a third time, it immediately goes to vote as per the voting alternative process and is passed if the majority approve it.

Voting Alternative Process

The voting alternative process is used under the following circumstances:

- any decision that is identified as a decision that does not require agreement from all members

- any decision if a decision has not been reached at three consecutive meetings

- for a required decision if a decision has not been reached after a single attempt

Aesthetics and Personal Preferences

Some topics are unlikely ever to achieve consensus, or at least not in a timely manner. Consensus invites people to hear and accommodate each other's different views on a topic. There is little space for that on matters of personal preferences or value judgments. Aesthetic decisions—for example, print fonts or design details—are notoriously difficult to reach by consensus or may require a lot of time if consensus is to be used. There are a great many aesthetic decisions in the development process, and time is precious! These decisions need to be managed to minimize complexity and control costs. Where possible, CDC framed such decisions to allow a degree of choice: Do you want this warm interior paint colour or that cool one? (We did have one group that easily agreed to a single wall colour!) These kinds of decisions do not require all members to agree, so some form of the voting alternative process such as dot voting may be used to identify two or three "winners" (two choices of wall colour, for example).

"I remember... you put posters of the various exterior treatments on the wall and then said something like '...this time, we are doing dotmocracy. Stick your dots on your favourite design. We'll pick the most popular and then we will move on. You've got five minutes.'"

LITTLE MOUNTAIN COHOUSING MEMBER

Required Decisions

An alternative to consensus was also needed during the development process for some decisions. CDC let groups know if the agenda item was a *required decision*. All time-sensitive decisions are classified as required because there are financial implications if the decisions are not made in a timely way. As project manager, CDC's job included liaising with professionals to identify the required decisions that had to be made so the project could move forward without delay, and indicating them in the general meeting's agenda.

Ideally, items were brought forward for discussion and decision many months before the decision was required, but once in a while arriving at a decision took longer than anticipated. The selection of a mechanical heating system is one example from a past project. A majority of members wanted one system that was more costly than some members could afford. It took many months to come to a solution that all members were willing to accept. A decision was required to begin preparing construction drawings to initiate the building permit application; financing costs are very high at this stage of development, so any delays have major cost implications. Most of the time such decisions are made by consensus, but the voting alternative process can be used when necessary.

Participation in the voting alternative process is limited to one vote per equity member household. The two levels of membership, *associate* and *equity*, are described in Chapter 6. The legal structure described in Chapter 8 includes some details about shareholding. When two or more members of a household jointly own a share, they can all participate equally in the consensus process (i.e., Normal Decision Process), but when using the voting alternative process each shareholding household has a total of one vote. If members of a household don't agree amongst themselves, they cancel out each other's vote.

Prior to 2020, CDC recommended that a super majority of 75 percent be required for the voting alternative process. Experience showed us, however, that the super majority requirement meant that 25 percent of the group could hold back the majority. This seemed unfair to us and the groups we served. We began recommending that groups require a *simple majority* as a voting alternative. The voting alternative was used very rarely, but when it was required, the members agreed that it was important to have a process in place that served the interests of the majority, rather than having progress potentially delayed by a small minority.

Delegating Decision-Making Authority

The voting alternative process is one way for a member group to make decisions under time pressure. Another way is to delegate authority so a few of the most qualified and prepared people are making decisions on behalf of the member group. Although the primary decision-making body remains the group as a whole at the general meetings, the members in a general meeting can authorize the community-building, design, or legal and finance committees to make decisions for a more efficient process in certain situations.

In addition, an individual or small group can be authorized to communicate with a professional for a particular purpose, to make decisions, or to have authority to sign something for the whole member group. *It is important to have clear records of such delegations of authority and for the extent and duration of the authority to be spelled out.* For example, in a group that wanted to have a community internet system in place at project completion, one member had more expertise about this than the professionals the group had retained. So the group delegated authority to that member to coordinate the design and installation of the system.

People with delegated authority are often members, as in the example above, but sometimes delegated authority is given to CDC or another professional. Here is an example from a project early in the construction process which had a few unsold units:

> Motion 20. To authorize CDC to select colour schemes for unsold units, based on what is most popular with existing members, and to select optional upgrades on the same basis. Approved by consensus.

Other professionals also can receive delegated authority, as when the architect is given authority to resolve a design challenge in the most cost-effective manner.

Other Tools to Support Collaborative Decisions

Role Selection

In a community led housing development, delegation and decision-making intersect in another way. The business of a general meeting includes more than discussing and deciding on actions; it includes selecting members for smaller groups in service to the whole community. Most often, the facilitator will call for volunteers, for example, to serve on a task group. The people who come forward are the most willing but not always the most qualified. Some form of election can help ensure that the people filling the roles have the community's confidence. This is especially important in selection for the more powerful roles, such as an agenda-planning team.

CDC supported some groups to successfully use the election process that experienced community facilitator Laird Schaub recommends for situations where a high level of trust is required. It starts with having a clear mandate for the committee and a clear definition of the qualities prospective members need to be effective on the committee. Those willing to serve identify themselves, but a paper-balloted election process determines who will serve from among the volunteers. This occurs over a period of days. Voters consider if the person can fulfill the mandate and has the qualities needed to serve. Prospective committee members are expected to work well together, so they are asked to let the election committee know confidentially if they might not be able to work with any of the other candidates.

Sociocratic Processes

Although some trainers advise against "cherry picking" sociocratic elements, CDC has borrowed some with success. We have found the sociocratic proposal-forming process very helpful. It gives teachable structure to how we work with groups to develop collaborative decisions. We also encourage groups not to aim for perfection but to remember the sociocratic mantra: Is this path "safe enough to try" or "good enough for now"? The sociocratic decision-making process of seeking consent, not consensus, also resonates with the structured way we use consensus. And we have found that the sociocratic role selection can allow for more transparency and authenticity than the election process described above. To learn more about this, Sociocracy for All's website includes detailed information that describes these processes and how to use them.[10]

What Matters Most

We believe that what matters more than *what* governance and decision-making system a group chooses is that *the system is easily understood and is followed*. For a community led housing project's success, a clear, transparent, and effective organizational structure is essential, and so is a consistent, formal decision-making process.

Building community connection through participation in consensus decision-making is an ongoing process, even in completed communities. CDC works hard to support groups to learn to use a consensus process during development, but the members themselves will do this work indefinitely after they move in, whether they continue with a consensus process, adopt a consent-based system such as sociocracy, or shift to another way of making decisions. So long as they continue to be a group committed to community connection, they will differ from conventional multi-family living. New households will need to be educated, indeed assimilated into the particular community's culture. Households joining the community usually are unfamiliar with this way of making decisions, even founding members can benefit from a review and tune-up, and it is normal for the organizational structure and decision-making process to evolve.

6

Building Community Membership

T HREE YEARS into one community-building process, a weekend of meetings ended with members complaining about the intensity and pace of the learning curve. In response, one household shared the following in an email to the group:

A Brief History of Cohousing Newbies

1   The big bang, first contact with the community, information session, Jan 2014. [Became Associate Members and] were allocated our buddy.

2   The rapid expansion, first meeting weekend, Jan 2014.

3   The primeval soup—we missed Feb meetings.

4   Towards a steady state. Equity members in May. We have attended all subsequent meetings, studied the web and emails and are still in the dark on some issues.

5   Beginning to see the light in June.

This chapter describes the structure of the membership phases and the process CDC has followed to find and educate new members so they could self-select whether to commit financially to a project under development. It also describes the community-building process during development to shape groups in support of their overall shared goal: successful completion of their project.

The outreach process that draws new members into the centre of an unfolding community led project is intense. A potential member might first discover the project's website. They might hear about the group from a friend or on the radio. They might read about it in a newspaper or see a local poster for an information session or a workshop about the project to be held in person or by videoconference. Curiosity self-directs this process and supports a steep learning curve as people read, ask questions, participate, and decide for themselves if they want to get involved. Integration into a two-level membership structure follows, along with deeper education about living in community and about the project. Members learn their responsibilities and obligations. In meetings and social events, they work through challenges together and build community connection long before project completion. The more clearly defined the group's values, intentions, and process are, the easier it is to attract and integrate like-minded people into the group.

The following provides recommendations on when each section in this chapter should be given greater consideration:

- **Membership:** Membership should be considered in the getting started phase. There needs to be some kind of agreement about how to collect money and what happens to the money if the project does or does not proceed. However, our recommendation is to wait until the development corporation has been determined before finalizing decisions about the legal and financial requirements for membership.

- **Power and Social Capital in Building Community:** It is important to be aware of the ways in which power dynamics and social capital come into play and to keep them in mind throughout the process of building, and living, in community.

- **Outreach:** The success of a project is dependent on effective outreach. There is a lot of information in this section, grounded in experience, that will help a group to develop a successful outreach program. You have only one opportunity to make a good first impression!

Membership

New projects need to attract members with the financial capacity to fund development and purchase a home. Members also need to have knowledge about the legal, financial, and organizational structures; the risks associated with development; the decisions that have been made; and the requirements for participating in the community. The group needs a structure for integrating new people and educating them about the process. It is essential to maintain a stable membership for the project to succeed and to ensure that the people making the key decisions are those who have made a commitment to the process.

All projects managed by CDC have followed the same recommended membership structure, as described here. This features two levels of membership: associate and equity.

Associate Membership

Associate membership is for anyone who is considering joining the community. Typically, people interested in membership are encouraged to attend an information meeting about the project (described later in this chapter). The purpose of associate membership is to provide an opportunity to get to better know the group as a member and determine whether they want to get more involved in the project. At this stage, neither the group nor the associate member is making any commitment other than time and a small membership fee.

Associate member households typically pay around $150 for a three-month membership. McCamant and Durrett's book *Cohousing: A Contemporary Approach to Housing Ourselves*, or Durrett's *Senior Cohousing Handbook* for senior groups, is reading CDC recommends to help educate new members about the concept. If the project they join requires a workshop, people will be encouraged to take it during their associate membership period so that what they learn in the workshop can contribute to their decision-making process.

CDC recommends pairing associate members with an equity member "buddy" to help answer any questions. This supports new members while they are brought up to speed and can be a good review for buddies. Providing guidance about the project to newcomers supports learning on both sides. Associate members are also given access to all of the community's decisions and documents. They are encouraged to become familiar with the decisions they care most about; for example, a pet owner would likely want to know the pet policy.

Within the three-month period, associate members are encouraged to attend community meetings. They actively participate in the planning, tasks, and decision-making; however, they cannot block decisions made by equity members. This gives them an opportunity to get to know the members, to educate themselves about the project, to develop a full understanding of the legal and financial responsibilities of membership, and to determine whether this lifestyle choice suits them.

By the end of three months, associate members must make a choice to do one of the following:

1 end their relationship with the community
2 become "friends" of the community
3 become equity members, if they meet the requirements

Friends of the community receive emailed updates and are invited to events (potlucks, milestone celebrations, etc.). They can informally advocate for the community and be part of its network, facilitating outreach to identify potential members. Friends pay no fees, and they do not have access to the private members website and do not participate in planning, tasks, or decision-making.

Sometimes an associate will make a request to extend their membership beyond three months; however, the time constraint serves a purpose: The project cannot proceed without equity members. People need to be decisive if they want to be a part of making the community happen and eventually living in it! For the CDC managed projects, the community-building committee had authority to make the decision about extensions and did so on a case by case basis. It takes effort to support associate membership, so the focus needs to be on supporting the people who are seriously interested.

Equity Membership

Equity members are people who have a strong desire to directly influence the quality and design of their home and neighbourhood, who have a vision about community that is different from what can be found in conventional developments, and who are willing to make time and financial commitments to realize their vision. Prior to committing, they need to have attended a certain number of meetings as an associate member; ensure they have the money to pay for a home in the community; be knowledgeable about the process, their responsibilities, and obligations; and meet any other requirements (e.g., take a workshop).

Typical equity membership requirements include but are not limited to the following:

- Pre-approval for a homeowner mortgage (unless the member intends to pay cash for their home or is already a homeowner), a statement of personal net worth, and any other information required by the financial institution to validate income and assets. This information is required to secure the financing for the development. For projects CDC managed, the development consultant collected this information on behalf of the company to maintain confidentiality among members.

- Provide some assurance that they have a good understanding of the group's social process and values, legal and financial obligations and responsibilities, and the design and development process. Often communities require a prospective equity member to have attended at least one group meeting (sometimes more). In projects CDC managed, equity members also had to sign a document saying they accepted all of the decisions the group made before they joined. They were expected to know how to find these decisions and other relevant documents on the private website.

- Be prepared to sign the legal agreements required to develop a project.

- Be prepared to make the minimum required equity investment.

- Sign a non-disclosure agreement indicating that all information provided during membership is to be used exclusively, during or after membership, by active members of the community for the purposes associated with developing or living in the community. Such an agreement will likely specify that no part of this information may be reproduced, stored in or introduced into a retrieval system, or transmitted in any form or by any means (electronic, mechanical, photocopying, recording, or otherwise) without prior written permission.

- Meet any other requirements specific to the community. For example, a community might require a workshop to build members' skills or support them to be a good fit.

Good legal agreements are an essential part of the development process, and it is very important to have agreements that are appropriate for the local context and well understood by the members. New equity members in each project have been required to sign such legal agreements; additionally, goodwill and trust are extremely important. No contract can cover every eventuality, which is why member education and integration is such an important part of the community-building process.

When to Introduce Two-Tiered Membership

A two-tiered membership allows time to familiarize oneself as an associate member at low cost before making a commitment to purchase a home in the community on completion. Without such a clear membership structure, new groups can languish in what some call the "potluck stage," where everyone wants a voice but too few are ready, willing, and able to put their money where their mouth is.

We recommend that groups create associate memberships as soon as the project has a clear, concrete vision and a practical objective. Often this is well before a formal legal structure is adopted. Potential members who are willing and able to invest will want clarity about the project, including what it takes to become a member. Some households involved in the very early days of a new project are likely to be more eager to commit money than others. Creating a category of "pre-equity" membership even before adopting a formal legal structure can build confidence in the project and encourage investment. Pre-equity members willing to take on early risk can receive a benefit if the project proceeds and the money invested becomes part of a down payment on the purchase of a home in the community. We recommend having members who invest more than the amount required for associate membership sign a document that sets expectations about what happens to the investment if the project does or does not proceed. Once a formal legal structure has been adopted, the pre-equity member agreement is no longer needed.

Power and Social Capital in Building Community

Typically, there are a few "burning souls" in every successful new group.[1] These founders are the initial leaders, the people with the vision and often the communication skills and entrepreneurial experience to coalesce a core group for a project. Ideally, these founders can understand complex material yet are aware when they don't know something and accept professionals' advice. In our experience, founders must be willing to spend money and, like all members, they must have enough funds to buy a home in the community. Founders are beacons for the project, attracting new members who want to invest in the shared dream and help to shape it.

As we noted in Chapter 1, the fabric of community connection is stitched together with a thread of consensus decision-making, beginning during development. In accordance with the organizational, legal, and decision-making structures described in other chapters, members collaborate and share responsibilities for building their community with every decision they make. This does not mean that power is evenly distributed—it never is—but power is shared through consensus decision-making. The commitment to consensus encourages founding members to listen as new members with fresh ideas build confidence and a sense of belonging.

Founders who earn each other's respect amass more social capital than other members. They likely exert more power in the group than others, but in a collaborative development process they need to see themselves as part of a team. CDC's approach to building community prioritizes collaboration in the structures and processes we recommend to groups. In community-building meetings, CDC often includes opportunities for members to work together to solve problems, make choices, and build community skills. New members are encouraged to participate in and even lead tasks. Some become part of a team of facilitators for the monthly meetings or learn to take minutes. Everyone learns to give and receive feedback.

Members agree at the outset that in a consensus process they know they will not always get their own way, but it can be difficult to let go gracefully. Some members who are successful in a conventional majority rule setting chafe at sharing power, but at least they become aware of it. As facilitators and authors supporting cooperative culture, Yana Ludwig and Karen Gimnig have observed, "Power in and of itself is not actually a bad thing. We *need* to exercise power in order to be effective and get anything done... So the goal is not to indiscriminately eliminate differences in power but to be conscious of where power is held, what impact it has, and whether the power difference is helping or hurting the group." They conclude that "power is most harmful when it can't be talked about."[2] Laird Schaub's blog is another good resource for information about power dynamics.[3] CDC supports groups to have authentic conversations that raise awareness of power differences, encourage clear personal boundaries, and promote power sharing.

Relationships with Landowners

Several of the groups for whom CDC provided project management purchased their sites from landowners who were eager to sell to the group and who became group members. Beneficial financial dimensions of these arrangements are described in Chapter 10, but the community-building aspects are worth mentioning here. The arrangements with the landowners reduced risk and enhanced the success of the projects in terms of community-building as well as financially.

Two of the sites featured attractive homes, each of which the members decided to retain as a common house. The homes were like magnets, drawing new members into the projects in different ways.

With lofty ceilings and spectacular views, the building itself seemed to recruit new members for one project in coastal BC. Potential members visiting in the winter from other provinces would open the front door featuring an ornate carving, walk into the wood and warmth of the common house, and head straight for the deck to experience the beautiful views and mild weather. Many signed up on the spot to become associate members.

At another project, the warm hospitality of the former landowners was very inviting to members. The development consultants enjoyed being part of the casual community-building that happened around the big dining table or near the barbeque over glasses of wine, delicious meals, and much laughter.

The degree to which these landowners were willing to share power in the community and let go of control contributed to the success of these projects. The fewer the conditions and concessions, the easier it was for members to appreciate the landowners as facilitating the development process.

Well-Oiled Machines

In keeping with our emphasis on collaboration, part of CDC's community-building process supports people to be highly effective team members with the project's professionals. The metaphor of a well-oiled machine is one way we conveyed to the later member groups how to work with each other and the professionals for efficiency and effectiveness.

Outreach

Effective outreach is an essential ingredient for a successful project. CDC's experience has been that a grassroots approach with minimal conventional advertising is what works best to attract members to a new cohousing community. In our experience, paid advertising does not generate the interest needed for success. The outreach is most effective when based on active member involvement. The members invest considerable time and effort until the last purchase agreement is signed. At the beginning, everyone needs to participate in outreach. As the group grows, it is still most effective when all group members take responsibility for performing tasks related to outreach. It takes the whole group to build the group! Potential members want to know not just what they are getting into but whom they are getting involved with financially and as neighbours.

Marketing community led housing is about invitation—inviting people to find out more, and if they are interested in the concept, inviting them to participate. Providing information and helping newcomers feel welcome are the most important ingredients. When potential members know and like what they are getting into, they will self-select, deciding for themselves if the project is a good fit.

A note about member selection: All the groups with whom CDC has worked have chosen to use the "self-selection" process. The more clearly defined the group's values are, the easier it is to attract like-minded people. Equity members will meet with a new member to review the agreements, responsibilities, and obligations to be sure the new member understands the requirements and expectations, and this provides an opportunity for an authentic conversation. In the end, however, rather than the group deciding who can join, it is those people who can satisfy the equity member requirements who are welcomed to join. We believe this process contributes to the development of a healthy and diverse community.

Outreach begins the moment the founders share a spark of an idea for a new community and invite people to join them. From the outset, clarity is important. What is this project? What is it not? One group found it helpful to think of their project as a box, then imagine what went in the box and what didn't. To support such clarity, we have encouraged founders to educate themselves about cohousing or whatever form of community led housing they want to create, then share what they learn with their networks and coalesce a core group that can name the project and agree on a shared intention.

Outreach Plan

One of the first steps for a new project is to create an outreach plan to identify who will be interested and why. What is the message the founders want to convey, and how will they reach their target audience? Few who learn about the project will go on to become owners, so it is important to create an outreach plan that reaches a lot of people to find those who are most likely to take the first steps towards full membership.

Responding to Inquiries

It is also important to respond promptly to telephone and email inquiries. Responding quickly and effectively shows competence and gives a good impression. However, responding to questions from interested people can be very time consuming. It is also difficult for an individual member to explain the concept fully and give a sense of what the community will be like without the help of the larger group and display materials. In the early days, the members may want to check with the consultants to ensure accuracy before responding to detailed questions about development.

Be careful what you say! There are many legal requirements that govern the promotion and sale of securities and real estate. It is important to make sure the message in any promotion or response to an inquiry is achievable and does not violate government legislation that has been enacted to protect the interests of the public. In real estate development, there are many risks and unknowns. You don't want to promise something you can't deliver.

The most successful approach is to encourage interested people to attend an information meeting. Let them know that many of their questions will be answered at that time and that it is really the best way to get an overall sense of the project. If someone is not willing or able to attend a meeting, it is very unlikely that they will ever become a member.

Information Meetings

Information meetings are hosted by group members as a way of directly connecting with people who are interested in the project. Holding information meetings before the regularly held member meetings can work well from a timing perspective. Anyone who joins at the end of such a session can immediately attend the member meeting and get familiar with the process and content of the project.

CDC recommends that many members take roles in information meetings as part of the community-building process. The variety of roles, from set-up to speaking to serving refreshments, allows members to exercise personal preferences. Taking on a role in the presentation supports members to learn more about that aspect of the project, organize their thoughts or learn a script for their part, and present to an audience. Having spoken in an information session, they might feel more comfortable facilitating a future session or doing more outreach. No single role is very large. This shares the burden, and joy, of outreach. It also emphasizes the collaborative nature of the development process and of community living as a way of life.

Groups in development need to balance the desire for more members with their ability to integrate newcomers, which takes time and energy. New members often need a few months to decide if they want to commit to full participation or leave. Groups with whom CDC worked sometimes closed their membership temporarily to process an influx of new members. Paradoxically, this tended to increase interest in joining the group—giving the implicit message that space is limited and you need to make up your mind if you want to be part of it!

The information meeting is a very important part of the outreach process. It is essential that the space where the meeting is being held is inviting and that as many existing members as possible attend. The size and diversity of the group helps to make the project feel real. Generally, the larger the member group in attendance, the easier it is to attract new members. A caveat is that the members need to focus on the visitors, not each other, and create a warm welcome. The fact that a newcomer has taken the time to attend generally indicates a fair degree of interest. A well-organized information meeting is the best opportunity for a forming group to attract new members.

New people "sell" themselves on each project, or not, without the group needing to do any "selling"; the enthusiasm of existing members, the simple fact of their commitment to the project, and the project's high level of organization are usually all that are needed. In CDC's experience, information meetings with relatively large numbers of existing members and small numbers of newcomers are the most successful. The best ratio depends on where the group is in its outreach plan, but ideally an effective information meeting includes at least one established member for every guest. In such a meeting, the newcomers have a good opportunity to meet, ask questions of, and learn from existing members. Everyone can establish personal contacts that invite deeper connections.

Internet Presence

Outside of a website or other internet presence, word of mouth, friends of friends, and media coverage of the project are highly effective outreach tools for marketing. Members often want to spend more money on outreach—for signage or print advertising, for example—but CDC's experience suggests that the internet is more effective in attracting people to attend information sessions or register for a workshop where they can learn about the project. It may be useful to spend some money on online promotions such as boosting Facebook posts. This is not an area of expertise for CDC, but we have found through experience that a presence on the internet is one of the best ways to attract interest.

A good website was essential to all the projects CDC supported. The site should provide information about the mandate, mission, and location of the project, brief biographical information about the members, and whom to contact. CDC created such websites as part of project management services. These same websites continue to serve some of the completed projects. Other communities chose to create their own websites during or after development. Every project needs a web presence. While this could be a Facebook page or other social media site, simple websites have historically worked well.

The Canadian Cohousing Network (CCN) offers another internet presence, to support outreach during project development and advertise resales once a project is complete, through a reduced membership fee for forming groups. In 2022, it was fifty dollars for the first year for forming groups, then twenty dollars per year for each committed household (however the group defines that) up to a maximum of $500 per community. CCN's website (cohousing.ca) gives a new community an immediate connection with established, successful communities. Member communities are encouraged to post a descriptive listing that links to the project's own website and email address. Classified ads are free with membership and are an effective way of reaching potential buyers during construction and after move-in.

Workshops

CDC encourages groups to hold skill-building workshops during development. The shared experience of these workshops nurtures a sense of community among members and develops their skills in such areas as facilitation, conflict management, decision-making, and communication. CDC offers some mini-workshops on these topics within or in addition to the project management scope of service but recommends that groups also contract with others who specialize in this work for day-long or weekend training. Such workshops build capacity within the groups and encourage members to share power collaboratively.

Furthermore, it is important for groups to specify and develop workshops required for equity membership. Such a workshop was part of three of the projects CDC managed: Harbourside, West Wind Harbour, and Ravens Crossing. The course, open to anyone who wanted to take it, was recommended for associate members but was required in order to become an equity member of these communities. The reasoning was that experiential learning could support people to self-select, deciding for themselves whether living in this community would suit them and whether they would be a good fit for the community. A major goal of each new project is to sell all the units by construction completion. The addition of equity members is crucial and so is member retention. The course is one resource for achieving these goals.

To prepare potential members for life in a senior-focused community, Harbourside required in-person attendance at a workshop called "Aging Well in Community" (later called "Dare to Age Well"). Impressed by Charles Durrett's *Senior Cohousing Handbook*, Margaret Critchlow and another Harbourside founder trained with Durrett in California in April 2011. They learned how to offer the ten-week course Durrett called "Study Group 1." With Durrett's approval, they reframed the curriculum as a two-day workshop, which they offered independently and through Royal Roads University. Between 2011 and 2015, they offered this workshop thirteen times to groups ranging in size from five to twenty-five. They trained others to offer a similar workshop through Simon Fraser University.

In the spring of 2016, as both West Wind Harbour and Ravens Crossing began to take shape, Margaret Critchlow developed a new course called "Is Cohousing for You?" This experiential weekend workshop was required for equity membership in either of the two communities under development. It was offered at least quarterly for a total of nineteen workshops before Covid-19 restrictions prevented in-person gatherings in March 2020. The next two weekend workshops were held on Zoom, and the last equity members of both groups completed half-day versions of the workshop on this video-meeting platform.

These workshops supported the community-building process in the new groups. They encouraged new members to better understand what they were getting into. A willingness to pay for and attend a workshop was itself a measure of serious intent. The content of the workshop built members' skills; it introduced consensus decision-making, supported communication skills, and prepared people to participate in meetings during the development phase. Less tangibly but perhaps more importantly, participation in the workshops gave people a taste of what it could be like to live with others in community. The workshop evaluations included frequent comments such as these:

"I learned so much about the social aspects of living in cohousing."

"It was a crash course in community psychology."

"Fellow participants were awesome! I learned not only with them but through them."

Even some "uncomfortable" exercises in communication and expressing fears were generally seen as useful and important for developing skills to live well in community.

One measure of the workshops' success is that some ended up answering no to the question in the workshop's title and were grateful for the clarity their experience of the workshop provided. One participant said the course made it clear: Consensus decision-making was not for him. Of the many who answered yes, only about half became equity members. The workshop was very helpful to the community-building process. Not only did it support individuals to make informed choices about committing to a group, it nurtured a nascent sense of community for each project.

Prioritizing Household Types in Community-Building

Many groups want to include younger participants with families in the membership, but this can sometimes be very challenging to do. Including young families was already a priority for one group where the municipality required a "no age restriction" covenant to be registered on title and 10 percent of the homes to be designed as three-bedroom units suitable for families. While the member group included many people over the age of fifty-five, they did not want to be "senior-focused," so they did everything they could to attract young families. Their online presence and printed flyers were targeted. They did outreach in local parks and fairs. At one point they closed their associate membership to people over fifty-five and prioritized younger households to see if they could change the trend. It was disappointing, but not surprising, that this strategy yielded no results given the site location, which was in a town with a predominantly senior demographic and housing costs that reflected the high desirability of the area. A few months later, the group reopened to all ages and filled their membership before construction completion, mainly with people in the second half of life. After completion, two younger households became tenants, which shows how having the ability to rent out homes can contribute positively to diversity in community.

One community was particularly successful at attracting young families. They had a number of families who were founding members, so from the start the meetings were "family friendly," and a third of the homes were priced at 25 percent below market, which made them financially viable for the families that were later attracted to the project. The homes have covenants in place to ensure they remain affordable in perpetuity. The legal and financial aspects of this non-market component are discussed in more detail in Chapters 8 and 9. These lower-priced homes made it possible for families to purchase housing of an appropriate size—three and four bedrooms in a city where the high costs would otherwise have forced them into one- or two-bedroom homes. As a result, the community includes a greater number of young families than is typical for that area.

During the design phase, if all the membership is not yet in place, the existing members need to look carefully at who is likely to be most attracted to the community when they are finalizing the decision on the mix of housing types and sizes. The risk of having homes unsold at completion needs to be balanced with the desire to attract a certain kind of member. If, for example, the demographic in a particular area indicates that the location is not generally attractive to young families, the likelihood of having unsold homes at completion increases if the unit mix favours that demographic.

7

Design and
Development

THIS CHAPTER IS INTENDED to provide an overview of the process. There are other books available with more detailed information about the design principles that contribute to making a project successful and that can help to guide an architect engaged to provide design services. A recommended reading list is included on the CDC website, CohousingConsulting.ca.

Forming groups (and potential architects) are encouraged to visit completed communities and experience the elements that are unique to each community. This can stimulate design ideas as well as give a sense of what might be possible and realistic to achieve.

The following provides recommendations on when each section in this chapter should be given greater consideration:

- **Priorities for Design:** Priorities should be considered in the getting started stage. The decisions that are made about design priorities should be part of the statement of shared intention or project objective. The group may refine this over time, but the prioritization that is made about these aspects will shape the project and the people who are attracted to it.

- **Affordability:** If affordability is going to be a focus, then this needs to be identified early in the process. Again, any decisions about it should be included in the statement of shared intention.

- **Designing for Community Rather Than Individuals:** It should be clear from the onset that the design of the community is for the benefit of the larger collective, not focused on individual interests. Although it is important to consider the individual, their interests cannot be paramount.

- **Working with Design Professionals:** Our recommendation is to have the development consultant engaged before determining the most effective way of working with the design professionals.

- **Preliminary Programming:** It is most effective to have a professional involved in the creation of a design program during the site search phase; however, it is worthwhile considering these aspects when preparing the statement of shared intention in the getting started phase.

The last five sections of this chapter are all focused on what needs to happen after a site has been secured and the project has entered into the design and development phase. Our recommendation is to have the professional team in place by this time, and the information in this section is intended to support the professionals to facilitate an effective development process.

Priorities for Design

In a custom-designed neighbourhood where the future residents make the decisions, it is all about finding a way to balance the values of aesthetics, affordability, environmental sustainability, and design principles that support community connection. The values and priorities of the group have a big impact on the final cost of the homes.

During development, in the organizational structure that CDC uses, design decisions are made by consensus by the membership at general meetings, unless the decision is delegated to a smaller group. The design committee does research as required and prepares for the discussions in the larger group. The general membership identifies the priorities they would like to explore, and the development consultant works with the group to support the decision-making process.

The desire is always to meet the needs of all the members as much as possible, but it is not possible for everyone to always get exactly what they want. Consensus is not about having everyone agree with the decision; it is about finding a place where members are willing to accept the decision. A consensus process does consider the interests of the minority; however, the final decision must be one that best meets the needs of the larger group.

In our experience, all members want an aesthetically pleasing, environmentally sustainable building that balances privacy and community, supports spontaneous connection, and has extensive common amenities for shared use—all at an affordable price! In other words, they *want it all*.

These goals, however, are sometimes in conflict with each other. The design principles that support community connection tend to take precedence in the decision-making because community connection is why most people are involved, even though a layout that supports this aspect may not be the most affordable or environmentally sustainable option.

The following provides an overview of what we mean when we use certain terms:

- **Aesthetics** in this context means a person's idea about what is beautiful, attractive, or pleasing. As we know, there can be a lot of difference in what people think of as beautiful!

- **Affordability** is a relative term. The goal is to ensure that the end product is financially feasible for all members of the group. When the group is diverse, then what is affordable is strongly influenced by the members with the most limited resources. Even though some choices have a long-term benefit resulting in reduced costs, the increase in capital cost and whether all members can afford the final unit purchase price need to be considered.

- **Environmental sustainability** in this context means a material or method that has a low to zero negative impact on the environment in its manufacture, use, and eventual disposal. Durability is also often considered when looking at environmental sustainability.

- **Community connection** refers to the amenities that are designed for common use (both indoor and outdoor) and the principles that support spontaneous connection among residents and the balance of privacy with community.

For each of us there is generally one aspect of the first three that will have a bigger influence when we are making decisions on our own. Sometimes our priorities will change based on the situation, but each of us tends to have a preference. When looking to purchase a piece of furniture, sheets or towels, or kitchen appliances, for example, it is good to be aware of which of these factors influences our decision the most: Is it cost? Or what it looks or feels like? Or is it based on what is most environmentally sustainable? It is helpful to be aware of our own preferences when entering a discussion that involves making decisions with others. Sometimes it is hard to understand how anyone could see things differently from how we do! When decisions are made by consensus, the differences are acknowledged and the attempt is made to arrive at a solution that gives "the most of what the most people want the most" and one that will support an effective and caring community!

In CDC's experience, these values are generally pretty evenly distributed among members with no one value standing out as a priority, which makes it more challenging to establish group priorities. Still, the group should, ideally, set priorities early in the process and use this as a guide when making decisions. What follows are a few examples (from different communities) of the conflicts that can arise.

Community connection and affordability vs. environmental sustainability— community layout: Environmental sustainability was a high priority for a group that had purchased a multiple-acre site, and they wanted to maximize the potential for passive solar in the design. The land use designation was duplex or single family, so they were working with a low density housing form in order to stay within the municipal requirements. However, when the architect showed the members what the impact would be on the site layout to incorporate passive solar, they discovered this conflicted with the values of community connection and affordability. As a result, the group chose to focus on creating a layout that facilitated better opportunities for community connection and reducing the overall development footprint, which contributed to both affordability and environmental sustainability.

Aesthetics vs. affordability—window frame colour: Members had unanimously agreed on a custom window frame colour. Windows can have a big impact on the look of a building, inside *and* out, and everyone agreed that the custom colour was more aesthetically pleasing. However, when they found out that the cost of the custom colour would add about $1,000 per unit, there was a conflict between the values of aesthetics and affordability. They decided to go with the standard colour because they had identified affordability for all members as a higher priority than aesthetics.

Aesthetics vs. environmental sustainability—flooring: Members had identified two flooring products that met all their requirements for durability, affordability, and low maintenance. One product was very environmentally sustainable, but many did not like the look. The other product was more attractive, but it was not environmentally sustainable. There were no options that met both these values at a price point the members could afford. In this case, the group decided to allow both options, which meant that the flooring was somewhat less affordable because of the lower volume. This decision was an attempt to balance the three values of aesthetics, environmental sustainability, and affordability.

Affordability vs. environmental sustainability—insulation: Stone wool, also known as mineral fibre insulation, is a more sustainable product than fibreglass insulation for a number of reasons, but it is also more expensive. One group had planned to use this material, but when they found out what the additional cost would be, their value of affordability took precedence over sustainability.

Affordability

Affordability is a spectrum and has many different definitions. For the projects that CDC has managed, we have chosen to use the term *non-market* to refer to the homes that were subsidized in some way. Creating non-market homes that have been generated by a means such as increasing density or by financial grant or self-subsidy (strategies 2, 3, and 4 noted below) is one way of creating greater diversity in the group and contributing to the affordable housing continuum. To ensure affordability for perpetuity, it is important to register housing agreements on title to restrict the value over time. If the regulatory authorities require a non-market or rental component as a condition of the rezoning, then it becomes an unavoidable cost of doing the development. If it is not a requirement, the implications of pursuing a non-market or rental component warrant careful consideration; their inclusion will add to the cost of the remainder of the (market) homes.

Providing non-market homes for purchase with housing agreements requires an organization to manage the resales. In the four CDC managed communities that included a rental and/or a non-market for purchase component, the members manage the rental and resale program according to predefined requirements. More information about creating and managing non-market homes is included in Chapters 8 and 9.

Strategies for Enhancing Affordability

The following strategies are ways to contribute to affordability during development and should be discussed when establishing the priorities for design. It is important to make decisions about this early in the process because it is very challenging and costly to go back once the design has progressed.

1 **Work Efficiently:** Once a site has been purchased, the monthly costs are typically many thousands of dollars—time is money. The faster a project can move through the design and development stage, the more will be saved on carrying costs and the lower the final home purchase prices will be. So, moving forward as quickly as possible and being efficient in the decision-making contributes to affordability.

2 **Increase Density:** Including more homes per acre results in lower land costs per unit. In an urban context this may not be practical because of site size or zoning restrictions, but this is how affordable homes (non-market with registered covenants) were

developed in partnership with the local municipalities on two of the projects that CDC managed. In those cases, the density was increased beyond what normally would have been allowed in that location. Then it becomes a question of how much density the members are willing to accept. In addition, attached or stacked homes (as opposed to single-family homes) save construction costs as well as long-term energy costs.

3 **Secure Government Subsidies:** Government subsidies by means of grants or reductions in development costs, although rare, can contribute to providing affordable housing for perpetuity. For one of the CDC-managed projects the municipality waived the substantial community amenity contribution fee in order to support the development of non-market housing, which contributed hugely to the group's ability to include more young families in the community.

4 **Self-Subsidize:** To create greater affordability, some members in a group, or the group itself, may choose to subsidize the cost of some of the homes or may include homes within the community that are available for rent. For one of the projects that CDC managed, a housing unit was subsidized by the group to support a long-time member who could not have afforded to purchase there otherwise. If a decision is made to create some affordable homes for purchase or rental, then this needs to be considered in the financial planning.

5 **Take On Risk:** Assume as much of the financial risk as possible. The more it is assumed by the members, the greater the potential cost savings are likely to be. Developer partners want to see a profit, so working with them increases the project costs unless the developer partner can contribute substantial efficiencies.

6 **Standardize the Design:** A major way to achieve greater affordability is through standardization. This cannot be emphasized enough because it is such an important aspect and groups tend to lose sight of it in the excitement of the design process. Keep the number of floor plans to a maximum of four or five. Standardize

kitchen and bathroom layouts as much as possible. Keep *all* customization to an absolute minimum to maximize efficiency during construction.

7 **Pursue Compact Design:** Although the construction cost per square foot is higher for smaller homes, the total cost can be less if the home is compact and efficiently planned. Reducing the number of bathrooms also makes the home less costly to construct.

8 **Avoid Complexity:** Keep things simple. Complexity of all types adds to the cost.

9 **Embrace Environmental Sustainability:** Employ life-cycle costing and energy efficiency. While capital costs may be greater, lower operating and maintenance costs will make the project more affordable in the long term, and this all needs to be considered when looking at affordability.

10 **Use Space Efficiently:** The common house should be no larger than it needs to be. Thoughtful, efficient use of space contributes to affordability. Design and furnish common spaces to function for multiple uses. For example, a common room can function as a meeting space during the day and guest sleeping space at night. Or the main dining room can accommodate yoga or dance when it is not being used for common meals.

Designing for Community Rather Than Individuals

Although it is important to keep individual needs in mind, the purpose is to create a design that best meets the needs of the group as a whole—to create a community. It is sometimes challenging to clearly define the needs of this larger collective; individual voices can be distracting and sometimes overpowering. At the completion of every design workshop, it is important to prepare directions for the design team that are approved by the group as a whole. Ensuring that the design team only works with the group-approved decisions keeps the team focused on the community's needs rather than the needs of individuals. CDC believes it is important for the whole group to be involved in the major design decisions for homes and common spaces, and that is how we've proceeded on the projects that CDC has managed.

Customization and Optional Upgrades

As noted above, one of the ways to contribute to affordability is through standardization. When the number of home designs is limited to four or five, there is less opportunity or temptation to customize in order to meet the specific needs of an individual or small group of member households. Though it is challenging to put an exact dollar figure on it, it costs more to have many different unit layouts and sizes. Suffice to say that it reduces constructability and increases complexity and cost. The term *constructability* defines the ease and efficiency with which structures can be built. The more constructable a structure is, the more economical it will be.[1]

Another challenge with supporting customization is the impact it has on member relationships. The consequence of customization is that it allows individual interests to take precedence over the interests of the group. It further contributes to the challenge of working towards a common good, which is already difficult in our Western culture where individualism is so highly valued.

In CDC's experience, including some optional upgrades (features that members can choose to select or not) contributes to greater owner satisfaction when there is a diversity of needs in the group; however, it is valuable to only select things that are impactful yet cost effective to manage. Determining whether optional upgrades are needed, and if so what they will be, should occur near the end of the design process and prior to going out to tender for the construction. Appendix D includes examples of possible optional upgrades and identifies the challenges associated with them.

Working with Design Professionals

CDC worked with the design professionals to plan a formal design process to facilitate the group's input. The intention was to create an efficient system for communicating input from the members as a whole. Around seven workshops with the design professionals of about five hours each have typically been sufficient. The topics for the workshops will depend on the type of development (single-family, townhouse, multiple story), but an overview of what needs to be considered has been included later in this chapter. At the completion of each workshop, it is important to identify what decisions are needed to keep the process moving forward in a time- and cost-effective manner.

Preliminary Programming

As noted in Chapter 2, one of the recommended first steps after involving a development consultant is to prepare a financial development strategy. Certain assumptions will need to be made about the nature of the project, which is required to estimate the costs. These assumptions need to be tested against the decisions the group makes about the design, and the financial analysis needs to be updated on a regular basis to help identify the impact on the bottom line and keep the project grounded in reality. Maintaining costs within the range of current market value for conventional housing in the area helps to ensure financial viability.

There is value in starting the design process before a site has been secured (but after a feasibility study has been completed) in order to be prepared for the time constraints associated with a cost-effective development process. Design is an iterative process, so any work done in the early stages is built upon in the later phases as the project proceeds. However, until a site has been secured, groups need to be aware that any money spent, on professional services or otherwise, may not see fruition in the development of the project. The feasibility study should identify the likelihood of securing a site in the desired location, which reduces the risk somewhat, but it is important to keep costs as low as possible during this stage.

The following provides an overview of the steps that can be taken prior to the formal design workshops, which are generally held once a site has been secured. If a site is secured sooner than expected, this work can also happen concurrently.

Clarify Expectations, Establish Priorities for Design

As noted above, identifying the priorities for community connection, aesthetics, environmental sustainability, and affordability is an important first step. But there is also a need to clarify expectations about the design process, how members can participate in that process, and what is possible. At one end of the design spectrum is the "custom-designed dream home." At the other end is the developer project where there is very limited involvement (i.e., buyers might have the ability to choose from two colour palettes for a new conventional building). Community led housing cannot be custom-designed dream homes when meeting diverse needs means being economically viable for all members, so the final product needs to be closer to a developer project on the design spectrum. There is certainly more opportunity for feedback than there is in a developer project, particularly as it relates to the overall layout and common spaces; however, there will still be a need to compromise and to be mindful that complexity adds to costs.

Influences on Design and Desired Density

Understanding the regulations and constraints that will impact development in the desired neighbourhood is essential to support the members to participate effectively in the design process. There are often requirements associated with green building, affordability, universal accessibility, parking, building heights, setbacks, and density, which may include density exemptions for certain kinds of amenities. For example, in many BC municipalities, a percentage of the total building area is exempt from the density calculations when common spaces for shared use by the residents are provided. Appendix E includes an overview of some of the municipal policies that have been supportive of cohousing that may exist in your municipality and are worth discussing with your municipal planner.

Other considerations and influences on site design such as weather, noise, solar access, shading from adjacent buildings, vehicular and pedestrian access, views, site grade or slopes, and subsurface soil conditions also need to be considered. And, as much as possible, the costs and risks of all choices need to be elucidated. At this stage, ideally, the professional team will organize activities that will help members to understand how these different aspects will impact the design. The aim of this phase is to determine members' ideal density and building form, grounded in practical reality.

Preliminary Design Programming for Outdoor Activities

The recommendation for this stage is to have members provide images to inspire design ideas for outdoor living and activities. These may include outdoor cooking and/or eating areas, gathering spaces, bike parking, gardens, composting, children's play areas, private outdoor spaces, places for hanging clothes to dry, quiet spaces, water features, or any other features the group may want to include. Organizing the information into categories and identifying the order of importance will help the design team to prepare a preliminary site layout and determine whether a site will meet the needs and desires of the members. It will be important to remain practical in the process and to think in terms of the reality of what a potential site can accommodate. Small urban sites, for example, do not have the capacity to include a lot of specialized outdoor areas, so it will be important to identify uses that are complementary and can be incorporated into the same space.

Preliminary Design Programming for Indoor Common Spaces

Indoor common spaces as a minimum typically include a common kitchen and dining room, guest suite, common laundry, storage, and garbage and recycling. Some also include a children's play space, community office, meeting room, library, additional guest rooms, workshop, and rooms for art, music, and exercise. It is really up to the group to decide what they want, keeping in mind what they can afford! Similar to the outdoor activities, organizing the information in order of priority and considering complementary uses and multifunctional space will provide valuable preliminary information to support an efficient design process once a site has been secured.

Preliminary Unit Types and Mix

As noted previously, it is important to keep the number of unique floor plans to a minimum to support the economic viability of the project. Members with similar desires for number of bedrooms, bathrooms, and format (one or two levels) will need to work together to refine the home type attributes that are desired (ideal number and size of rooms, bathroom requirements, whether laundry facilities are required, etc).

Once the types of homes have been identified, an assessment needs to be made on the mix. If all the members are not yet in place, which is usually the case at this stage, then it is worthwhile to look at market trends—what home type is most popular in the neighbourhood of choice? Smaller homes are usually easier to find buyers for, so having more smaller homes is generally less risky than having larger homes that have not been spoken for. The risk of having unsold homes at completion is something that should be considered when establishing the mix. Chapter 9 includes an overview of what happens if there are unsold homes at completion, and the section on the elements of a feasibility study in Chapter 10 describes what information is required to understand the potential risks.

Preliminary Parking Needs for Automobiles and Bicycles

Survey members to identify the number of bicycles and automobiles that will require parking on site. The local jurisdiction will have minimum requirements that need to be considered. Automobile parking is costly from a land-use perspective and is also costly to construct. Parking can have a big impact on the design and must be considered early in the design process. Ideally, the group will look for ways to reduce the number of automobile parking spaces required. Local jurisdictions may be willing to relax the parking requirements if the group is able to provide and commit to a viable car-share program.

Environmental Sustainability

Once the priorities for design have been established, the members will need to identify what sustainable building options they want to consider. In addition to the higher-cost systems and finishes, there are many low- or no-cost options that can easily be incorporated. CDC recommends working with a knowledgeable professional to get the most accurate and up-to-date information on the costs and benefits of the many options to ensure decisions are in line with the agreed-to priorities. Most of the groups that CDC worked with chose to pursue Built Green certification. Built Green is a non-profit organization committed to working with builders and developers interested in responsible sustainability practices in the residential building sector. Working with the extensive checklist that is available to registrants in the program can be a cost-effective way to identify the sustainable building materials and methods that are best suited to the project.

The Design Workshops

Once an offer to purchase is made on a property, there will be little time to undertake due diligence. (In a high demand market, thirty days is typical.) During this period, the professional team gathers site specific information on the conditions and costs that can be expected with developing there. The project architect will need to have had design direction to apply to the potential site so they can prepare a preliminary concept plan. The more clarity provided, the better able the professional team will be to assess if the potential site is a good fit. Once the site has been purchased, it is important to have a time-efficient design process to keep costs under control.

Though the exact topics for each design workshop will be influenced by the type of development, as noted above, the following provides a big-picture overview of the typical topics for design workshops to hold once a site has been secured:

- site layout and landscape design programming
- common house programming

- site layout, landscape, and common house design concept plans
- homes and unit mix programming
- review and refine concept plans
- detailed design and material selection (including the selection of optional upgrades, if there are any)
- completion of design

Land Use Designation and the Regulatory Process

Ideally, a site will be selected that has a land use designation in place to support the form of development that is desired. However, CDC knows, based on experience, it is rarely possible to secure a site that does not require some kind of change to accommodate a development that has a focus on creating community. Appendix A provides information about the land use designation and development statistics for each of the projects that CDC has managed. Note that terminology used to describe land development can vary from one location to the next.

Chapter 10 discusses some of the aspects that should be investigated with the local municipality prior to site search. Once a site has been identified, the site feasibility study should elucidate the opportunities, risks, and costs associated with making an application for a change in the land use designation. Depending on the circumstances, the process can range from being fairly straightforward and understandable to being an incredible journey into the unknown. It is essential to have well-seasoned, knowledgeable professionals guiding this process—it can so easily go off the rails, which will have *huge* financial consequences, particularly in areas where land values are high and the approval process is long and arduous.

It is not within the scope of this book to provide education on the different land use designations and how to make an application for a change. Suffice to say, it is *essential* that someone knows what they are doing before starting this process—there be dragons!

Working with Municipal Staff and Officials

CDC believes it is important to maintain a collaborative approach with *all* the people who are involved in a development process. Connecting with municipal staff and officials early in the process, to educate them about the concept and the benefits of cohousing or other forms of community led housing, helps "set the stage." CDC believes it is best to take a humble approach—even though we may think (*know*, even) that community is what the world needs now, in our experience this attitude does not work well when dealing with jurisdictional agencies. We have found it is most effective to make the effort to identify a path that gets everyone working together towards a common goal. Having a professional land use planner on the team is essential.

For many of the projects CDC worked on, a copy of McCamant and Durrett's *Cohousing: A Contemporary Approach to Housing Ourselves* was given to each staff and council member involved in the development.[2] We love this book because it is beautifully published with many evocative colour photos; unfortunately, it is no longer in print. There are other options available, so it is a matter of selecting something that is most appropriate to the group's situation (whether the community is senior or intergenerational). The point is to find a way to support staff and officials to see why they would want to have this kind of project in their jurisdiction.

Once municipal staff and officials understand the concept, in our experience they are typically very supportive and will try to be helpful; however, there are limits to what they can do. Unless cohousing, or other forms of community led housing, has been identified in the municipal bylaws as deserving special treatment, staff and officials are obligated to follow procedure and treat the project the same as every other housing project.

Working with Neighbours

Once a site has been secured, it is particularly important to connect with the neighbours located in close proximity to the site. It is not always easy, as they can be unhappy and afraid of the changes that will occur as a result of the new development, but it is essential to reach out. There is value in offering some benefits (a new fence, paved driveway, etc.) to help alleviate some of the challenges of having a new construction project in their neighbourhood. CDC recommends having a professional land use planner connect with each of the neighbours to identify the impact as well as ways to ameliorate the effect. Again, it is all about collaboration and finding a common goal.

It may seem like a lot to spend $2,700 to replace trees, for example, but having the neighbours onside when applying for a change in land use designation is worth its weight in gold! It will cost a *lot* more to deal with delays that can result when neighbours rally against a project. Knowing the right balance, how much to give and where to stand your ground, is something that an experienced land use planner can help with.

It pays to have good relationships with the municipal staff because they can help with neighbour relations. The following is a quote from the land use planner on one of the projects CDC led that provides a great example of fostering goodwill with neighbours while working closely with the city: "As per the email from the municipal staff member, the retaining wall is now permitted to be located on the city side of the property line. Constructing the retaining wall on City Right of Way means a lot to the neighbour (as it will save several shrubs and trees that are dear to her). This will help us greatly to maintain good neighbourly relations."

Developer Information Meetings and Public Hearings

Familiarizing neighbours with the project is an important step in the development process. (In this case, we are referring to folks living in the larger area as opposed to just the immediate neighbours.) If a developer information meeting is a required part of the land use application process, then the local municipality will have a prescription for how to conduct it and requirements for advertising (notice board on site, newspaper ad, flyer mailed to neighbours within a certain distance of the proposed project, etc.). A developer information meeting is different from a public hearing in that it is organized and managed by the developer (in this instance the community led housing group) rather than the local municipal officials (as is the case for a public hearing). If the developer information meeting is not required, then it will be up to the group, working together with the professional team, to determine how best to generate neighbourhood support for the project.

It is important to have garnered neighbourhood support well before the public hearing. Ideally, neighbours will give enthusiastic support and welcome the new project into the local community at the hearing! This may be possible if the groundwork is done beforehand. But it may be that, despite best efforts, neighbours come out of the woodwork and express concerns that are not expected. If the group has done the work to get the local elected officials and local government staff onside, then a few voices against the project will not have a major impact. In our experience, local officials are looking to make decisions that are in the best interest of the larger community, and if they believe the project is supporting that goal, then it is likely it will be approved even if there are some detractors. Nevertheless, it is important to try to generate as much support as possible and to make sure those people who support the project are available to speak at the public hearing or provide letters of support beforehand.

8

Legal Structure
and Agreements

T HE LEGAL STRUCTURE is one of the backbones of the development process. It needs to meet the requirements of government legislation and regulations while facilitating the flow of money and the growth of membership from inception to completion. Clear and transparent decision-making processes that are codified in the legal agreements support outreach endeavours. A legal entity is required to buy land and enter into contracts. Legal agreements need to be in place to secure member investments and other financial commitments and allow for the transition from development to a completed project.

In the development process that CDC has facilitated, there are two distinct phases, each requiring different legal structures. The first phase requires a structure that will support a group of individuals to legally join together for a period of time to purchase land and design and construct the buildings that will make up the community. Once the construction is completed, the legal structure needs to transition to a second phase that allows for individual tenure.

The following provides recommendations on when each section in this chapter should be given greater consideration:

- **Government Legislation:** Understanding the different acts that govern the development and sale of real property will help members during the getting started phase to have a realistic perspective on what needs to be considered when deciding on the legal structure for the project.

- **Selecting a Lawyer and Legal Structure Overview:** The ability to finance the construction and eventual home purchase (for those needing homeowner mortgages) will be impacted by the legal structure that has been chosen. The group will need to make decisions about this early in the process.

- **Legal Structure for Development and Legal Structure for Home Ownership:** Once a site has been secured, the legal entity for the development needs to be in place. Once the development has been completed, the legal structure needs to allow for individual tenure. These sections provide information about what needs to be considered.

- **Legal Agreements and Considerations and Setting Up the Development Company:** These sections provide details that will support setting up the legal structure.

- **General Administration and Record-Keeping:** This section provides information about some of the tasks that need to be considered when determining responsibilities associated with general administration and record-keeping.

- **Disclosure Statement:** In British Columbia, once the development approvals are in place, a disclosure statement is required before the members can enter into agreements to purchase the homes they have selected. Regardless of whether this section is applicable to other locations, it provides information about how purchasers, who have not been involved in the early stages of the project, should be informed prior to entering into an agreement to purchase a home in the community.

- **Purchase Agreements:** Although it is important to have an understanding early in the process of how the transition from development entity to completed project will happen, it is not essential to have the details of the purchase agreement in place until the development is at a stage where the members can enter into a legally binding agreement to purchase their home in the community.

- **Non-Market Housing Agreements:** This section includes a high level of detail that is intended to support negotiations with local municipalities to include non-market housing in the development.

- **Transfers Prior to Completion:** Life circumstances can change in the process of developing a community led housing project. This section provides information about some ways to deal with those changes as the project nears completion.

- **Transition at Completion:** The end of the development road, and the beginning of the journey of living in community!

Government Legislation

In Canada, each province has its own legislation, often referred to as acts, that governs the development and sale of real property. Anyone contemplating creating a community led housing development needs to engage a legal professional, in the project's home province, who can provide the expertise necessary to prepare agreements that will comply with the legislation. How to identify appropriate legal counsel for a development of this kind is included in the following section on selecting a lawyer.

In general, any acts that may be applicable need to be considered when determining the legal structure for the development; such acts include: company or corporations acts, securities acts, strata property or condominium acts, cooperative housing acts, human rights acts, and any acts regulating the marketing and sale of homes in a project under development. These acts are different for every province or state and can change at any time. Anyone contemplating development needs to be aware of the current local legislation.

Company or Corporation Legislation

The company or corporation legislation covers the various laws that govern the formation, dissolution, and management of companies. A developer (whether conventional or not) needs to generate funds and enter into contracts to purchase land and construct homes. To serve this function, conventional developers in Canada typically set up a limited liability company, which may also be referred to as a corporation. This structure limits liability for the owner, is flexible, and is the most easily recognized by lending institutions, which has an impact on their willingness to lend money.

Companies are owned by shareholders who share in profits and losses generated through operations. A company is a legal instrument that allows a group of individuals to pool resources together to buy, sell, or enter into contracts. A company and its owners are limited in their liability to the creditors and other obligors only up to the resources of the company, unless the owners have given personal guarantees, covenants, or indemnities. For the projects CDC managed, the groups constructed dwellings for themselves at cost, so there was no profit.

Securities Legislation

The securities legislation regulates trading in securities (shares) within a province. If the company or corporation legal structure is used, then there is an opportunity to issue and sell shares, in which case the requirements of the securities legislation apply. Every province and territory in Canada has a securities commission or equivalent authority with its own provincial or territorial legislation. CDC is familiar with the requirements of the Securities Act for the province of BC, but since every province has its own authority, the requirements of the legislation will vary. The intention of the securities requirements is to ensure that all investors are fully informed about the potential risks prior to making an investment.

The British Columbia Securities Commission (BCSC) describe themselves as "guardians of the province's investment marketplace, striving to make BC a place where people can invest with confidence and companies can flourish."[1] They issue publications that can support businesses and investors to understand the requirements. Under the BC Securities Act, companies are required to file a prospectus with a securities regulator for review and receipting before it can sell shares to the public. This can be a lengthy and expensive process, so securities regulators provide exemptions from the prospectus requirement to raise capital more quickly and efficiently without compromising investor protection. For groups in BC, it is important to make sure that the company organizational structure, shareholders agreement, and subscription for share agreement meet the requirements of the Securities Act for the province. This is discussed in more detail later in this chapter. Although other jurisdictions may have more or less stringent requirements, it is very important to ensure the company agreements are in alignment with the regulations.

Strata Property or Condominium Legislation

The strata title or condominium legal structure allows for multiple owners of a building or property. The strata property, or condominium legislation, provides a framework for the creation and operation of these multi-unit developments and sets out the guidelines under which the owners must operate. All of the owners make up the "strata/condominium corporation," and the legal structure is formed when the strata/condominium plan for the newly created development is registered at the provincial land titles registry.

Cooperative Housing Legislation

The cooperative housing legislation governs the formation and operation of many kinds of cooperatives. In a housing cooperative, the cooperative owns all the homes. Members of the cooperative purchase shares, which gives them the right to occupy a home.

Human Rights Legislation

The human rights legislation protects people from discrimination. Although it is unusual for issues of human rights to come up in a development process, it is important to be aware of the criteria that are protected from discrimination.

Real Estate Development Legislation

The Real Estate Development Marketing Act (REDMA) in BC regulates the sale of homes in a project under development and defines the marketing requirements and responsibilities of the developer. There may or may not be legislation in other provinces that regulates this, so a legal professional in the province in question would need to be consulted.

REDMA is intended to protect the public by ensuring the necessary steps are taken for the development of the property, that the developer has sufficient financing to ensure the title and services will be in place at the time of transfer, and that the developer deals with purchasers' deposits appropriately. Additionally, REDMA protects the public by requiring developers to disclose specific information about the development to prospective purchasers, requiring developers to file a disclosure statement with the superintendent of real estate and provide a copy to prospective purchasers before marketing lots or homes for sale.

Filing a disclosure statement may be voluntary in some provinces, but it is mandatory in BC to file prior to marketing homes for sale, even for groups that are self-developing. Groups in BC need to be careful how they promote themselves prior to filing a disclosure statement because the superintendent of real estate has a number of rules regarding the sale of homes prior to construction completion. Legal considerations for outreach are discussed in more detail in the section below.

CDC has worked with lawyers to try to get this requirement waived for projects that are self-developed, but to date that has not been possible. The reason given is that the development company is a different legal entity from the individual purchasers, even though the company shareholders are the same people as the purchasers. It may seem redundant to disclose information to the people who made the decisions, but in our experience it is rare to have all the shareholders in place prior to the filing of the disclosure statement. We have found the document to be a very useful way of providing information to new shareholders who were not involved in the original decisions. Also, because of the documentation that is required for filing, the members make decisions about the community governance and finance well before move-in, which helps with the organization and transition to a completed community.

Be careful what you say! Remember this earlier advice? There are many legal requirements that govern the promotion and sale of securities and real estate. It is important to make sure the message in any promotion or response to an inquiry is achievable and does not violate government legislation that has been enacted to protect the interests of the public. In a real estate development, there are many risks and unknowns. You don't want to promise something you can't deliver.

Selecting a Lawyer

As noted in Chapter 3, it is very helpful if the law firm that is engaged to provide legal counsel for the project has experience working with a community led housing group. They are more likely to understand the relationships, attitudes, and legal requirements than someone who has only worked with conventional developers. Although the scope of work is in many ways similar to a conventional residential development, there are some differences when the future residents are the developer. For example, the transfer of ownership and payout of the construction loan at completion of a community led housing development can be quite different from that of a conventional development. Because it is possible to arrange for closing (transfer of money) to occur within a two or three day period, this can support a lump sum payout of the construction loan rather than incremental payout, which saves money by eliminating the individual payout fees.

Legal Structure Overview

As noted in the introduction, cohousing, as well as other forms of community led housing, is not a particular legal structure. When CDC started working with groups in 1996, we looked at the different potential structures for development and ownership. We determined there were essentially two options for a project that is creating individual self-contained homes. One was to set up as an incorporated company during development and then convert to a strata or condominium at completion. The other was to incorporate as a cooperative.

At the commencement of the project, the group will need to determine what legal structure they want to use at the completion of the development. Appendix B includes a document titled "Legal Structures and How Cohousing Fits" that attempts to clarify what we mean when we use these terms. In BC a strata title home is referred to as a *strata lot*, and in some jurisdictions in Canada it is called a *condominium*. We provide this example of varying terms to emphasize the importance of working with a local legal representative to ensure the terminology and agreements are appropriate to the local context.

> In the majority of cases, the strata lot or condominium boundary is the midway point of a shared wall; the strata lot is the defined area of the unit or home, and everything else is classified as *common property*. Single-family homes, on individual lots, can also use the strata title or condominium legal structure. In BC, this is called a *bare land strata*—so, in this case, a strata lot is a defined area of land.

For the past twenty years, there has been no financial benefit to setting up as a cooperative in BC and, in fact, there are many barriers. In the early years of cohousing in Canada, a group (that CDC was not involved with) set up their development company as a construction cooperative. One of the founding members reported that this unconventional legal structure inflated the legal and financing costs by as much as $200,000 at that time. There continue to be many challenges to securing homeowner financing at completion, which not only makes the homes less affordable, but makes them less accessible. This is discussed in greater detail in the upcoming section on legal structure for home ownership.

Legal Structure for Development

A developer (whether conventional or not) needs to generate funds and enter into contracts to purchase land and construct homes. Conventional developers in Canada typically set up a company (also referred to as a corporation) to serve this function. This structure limits liability for the owners, is flexible, and is the most easily recognized by lending institutions, which has an impact on their willingness to lend money.

Companies are owned by shareholders who share in profits and losses generated through operations. A company is a legal instrument that allows a group of individuals to pool resources together to buy, sell, or enter into contracts. A company and its owners are limited in their liability to the creditors and other obligors only up to the resources of the company, unless the owners have given personal guarantees.

Although the company is not a registered non-profit, the purpose of the company can still be "not for profit," which is typically the case for community led housing groups since the group intends to construct dwellings for themselves at cost. Each of the completed projects that CDC has managed incorporated as a company during the development phase. We have found through experience that the closer the legal structure is to a conventional development, the more likely the legal and financing costs will be competitive with the general market.

If the final legal structure for home ownership is cooperative, then it may be advantageous to set up as a cooperative during the development phase. However, since none of the projects that CDC has managed to date have used the co-op legal structure, this is not something we are familiar with. A professional that specializes in cooperatives would need to be engaged if a group wanted to explore the pros and cons of co-op versus strata/condominium ownership.

Legal Structure for Home Ownership

Once the development is completed, the legal structure needs to allow for individual tenure of the homes and shared ownership of the common property. Either the co-op or strata title/condominium structure can support this, and either can be set up to provide rental accommodation or market or below market ownership. In addition, both legal structures can accommodate any housing form: single-family units, duplexes, triplexes, fourplexes, townhouses, apartments, or a combination of these.

Shared ownership of the common land and facilities is not unique to cohousing! Strata title/condominium developments are legally structured the same as cohousing; it is just that the type of amenity spaces are often different. The focus in cohousing is to support connection with neighbours; however, cohousing can include amenities more typical of conventional developments such as pools, gyms, or party rooms. It is up to the group to decide what they want and what they can afford.

Lending institutions consider the cooperative legal structure for home ownership to be higher risk than that of strata title/condominium for a number of reasons. The main reason is the lack of individual titles in the conventional co-op structure (see more below), but the other risk is related to the restrictions on resales that are possible in a co-op but not generally legal in a strata title/condominium. When CDC investigated the financing options for a group forming in Vancouver who wanted to convert a rental building into a cooperative, we discovered there were very few institutions willing to provide financing. At the time, the financial institutions that were willing to finance co-ops required a minimum 35 percent down payment, whereas conventional home ownership was possible with a down payment as low as 5 percent of the value. As well, interest rates tended to be substantially higher for the mortgages for co-op units. Both of these factors contribute to making newly constructed co-ops less affordable than strata title/condominiums. The high down payment requirement and higher interest rates make the homes less accessible for young families, who typically have minimal equity when purchasing their first home.

Because the cooperative structure is more difficult to finance, the market value tends to be lower, not because it costs any less to build but because there are fewer people interested or able to purchase. If it is more difficult to secure financing, requiring a higher down payment and higher interest rates, that in itself will eliminate some purchasers from the market and thus reduce the demand. Market value for real estate is driven by demand. If the demand is low, the values are lower, regardless of the replacement cost. The cost to construct and maintain a co-op is the same as the cost to construct and maintain a strata title/condominium. So, unless there are major government subsidies, like there were in Canada in the 1980s, the co-op ownership structure does not contribute to affordability.

In the strata title/condominium ownership structure, each owner has separate title to their own home and together with the other owners have ownership of the common land and facilities. The individual titles are created once the construction has been completed, the strata title/condominium plan has been prepared, and an application has been made to the land title office to register the plan, which essentially subdivides the property into separate titles for each home.

Having separate titles makes it possible to register a mortgage and ensures that homeowners are individually responsible for the financial obligations. Having the ability to register a mortgage provides the lender with an asset in the event that a homeowner defaults on their payments, thus providing security for the loan. In BC, there is no legal way to create separate titles for a co-op. The cooperative owns the home. Members purchase shares, which gives them the right to occupy the home. The strata title/condominium ownership form works well because it provides for the shared ownership of the common land and facilities along with private ownership of a home that can be mortgaged. It is also possible to create below-market homes for rental or ownership, that remain affordable for perpetuity, with a strata title/condominium structure. This is discussed further in the section on non-market housing agreements.

As a result, the projects whose development CDC has managed have used a strata title/condominium structure for home ownership at completion. The development company is closed down once all the homes have been sold and it is no longer required. In BC, because of the new home warranty obligations (discussed in Chapter 11), the development company needs to be retained, with a budget to cover company expenditures, for at least five years following completion.

Legal Agreements and Considerations

The membership structure that CDC has used is discussed in Chapter 6. In summary, associate membership is for people considering joining the group, and equity membership is for people who are willing and able to make the legal and financial commitments.

In the initial stages, prior to securing a site, CDC recommends working with a very simple structure to avoid the legal costs of having members become directors and shareholders. Once a company is incorporated, one member of each household consents to act as a director, and each equity member household purchases a share in the company (and owns the share jointly if there are two or more members of the household). Each share represents one home in the development. If a member household intends to purchase multiple homes, they will purchase an equivalent number of shares. The shareholders make loans to the company during the development phase, and at the project's completion these are credited against the purchase price of the homes they are buying. The type and amount of the loans is discussed in more detail in Chapter 9.

CDC has worked with lawyers to generate legal agreements to address the requirements of the legislation that governs the development and marketing of real estate, particularly focused on BC. As noted in the introduction, BC is a highly regulated jurisdiction, so legal agreements needed to be tailored to address this. CDC's philosophy has been to create documents that address the requirements as succinctly as possible, while giving directors and shareholder flexibility to deal with the unpredictable. No one can know what future challenges will arise. The intention of the agreements is to provide enough structure to support a universal understanding but not be so rigidly prescriptive as to prevent innovation—essentially, attempting to incorporate Occam's razor: simplicity is preferable to complexity.

The agreements that members signed when they became equity members, prior to the issuance of a disclosure statement, will have included a consent to act as director, risk acknowledgement forms, a subscription for shares, and a shareholder agreement. The associate member agreement is intended to clarify expectations; for the stability of the project, it is essential that the equity member agreements are legally binding.

The consent to act as director and risk acknowledgements that CDC used are standard forms for BC. The subscription for shares is designed to succinctly address the province's securities requirements. The shareholder agreement is intended to clarify and govern the rights and responsibilities of the shareholders and is probably one of the most important documents that shareholders need to understand and agree to.

As noted above, CDC attempted to create documents that were just the right level of detail—not too much and not too little. Our goal was to provide an agreement that was good enough to cover the essential aspects and leave the details to the day-to-day operation, which can be influenced by many variables. We are aware that this is not the typical perspective of the legal profession, which is to try to foresee all possibilities and include that information in the documentation. For example, in the shareholder agreement that CDC used, the schedule B decision process is a single page that identifies the high points but does not discuss the details of how the process works in practical application.

In addition to the aforementioned legal agreements, it is also important to have agreements that cover the day-to-day expectations associated with working collaboratively. We recommend including something with the formal legal agreements that a new member signs when they commit to equity membership, which clearly identifies, in plain language, the expectations of equity membership. Later in the process when memories may have faded, the document can be a useful reminder of what members have agreed to.

The equity members need to have a good understanding of the responsibilities and obligations associated with the legal agreements they are signing. One of CDC's roles was to meet with potential equity members to review the agreements and respond to questions. We encouraged members to engage their own legal counsel prior to signing the agreements if they had any additional questions or concerns.

Under the BC Securities Act, a company is classified as a private issuer if there will be no more than fifty shareholders. None of the developments that CDC managed had more than fifty shareholders. As a result, the companies could qualify for exemptions from regular reporting requirements. The Companion Policy 45-106CP Prospectus Exemptions is available to download from the British Columbia Securities Commission website and is an excellent resource for groups in BC. Similar statements with respect to other provinces' exemption policies are also available online.

The current exemptions assume that if someone is a director, they have some control over the company decisions and will have access to all the information they need to make an informed decision about investing. As well, there are exemptions for family, close personal friends, and close business associates of directors as well as for accredited investors. If someone is family, or a close friend or associate, they are assumed to have enough personal relationship with the issuer to know the risks. And an accredited investor is assumed to be sophisticated and wealthy enough that they do not need the protection of the securities commission as they understand the necessary due diligence to investigate an investment opportunity prior to becoming involved.

Even though potential members would spend time with the group, sharing experiences and potlucks and outings, and have access to all the information about the development that all the other members had, we concluded after a period of time that this may not be enough to classify a potential member as a close personal friend as described in the Companion Policy 45-106CP Prospectus Exemptions. We found that it was rare for members to meet the accredited investor status. As a result, we found it was simplest in BC to set up the company structure to include one director from every household. Therefore, in the projects that CDC managed in the later years, if a potential member did not easily qualify for either of these other exemption categories, they would consent to act as a director for a period of time prior to becoming a shareholder.

During the development phase, the members are shareholders of a private company, and new members need to be informed and meet certain qualifications before becoming shareholders. As discussed in Chapter 6, CDC recommends using a self-selection process during development. If a strata title ownership form is used after completion, there is no option but self-selection (see more below); however, the corporate structure during the development phase requires the equity members to approve new directors and shareholders. For reasons that cannot be construed as personal characteristics as defined under the Human Rights Act, existing members can choose not to accept a new director or shareholder. However, CDC believes that transparent and authentic communication, equal access to information, clear guidelines, and effective boundaries are essential for a healthy community, and employing these principles will support a robust self-selection process.

Under the BC Strata Property Act, owners must adhere to the bylaws and guidelines, but such bylaws and guidelines may not prohibit or restrict the right of the owner to freely sell their strata title home; although our experience outside of BC is limited, we expect that this is likely the case in other provinces as well.

One of the concerns groups often have with the right of an owner to freely sell their home is how to ensure the purchasers are people who are in alignment with the community values. CDC has found that this can be done without having the right to screen purchasers. It is most important to ensure that prospective members or purchasers are educated about the social, legal, and financial responsibilities of ownership and are made aware of all bylaws, guidelines, values, and governance prior to purchasing a home. And if they are attracted to the community after a comprehensive education, then they are likely a great fit!

Setting Up the Development Company

It is important to have the company incorporated and goods and services tax (GST) registration in place before closing on the purchase of land, but these do not need to be in place to make an offer on land. GST paid during the development phase is recoverable if the company is registered, although purchasers have to pay GST based on the final home cost at completion. This is discussed in more detail in Chapter 9. There are costs associated with incorporating and setting up the ancillary paperwork (such as preparing a shareholders agreement), so we typically do not recommend setting up the company until the project is at a stage where it seems likely that it will proceed.

General Administration and Record-Keeping

There are a number of tasks associated with general administration and record-keeping that need to be considered. Keeping accurate and complete corporate records is important in the event that there are ever any legal issues or the company is audited.

Someone who is involved in the day-to-day operations of the company needs to act as the liaison with legal counsel to manage corporate records such as preparing resolutions for the annual company report, changes in directors and shareholders, transparency register, and any other resolutions required to ensure legal compliance. The legal counsel typically maintains the company minute book, which includes hard copies of all the corporate records and the issued share certificates.

At the commencement of the project, it is important to set up a filing system for the project general record-keeping, including bank statements, invoices, financial statements, equity member agreements, correspondence with government agencies, contracts with professionals, etc. Subject to any changes in the Income Tax Act (Canada), this information needs to be available for no less than seven years in the event of an audit by the Canada Revenue Agency.

Disclosure Statement

When a buyer enters into a contract of purchase and sale to buy a new strata titled home from a developer in the province of BC, the buyer *must* be given a disclosure statement—as noted previously, this is a requirement. The superintendent of real estate can impose fines on anyone who does not comply and can issue a cease marketing order. The disclosure statement is a package of documents that a developer prepares and gives to the buyer when they sign the contract of purchase and sale. It is an information package, not a marketing document. Any marketing material is produced separately. The Real Estate Development Marketing Act (REDMA) provides a buyer with a seven-day cooling-off period to review and be satisfied with these documents. Once the cooling-off period has expired, the buyer is bound by the terms of the contract.

The disclosure statement contains a narrative description of the project's most important features. The superintendent has prescribed in the policy statement the information that must be included in a disclosure statement. It will include, among other things, a table of contents, copies of the proposed declaration, bylaws and rules, and other information that REDMA requires. The disclosure statement will also include the proposed budget; common expense amounts; proportionate shares upon which common expenses are calculated; building plans setting out the units, the common elements, the exclusive use common elements, and restricted access areas; property management agreements; and any insurance trust agreements. The disclosure statement is lengthy and comprehensive.

A disclosure statement cannot be filed until the development permit for the project has been obtained by the developer. Once the disclosure statement has been filed, purchasers will need to sign documents acknowledging receipt. As noted above, in BC it is not legal to market or sell residential homes in a development that is not yet constructed until a disclosure statement has been filed with the superintendent of real estate. Therefore, a cohousing group needs to be careful about how they promote themselves prior to filing the disclosure statement. They can invite the public to attend information meetings to find out more about the project, but it is not legal to advertise homes for sale or discuss terms of a sale.

Since the disclosure statement is a legal requirement, ultimately it should be prepared by a lawyer. However, someone will need to provide the lawyer with the information needed to prepare the statement, and even gathering the information takes a lot of time and effort. The following provides an overview of some of the items typically required for filing.

Information about the Developer

The development company's incorporation information, purpose, address, directors' names and backgrounds, and any potential conflicts of interest need to be provided.

Typically, in a community led housing development, none of the directors has any background in development, so this needs to be disclosed. The following is a sample clause that has been used on other projects to this end:

> The Developer and its officers and directors have no experience in the development industry. The Developer is relying on the expertise of the Developer's project manager, legal counsel, architect, engineers, general contractor, and other professionals who have been hired to provide advice and assistance with respect to the Development.

As well, the directors are required to confirm they have not been involved in any development that had previously been subject to penalties or sanctions, and that they have not declared bankruptcy within the previous five years.

The directors also need to identify any potential conflict of interest; since the directors are also the future purchasers, the conflict of interest is inherent. The following provides a sample clause that has been used on other projects to explain this conflict of interest:

The Directors of the Developer are also purchasers of some of the Strata Lots and thus are inherently in conflict with respect to their duties as Directors of the Developer and their personal interest with respect to their respective Strata Lot purchase(s).

General Description

A descriptive overview, number of buildings, number and size of homes, type of construction, finishing materials, mechanical and electrical systems, site infrastructure, permitted uses, and whether or not the development is a phased strata are some of the things that need to be described in this section. Essentially, this section needs to provide full and complete information about the proposed constructed development.

Strata Information

This section describes the unit entitlement, voting rights, common property and amenities, limited common property designations, highlights of the strata bylaws and rules, parking, furnishings and equipment, operating budget and estimated strata fees, utilities and services, management contracts, insurance, and rental disclosure statement.

A preliminary strata plan based on the architectural construction drawings is required. Engaging a qualified surveyor to prepare the preliminary strata plan contributes to its accuracy. The strata plan is updated once the construction has been completed and the surveyor can take actual measurements of the constructed building. This plan is filed at the land title office at completion of the project.

The Government of British Columbia website provides more information regarding unit entitlement (the share of common property belonging to each strata lot, key in identifying the liabilities and expenses of each strata lot owner), but in short it is determined by one of three methods: a whole number based on habitable area (what can be lived in, but excluding patios, balconies, garages, parking stalls, or storage areas other than closet space, as determined by a surveyor); a whole number that is the same for all residential strata lots; or an equitable number approved by the superintendent of real estate.[2]

Prior to filing the disclosure statement, the group will need to determine how it wants to allocate the unit entitlement. Under the BC Strata Property Act, a strata lot owner owns the common property and common assets in a share equal to the unit entitlement of the owner's strata lot divided by the total unit entitlement of all the strata lots. In BC, strata fees are calculated based on unit entitlement unless they are calculated by using another formula that has been unanimously approved by all owners at an annual general meeting and is registered in the land title office.

Because of the extensive common amenities that are shared by all owners, the cost of maintaining the common areas is a big part of the operating budget. Therefore, many groups that CDC has worked with have chosen to assign the unit entitlement as one (an equal share) rather than based on the habitable area (unit size) with the understanding that the formula for calculating the fees would change immediately after completion. When there are extensive common amenities serving a relatively small number of homes, as is the case for cohousing, using habitable area as the means for calculating strata fees requires that the owners of the larger homes (often young families) pay a larger share to maintain the common areas. But basing the fees on equal unit entitlement means that smaller homes pay a larger share to maintain the common spaces. So, neither system that is allowed under the Strata Property Act in BC works particularly well for cohousing. To create a more equitable system for calculating strata fees, the members would develop some kind of hybrid fee structure that takes into consideration the differing maintenance requirements of the different unit types and sizes. As long as all members have agreed to the fee structure during the development phase, in our experience it is possible to get unanimous agreement on a revised fee structure at an annual general meeting held immediately after completion.

If habitable area is the method for calculating unit entitlement, then a qualified surveyor needs to prepare a preliminary schedule with estimated habitable areas based on the architectural drawings.

Choosing an equal share method eliminates the need to have a qualified surveyor prepare the schedule of unit entitlement.

Common property is anything that is not an individual strata lot. Limited common property (LCP) is common property that is designated for the exclusive use of one or more strata lots. LCP is registered on the strata plan, and although it can be changed, it requires unanimous approval and an amendment to the strata plan. In the projects that CDC has managed, the decks, patios, or yards were designated as limited common property. Storage lockers, parking, and everything else was designated as common property. This allows for flexibility over time in the assigning of lockers and parking spaces and keeps the control of these amenities in the hands of the community rather than individuals.

Whether the project has been set up as a co-op, some other form of share structure, or strata/condominium, bylaws that describe the governance after completion will be needed. The purpose of bylaws is to provide for the administration of the community and for the control, management, maintenance, use, and enjoyment of the homes, common property, and common assets. When preparing the bylaws, it is important to ensure they are enforceable under the applicable provincial legislation. In BC, a set of standard bylaws has been developed by the provincial government. The standard bylaws are the "default" bylaws for a strata corporation unless the owner developer files a different set of bylaws with the land title office. If a group wants to revise the standard bylaws, they can do so and include those in the disclosure statement. The revised bylaws will be filed at completion when the strata plan has been registered and the titles to the homes have been created. Generally, the bylaws are customized to fit the needs of the members; however, it is essential to ensure that the bylaws comply with the applicable legislation. Bylaws that are unenforceable (because they are not supported by the legislation) can impact the quality of relationships among the members as well as impact the ability to get homeowner financing.

A budget with estimated strata fees for the first year of operation needs to be prepared. The operating budget should include an estimate of all expenses that will likely be required to manage and maintain the community. The budgets for multi-family developments typically include financial management, bank charges, office expenses, insurance, common area utilities, garbage collection and recycling, general building maintenance and repairs, window and gutter cleaning, janitorial services for common areas, some landscaping (much is done by volunteers), web hosting, community development and member education, babysitting to support attendance at community meetings, local area network (community Wi-Fi), regular building envelope inspections, and memberships in organizations such as the Canadian Cohousing Network that support the community.

For at least the first year after completion, CDC typically recommends engaging a property manager to provide financial management and support the owners to understand and adhere to the strata property act.

Title and Legal Matters

This section includes information about the legal description, ownership, existing legal notations, charges or encumbrances on title, proposed encumbrances (such as covenants required by the local municipality), outstanding liabilities, and environmental matters including site contamination and geotechnical reports.

Construction and Warranties

This section includes information about the estimated construction dates for commencement and completion, and any construction warranties that may apply.

Approvals and Finances, Miscellaneous

This section includes information about development or rezoning approvals, construction financing, deposits, purchase agreements, developer commitments, and other material facts. More detailed information about purchase agreements is included below.

Risk Factors

It is also a requirement to include a section on risk factors such as information about real property ownership, mortgages and interest rates, warranties and no guarantees, general socio-economic and political conditions, tax considerations and related risks, government regulations, environmental risks, insurance losses, litigation risks, and a disclaimer relating to marketing materials.

List of Exhibits

Included with the text of the disclosure statement will be a list of exhibits. The following items are typically included:

- architectural plans/drawings
- green building checklist of items included in the development
- municipal requirements relating to the development
- schedule of unit entitlement
- landscape plan
- preliminary strata plan
- strata bylaws if customized
- proposed operating budget and strata fees for the first year
- municipal covenants relating to the development
- geotechnical and site contamination reports
- rezoning, development, and building permits
- purchase and sale agreement

Purchase Agreements

During the development phase, the development company is the legal entity that owns the land and buildings. Each equity member household will need to enter into a formal written purchase agreement with the development company in order to legally secure their interest in a particular home. The financial institution providing the construction loan will typically require a certain number of pre-sales as a condition to advance loan proceeds for construction, so copies of the signed purchase agreements will need to be made available to them. As well, anyone requiring a homeowner mortgage at completion will need to show evidence of having entered into an agreement to purchase in order to make the mortgage application.

In the event of an audit, the Canada Revenue Agency will ask to see copies of the purchase and sale agreements. To avoid misunderstanding, we have found that it is in the best interest of the members for the purchase agreement wording to be as similar to a conventional agreement as possible.

Assignment

An assignment is a sales transaction where the original buyer of a property allows another buyer to take over the buyer's rights and obligations of the agreement of purchase and sale before the original buyer has closed on the purchase of the property. The official website of the Government of British Columbia defines the requirements for the disclosure of assignments, which are onerous.[3]

As a result of this regulation, the BC groups that CDC worked with included a "no assignment" clause on the purchase agreements, thus eliminating the need for reporting.

This BC requirement provides a good example of why a group needs to work with a lawyer in the province where they are planning to develop the project. It is legal counsel's responsibility to keep their clients informed about any new legislation or regulations that may impact them.

Non-Market Housing Agreements

As noted in the chapter on design and development, CDC managed four projects that included a non-market component: homes for rent and/or for sale at below-market rates. What follows is a comparison of the non-market home ownership programs for the four communities: Belterra Cohousing, Bowen Island, BC; Quayside Village Cohousing, North Vancouver, BC; Harbourside Cohousing, Sooke, BC; and Driftwood Village Cohousing, North Vancouver, BC. More information about the financial structure for the non-market homes is included in Chapter 9.

It is important to ensure that any non-market agreements that will be registered on title are acceptable to Canada Mortgage and Housing Corporation (CMHC) as well as conventional financial institutions. At the time of completion for Driftwood Village (July 2021), the non-market housing agreements did not impact the ability of the purchasers of those homes to secure homeowner financing.

Non-Market Home Ownership Programs Comparison: Municipal Requirements

Belterra: Five homes for purchase at approximately 25 percent below market with housing agreements were provided in exchange for a higher density than what the original zoning allowed. The municipality had a prescribed affordable housing strategy that was developed by Tim Wake, affordable housing consultant. If the non-market homes are ever sold at market value, the difference between the non-market and market price must be paid to the Bowen Island Municipality.

Quayside: Four homes for purchase at 20 percent below market with housing agreements and one non-market rental unit were provided in exchange for a higher density than what the original zoning allowed. The agreements were developed in collaboration with the City of North Vancouver and were used as a template for the Harbourside and Driftwood Village projects. If the non-market homes are ever sold at market value, the difference between the non-market and market price must be paid to the City of North Vancouver.

Harbourside: The District of Sooke viewed the entire project as a more affordable option for seniors and thus there were no municipal requirements to provide non-market housing. However, because Harbourside members wanted to support a long-time member who could not have afforded to purchase a home otherwise, they created one home at 20 percent below market using the Quayside agreement as a template. If the non-market home is ever sold at market value, the difference between the non-market and market price must be paid to Harbourside.

Driftwood: Eight homes for purchase at 25 percent below market with housing agreements were provided in exchange for cash community amenity contributions that would have been required to secure the higher density for the development. The agreements are essentially the same as the ones that were registered on title for Quayside, as noted above.

Non-Market Home Ownership Programs Comparison: How Initial Value Was Established

Belterra: The maximum initial price was set by Bowen Island Municipality in consultation with the developer during the development approval process.

Quayside, Harbourside, and Driftwood: The maximum initial price was based on the purchase price of the market units at completion, essentially fair market value, minus 20 percent for Quayside and Harbourside, and 25 percent less for Driftwood.

Non-Market Home Ownership Programs Comparison: How Resale Value Is Established

Belterra: The resale value is based on a formula using the increase in the Core Consumer Price Index (Core CPI) for Canada between the initial purchase date and the sale date. If the Core CPI decreases during the ownership period, the resale value remains the same as the initial purchase price.

Quayside, Harbourside, and Driftwood: The resale value is based on the fair market value of a designated unit, determined by a professional appraisal, less 20 percent of that value for Quayside and Harbourside and less 25 percent for Driftwood. The value of the non-market homes for purchase float with market value, always remaining at 20 to 25 percent below market.

Non-Market Home Ownership Programs Comparison: Restrictions on Size, Design, Etc.

Belterra: There were no restrictions, but the following guidelines were encouraged, all of which were met: a mix of housing types and sizes; within walking distance of amenities, transit, and services; compact, accessible units that meet the Green Building Standards set out by Bowen Island Municipality.

Quayside and Driftwood: There were no restrictions from the municipality other than the council needing to approve the proposed mix of unit types and sizes. The focus for both of these projects was to create affordable housing for families.

Harbourside: There were no restrictions other than the ones imposed by the members involved during the development.

Non-Market Home Ownership Programs Comparison: Managing Organization

Belterra: Bowen Island Municipality had hoped to have the Bowen Island Housing Corporation set up to handle this, but that had not happened by project completion. Therefore, the application and resale process for the non-market homes at Belterra is managed by the community based on a prescribed process that is defined in the registered agreement.

Quayside and Driftwood: Both communities are the managing organization and, like Belterra, manage resales based on the prescribed process. The registered agreement includes an option to transfer the obligations to a non-profit organization approved by the City of North Vancouver if they choose to do so in the future.

Harbourside: Since the municipality was not involved, the community has full control over the management of the non-market home and can decide to change the status in the case of a resale.

Non-Market Home Ownership Programs Comparison: Eligibility Criteria

Belterra: The following eligibility criteria were mandated by the Bowen Island Municipality:

- Must be a resident, permanent employee, or retiree who has not owned any interest in real property anywhere in the world, for at least five years prior to the purchase of a resident unit, whereas *permanent employee* means an individual who can demonstrate that they have secured full-time permanent employment for more than one year with a business that operates on Bowen Island; *resident* means an individual who can demonstrate that their current permanent residence has been on Bowen Island for a minimum of one year; and *retiree* means an individual who has ceased employment and who was a resident within the boundaries of the Bowen Island Municipality for five of the six years immediately preceding the date on which the individual ceased employment.

- The applicant will be required to obtain a mortgage pre-approval through a financial institution or a mortgage broker.

- The managing organization may approve an applicant who does not meet all qualification criteria if a clear majority deems the applicant to have special circumstances.

Quayside, Harbourside, and Driftwood: The criteria were established in negotiation with the City of North Vancouver during the Quayside rezoning process and adopted for both the Harbourside and Driftwood agreements:

- A qualified purchaser shall only be a person where 27 percent of the gross annual aggregate income of the purchaser and their household in the preceding calendar year does not exceed the sum of:

  1 Any municipal and other property taxes levied in respect of the designated unit for the immediately preceding calendar year;

  2 All strata maintenance fees and other charges levied by the strata corporation in respect of the designated unit in question for the immediately preceding calendar year;

3   The monthly blended payment of principal and interest required to service a mortgage having a principal amount equal to 90 percent of the price of the designated unit at an interest rate equal to the then current interest rate offered by a Canadian financial institution for a conventional residential mortgage having a term of three years and an amortization period of twenty-five years, multiplied by twelve;

4   Such other criteria as the developer may require the prospective purchaser to meet. For Quayside and Driftwood, the following addition to this clause was required: "as such criteria has been approved in advance by the City of North Vancouver, and is restricted to criteria regarding gross annual income, gross annual aggregate income or other matters relating to the financial situation of the prospective purchaser and his or her household)."

To help facilitate negotiations with the City of North Vancouver for the non-market homes at Driftwood Village, a member of the CDC team who lives at Quayside Village prepared an overview of the experience with affordable homes in Quayside. Quayside was completed in 1998, and they have successfully managed the resales of the non-market homes since that time. The document states "the affordable homes have helped to create greater diversity in the community" and "handling extra steps in the sale of an affordable home is relatively easy to facilitate, as it is an extension of an established marketing system."

CDC prefers the program where the non-market home value increases or decreases with the market over the one that increases based on the Core CPI. The homes remain more affordable over time with the Core CPI-based program; however, because there is no real lift in the value, homeowners can be reluctant to participate financially in community improvements. Whereas in the option based on market value, owners of the non-market homes have the same financial incentive to invest in the community as the other members. As well, if the home values are consistently decreasing over time in relation to market value, which is what has been happening when the increase is based on Core CPI, then it becomes more challenging for the non-market homeowner to afford different accommodations when life circumstances change. Other housing options become less accessible.

Transfers Prior to Completion

The shareholder agreement that CDC recommends using includes the following clauses:

> Each Shareholder shall take up the number of shares, make the capital contributions, and make the Required Shareholder Loans [this term is defined in Chapter 9] to the Company, all in the numbers and amounts and on the terms indicated in Schedule "C" attached hereto and/or in the Subscription for Shares completed by the Shareholder in conjunction with this Agreement.
>
> No Shareholder shall demand repayment of his Loan.
>
> Notwithstanding any other provisions of this Agreement, no Shareholder shall be entitled to sell, transfer, or otherwise dispose of any of his Investment or any part thereof without first obtaining the prior written consent of the other Shareholders holding in the aggregate not less than 75% of the issued Shares of the Company, which consent may be withheld without giving any reason therefor.

In the event that a shareholder wants to leave the project prior to completion, CDC recommends they resign as a director and transfer their share back to the company, and that the company retain the full amount of the required shareholder loan as a genuine pre-estimate of the company's liquidated damages. This may seem harsh and unkind, but in CDC's experience it is extremely important for the legal and financial stability of the project that members do not leave the project prior to completion. We tell members that if they want to leave, they must close on the purchase of their home and sell it after the project has completed. However, in a case where all shares have been fully subscribed or all homes have been pre-sold, it may be possible to refund the full amount of the required shareholder loan in a way that serves both the individual and the community.

CDC used the following protocol on one project to support the replacement of a member who wanted to leave a few months prior to completion. This may not work in all situations—the context is important—it is only meant to provide an example of one possible solution to support the individual and the community.

- The departing member resigned as a director of the company.

- The departing member transferred their share back to the company.

- The departing member cancelled the purchase of the home they had selected (only required if they have entered into a formal purchase and sale agreement).

- The company refunded the full amount of the required and additional shareholder loans. (The refund on the additional shareholder loan would need to be paid once all home sales have completed and the money is in the company account unless there is enough equity in the project to cover the cost prior to completion.)

- The company paid a termination fee that was less than what the discount would have been if the departing member had completed on their purchase, but it provided some compensation for the money that was borrowed for the project development and compensated the company for the cost and effort of securing a new purchaser.

- The departing member remained a guarantor on the construction loan until project completion. (Based on past experience, the legal fees would have been approximately $8,000 to remove a guarantor.)

- The new member became a director and shareholder, contributed the required shareholder loan, and entered into a purchase and sale agreement at the same price as what the departing member had paid for the home.

This process allowed a new member household that was on the waiting list to purchase. It also saved the community and the departing member the hassle and cost of having to sell a home immediately after completion. As noted above, this is only practical and economically viable if all the homes have been pre-sold.

Transition at Completion

Once the development has been completed and the occupancy permit has been issued, the members close on the purchase of their homes (in other words, they pay the balance of the cost either by cash or a homeowner mortgage), the titles transfer to the purchasers, and the construction loan is paid out. This is the point when the CDC development management services contract was considered complete. Chapter 12 provides more detail about the company requirements after completion.

9

Financial Structure

IN A CONVENTIONAL RESIDENTIAL DEVELOPMENT, the developer must have the capacity to pay a minimum of 25 percent of the total project cost before financial institutions will lend the balance required to build the project. When the development is completed, the purchasers pay for their homes, the construction loan is paid off, and the developer hopefully makes a profit.

In the projects CDC managed, the developer was the member group. The projects typically started with a few households and continued to build membership throughout the process. There was no profit—homes were sold at cost. The members took the risk to make the project happen, funded the equity that facilitated the development, and were jointly liable for the construction loan. All of the groups with whom CDC has worked generated 100 percent of the development equity from their members and secured a conventional commercial loan for the construction.

Unlike a conventional purchase (where a developer takes responsibility for the costs and expects to generate a profit for doing so), the funds that were invested went towards paying for development costs (professional fees, permits, construction costs) and were not held in trust. If the project did not proceed for any reason, then money that had been invested to cover these costs would not have been recoverable.

On completion, the legal status changed to allow for individual home ownership, the members closed on the purchase of the homes that had been created through the development process, and the construction loan was paid off. All funds invested by members in the development went towards the purchase as part of the down payment on their home. Any remaining balance owing on the home purchase was either paid by cash or by an individual homeowner mortgage.

If there are homes (or lots) remaining unsold at completion, then the members continue to be jointly responsible for financing and carrying costs on the unsold homes. Assessing the risk of moving forward and identifying a financial plan in the event that all homes are not sold is one of the steps a group needs to take prior to starting construction. Thankfully, all of the projects that CDC managed beyond the feasibility phase completed successfully, and all but two were sold out prior to completion.

Experience has shown that the amount of equity that members are willing to invest during the development process is dependent on how secure they feel about the risk: The more financially sound the project appears, the more willing members are to invest. Having a good legal and financial structure is a key factor not only for generating the funds necessary to develop the project but also for attracting members with the capacity to purchase a home in the completed development.

Our recommendation is to make reading this chapter a requirement for membership in the community, particularly in the getting started phase. The following provides an overview of the information that is contained in each section:

- **Financing the Development:** It is important to have a general understanding of this right at the start.

- **Financial Phases:** This section provides an overview of the stages when different levels of investment are required to make the project happen. Understanding these phases will help ground the project in financial reality.

- **Estimating Project Costs:** This section has a high level of detail and is provided to support experienced development professionals prepare a financial plan for a community led housing project. However, it also provides information that can support members to understand what needs to be considered when estimating the cost of developing the project.

- **Home Pricing:** Making a decision at the commencement of the project about how the home pricing will be established supports members to have a better understanding of the eventual home costs.

- **Non-Market Housing Financial Implications:** This section provides information about projects that successfully developed some of the homes with a final cost that was below market.

- **Home Selection Process:** Determining the home selection process early on reduces the likelihood of members having unmet expectations.

- **Pricing and Paying for Optional Upgrades:** All members need to understand the implications of upgrading from the standard finishing.

- **Homeowner Financing:** This section goes over what needs to be considered to ensure homeowner financing is obtainable to help inform members who need the financing to secure mortgages at completion.

- **Furnishing the Common House:** This should be considered when planning the budget for the project.

- **Financial Management and Managing Cash Flow:** Determining how the finances will be managed needs to be done early in the process.

- **Dealing With Unsold Homes:** It is important to understand at the outset what will happen, and who will be financially responsible, if there are unsold homes at project completion.

Financing the Development

For all of the projects that CDC has been involved with, the development financing essentially came from two sources: member investments and conventional loans from a financial institution.

Member Investments

There is typically a diversity of financial capabilities within a group. The legal and financial structure that CDC used allowed for different levels of financial participation. Rather than everyone having to come up with the 25 percent equity that is required to finance the construction (which is often difficult for young families), in this structure a more modest initial investment was required by each household to become a decision-making member (director and shareholder). Members with the financial resources to contribute more than a minimum investment funded the remainder of the required equity through additional shareholder loans.

All members needed to show they had the financial capacity to purchase a home at completion and qualify for a mortgage if required. In order to ensure financial viability, potential members provided CDC with a statement of personal net worth disclosing their assets. The financial institution also required this disclosure to secure the land and construction loans for the development. If the potential member had enough assets to pay cash for the home, then a mortgage pre-approval was not required. CDC worked with a knowledgeable mortgage broker who understood the legal and financial structure and was able to provide letters of pre-qualification for members who needed it, then supported them to secure homeowner financing at project completion.

The minimum investment, referred to as a *required shareholder loan,* needs to be substantial enough for financial institutions to believe that all the purchasers have made a strong commitment, but also low enough to attract a diversity of members. Assessing the financial capacity of the members and creating a financial plan was one of the services that CDC provided. Working with the recommendations from CDC, the members made the final decision about what minimum investment was appropriate for their project to ensure commitment, facilitate diversity, and meet the equity requirements for development. The following provides an example of how the initial financial requirements were structured per household for one of the projects:

- $500 at the dreaming/forming stage—all members contributing

- increased to $5,000 during the site search phase (documented with a pre-equity member agreement)

- increased to $30,000 with the decision to purchase land and set up the development company (documented formally as a required shareholder loan)

Once the design was completed, home prices had been identified, the disclosure statement filed, and purchase agreements had been signed, the required shareholder loan was increased to 10 percent of the value of the home being purchased. It was easier for members to access financial resources at this stage because the project costs had been clearly defined. Although the required shareholder loan only funds a portion of the equity needed to complete the development, it enables a broad range of individuals to be involved, thus making it easier to generate the membership required to make the project happen. For this structure to work, it is essential to have enough members with the capacity to contribute the *additional shareholder loans* required to meet the equity requirements of the commercial lender.

Members who invested additional shareholder loans generated a cost savings for having financed the development and construction of their homes. The savings were realized as a discount on the purchase price of the home at completion. The discount amount for this additional investment is determined based on the perceived risk and current interest rates.

The rate of return was much less than what would have been required by an outside investor, but the benefits were substantial enough to attract these funds and compensate the investors for the risk. Having the return flow back to the members contributes to affordability for those who invest. In some cases, members who contributed additional shareholder loans chose to waive some or all of the discount and pass the savings on to members with lesser means in order to support diversity in the community.

CDC encouraged members to continue to invest during the construction phase if they had the financial capacity to do so, which replaced money borrowed from a financial institution with funds borrowed from shareholders. This reduced the project development costs for all members by lowering cash flow requirements and loan progress fees as well as generating savings for the members who had invested.

For the completed projects that CDC has managed, equity from members' current homes made up the largest portion of the development equity and was generated through a combination of equity financing (mortgage against the value of the current home) and/or the sale of members' current homes during development. In CDC's experience, financial institutions are generally willing to finance up to 44 percent total debt service for people with good credit and up to 80 percent of the home value when providing equity financing (options could involve refinancing an existing mortgage, securing a reverse mortgage, or a home equity line of credit referred to as a HELOC). In some circumstances, registered funds can lend money to qualified investments; however, past experience indicates that pursuing this option for development funding can be complicated and would require the assistance of a tax accountant.

For a number of the projects, members chose to provide a discount to some, or all, of the members who initiated the project in appreciation for the work and risks they took to get the project started. The *founding member discount* was applied to the purchase price of the member's home at completion, along with any benefits from the investment of additional shareholder loans.

Commercial Loans

We have found that both banks and credit unions have been willing to provide land loans and construction financing. Once the financial institutions understood the concept, they could readily see that the risk would actually be lower than it would be financing a conventional development. Their willingness to finance any project takes into consideration the legal and financial structure, the financial capacity of the shareholders, and the experience and quality of the professional team.

CDC preferred to work with credit unions (as did the groups we worked with) because their community-oriented values were in alignment. As well, even though the credit unions' interest rates were generally a little higher than the banks', the overall financing costs were typically less due to lower commitment fees, monthly draw charges, and other miscellaneous costs associated with a commercial loan.

At the start of the project, prior to land being secured, CDC would approach potential lenders to gauge interest. If it was a lender that CDC had worked with previously, there was no need to explain the concept. However, if we were talking to a lender that we had not worked with previously, we would refer to the project as an owner developed strata and focus on how it was essentially the same legal and financial structure at completion as a conventional development.

The loan application for every project will be somewhat unique and will depend on local circumstances, but the information that follows gives an idea of what is typically required.

Professional Appraisals

There are two purposes for an appraisal: to make the application for financing (land purchase, if required, and construction) and to support the members to make a decision about how to price the homes prior to selection.

A land appraisal is required if the group needs to borrow funds to purchase the property. The appraiser should be provided with detailed information about the property development potential so they can accurately estimate the land value. They will also want to see copies of the land purchase agreements.

For the construction loan, financial institutions will lend development money based on estimated cost or appraised value, whichever is lower. The appraiser will need to provide an overall project value, including land, and will identify the individual value of each home. They will consider home size, configuration, access to light and views, and floor level in a multi-family building (top floor is considered to be most valuable). They will need building plans, information on the finishing materials for the exterior and interiors, and any special features that are not typical for other developments, as well as detailed information about the shared amenities.

For the project to appraise at least at cost, the appraiser will require an understanding of how the common amenities provide added value. As well, the project cost will need to be within range of local market values. Ideally, the overall appraised value would be very close to the cost of the development. If the appraised value of the project is lower than the cost to develop, then the borrower will need to come up with the difference in cash equity. If the appraisal is higher than the cost, the equity requirements remain the same.

In CDC's experience, the Canada Revenue Agency (CRA) required the goods and services tax (GST) to be determined based on fair market value (FMV) before GST. The following is from the Government of Canada website.[1]

> Generally, the Department's position is that fair market value represents the highest price, expressed in terms of money or money's worth, obtainable in an open and unrestricted market between knowledgeable, informed and prudent parties acting at arm's length, neither party being under any compulsion to transact. For deemed self-supplies under section 191, three aspects of the FMV of real property are relevant: the methods used to arrive at a value, the factors affecting measurements of value and the objects of FMV appraisals. Professional appraisers have recognized practices on how to take into consideration factors or characteristics.

Even though legally the development company is a different entity than the individual members, CDC has discovered that the CRA does not consider the transaction to be "arm's length" because the future purchasers are directors and shareholders of the company that is selling the homes. Therefore, if the appraisal is higher than the estimated cost, in order to meet the requirements of the definition, the GST on the home purchase price needed to be based on appraised value rather than the cost.

The following provides an example of the wording for a decision regarding the payment of GST:

> In the event that the appraised value is greater than the unit purchase price including upgrades, the GST amount on the purchase and sale agreement will be based on the appraised value. In the event that the appraised value is lower than the unit purchase price including upgrades, the GST amount on the purchase and sale agreement will be based on the unit purchase price including upgrades.

The recommended pricing structure for the completed homes is based on the market model. Homes in better locations (for example, homes with views or located on higher floors) sell for a higher price than homes in less desirable locations. As well, the price per square foot to develop a small home is higher than for larger homes because bathrooms and kitchens are expensive to construct and in a small unit these rooms make up a greater proportion of the total square footage. The selling prices in conventional developments typically reflect this.

The goal is to ensure that all homes are as desirable as possible to attract members and successfully cover the construction costs of the project. So the pricing strategy needs to ensure that the less desirable locations are desirable because of the pricing. To support this, CDC recommends that members work with a qualified professional appraiser to determine the percentage of value that each home represents to the total cost and to use that percentage to establish the home prices.

Some people are willing and able to pay for the best location in the development, whereas others are willing to purchase a home in a less desirable location in order to get more square footage at a lower price. The strategy for pricing the homes needs to find the "sweet spot" that addresses the variety of needs and interests. This is what helps ensure that the homes not yet selected are as desirable as possible and that all homes are sold at project completion.

Land Purchase Loan Application

The loan application for the land purchase is made as soon as a property has been secured, unless the group has the ability to pay cash for the site. CDC provided the following information when making an application to finance the land purchase:

1   **Introduction:** description of the proposed development

- link to the project website

- property description, current zoning and land use designation, property titles

- description of proposed development and architectural concept drawings

- copies of land purchase agreements and any rental contracts on existing buildings

2   **About the Developer:** description of the company and the legal and financial structure

- description of development entity and copy of the incorporation documents

- information about number of current equity members and financial contributions to date

- copies of personal net worth statements for current equity members

3   **Development Overview:** description of progress to date, list of professionals engaged and qualifications, any relevant reports (geotechnical, environmental, etc.), as well as any supporting documentation from municipal agencies that confirms the development potential

4   **Development Timeline:** description of the estimated timeline for development approvals and the proposed construction process

5   **Preliminary Development Proforma:** financial description of total estimated costs

6   **Loan Request for Land Acquisition:** description of the borrower's equity, estimated rental revenues (as applicable), and loan amount being requested

7   **Conclusion:** final description of how the project is lower risk (high demand for this type of product, examples of past successes, completed communities typically have waiting lists, etc.)

Construction Loan Application

The construction loan application can be made once the construction budget has been finalized. It requires similar information to the land loan application, but it also needs to show proof that the project has everything that is required to commence construction in place. The following provides a list of the additional information that is generally required, as well as information specific to British Columbia:

- development plans
- geotechnical reports
- development and building permit approvals
- individual purchase and sale agreements for the homes
- construction contract
- construction budget and cash flow projection
- company year-end financial statement prepared by an accountant
- disclosure statement (BC requirement)
- confirmation of new home warranty insurance (BC requirement)
- course of construction insurance

Financial Phases

Every development is somewhat different. In the early stages, the cash flow and timeline are based on many assumptions. As the project proceeds and becomes more concrete, the cash requirements and timeline become more predictable. More information about how to determine the financial viability in the early stages is included in Chapter 10 on establishing feasibility.

The following provides an overview of the typical phases. Funds are invested by members as needed. In the early stages there are fewer expenses, but as the project proceeds the equity requirements increase. In order to secure a commercial construction loan at the commencement of construction, the full amount of the development equity needs to be in place, which is typically 25 percent of the total project value.

Forming

In the early stages, the group will have ongoing, miscellaneous expenses for things such as meeting materials, room rental, child minding, refreshments, printing, and outreach. There is no need to spend the money to set up a formal legal structure until a site has been secured. Therefore, as noted in the getting started section in Chapter 2, we recommend setting up a bank account as a community organization. The initial membership agreement should define the participation and financial expectations, but it can be simple and written in plain language. We refer to this as an *associate member agreement*. For this stage, we recommend having a small financial commitment that is non-refundable where members pay an initial fee and after a three-month period commit to paying a monthly membership fee. The funds that are generated from associate and monthly membership fees are used to cover expenses during this Early phase, which are typically very low. The initial fee for the CDC-managed projects was generally around $150 and then $25 per month, which was adequate. Early members will need to identify what the likely costs will be and set an amount for associate membership that will cover them. If room rental is high for example, then this needs to be considered in the budgeting. CDC recommends maintaining this account throughout the life of the project.

Site Selection and Feasibility

The process of finding a suitable site and confirming feasibility generally requires the services of professionals. The amount of money that is required depends on the local context, on how challenging it is to find an appropriate site, and on what is required to establish feasibility.

If the expenses exceed the amount that has been collected through associate membership fees, then additional funds will be needed to cover these early development costs. Chapter 6 discusses having a pre-equity agreement in the event that more funds are needed. A rudimentary bookkeeping system should be put in place to keep track of all expenditures and financial contributions. It is not necessary to set up more than one bank account at this stage, but CDC recommends accounting for the development expenses separately. If the project proceeds and if members continue on to become directors and shareholders of the company, the money they have contributed towards development expenses can be applied as a credit towards the required shareholder loan and the expenses transferred to the development corporation. The completed development is the valuable asset that is created as a result, and the money that has been invested forms the down payment on the home being purchased. If the project does not proceed, it is important for them to be aware that the money invested will have gone towards paying expenses and is not recoverable because no saleable asset has been created.

Design and Development (Pre-Construction)

Once the site has been secured with a contract to purchase and feasibility has been established, CDC recommends formalizing the membership structure, incorporating the company, and opening a corporate development account to cover the project costs and manage the funds generated from equity membership investments (shareholder loans). Then the design work and approval process can commence.

This phase can take anywhere from six months to many years depending on the approvals required to allow for the proposed development on the selected site. Total expenditures are dependent on when the site purchase is completed. If the vendor is willing to carry the property during the approval phase, then this will save the group substantial money. Financial institutions are generally willing to lend at least 50 percent of the land value in a mortgage as long they feel secure with the general viability of the project and the members can show they have the financial capacity to carry the loan. On average, about 35 percent of the development soft costs (not including financing) need to be paid during this period for architects, engineers, surveys, legal work, insurance, project management, and permit fees. Financing costs will depend on the land value and current interest rates.

Construction

CDC worked with a general contractor during the design phase, getting estimates at key points to help ensure the final building design is in alignment with the group's budget. Once construction drawings have been prepared, the general contractor can finalize the budget based on firm quotes—up to this point, everything has been estimated. However, if a knowledgeable contractor has been involved throughout the design phase, there shouldn't be any big surprises. Home purchase prices can now be determined, the equity members can enter into contracts of purchase for the homes they have selected, and the balance of the equity needed to commence construction can be collected from the members. The section on home pricing further on in this chapter includes recommended wording for a decision by the company directors and shareholders that will ensure the home purchase prices are based on final costs.

Assuming the project is fully built-out as quickly as possible, construction typically ranges anywhere from twelve to eighteen months, depending on the size and complexity of the development. The construction phase is generally considered to be the lowest risk, particularly if the construction contract is fixed price and at least 70 percent of the homes have been sold prior to the commencement of construction. Before financial institutions will begin funding draws for construction, they need confirmation that the developer's equity has been spent on the project.

Estimating Project Costs

Identifying potential cost is an important first step to grounding a project in the reality of current economic conditions. When a site is secured, one of the elements of the feasibility study involves estimating the cost of a completed home in the community. As noted previously, the development process does not of itself generate below market priced homes. Even though it does not include profit if the resident group is the developer, the homes are often higher quality with more green-built features then conventional housing, which makes them less costly to maintain and operate but contributes to higher construction costs. To ensure that the project is economically viable, it is important to keep cost in mind during every step in the process.

The Development Proforma

The development proforma is a tool used throughout the project to identify potential cost for a completed home in the community and is revised each time the understanding of costs becomes more concrete. The proforma needs to be prepared by someone with development experience, who is familiar with costs in the local area. It is typically prepared by a development consultant. The final cost for every project is subject to decisions the group makes about site selection, design, quality, finishing, common house size, amenities, and environmental features.

Each project is unique, and the local context must be considered when estimating costs. Every development consultant will have a different way of organizing and presenting this information. Appendix F includes an example of a development proforma that was prepared once the site had been secured for a project that CDC managed. The project location has not been identified for reasons of confidentiality. This is meant to give information about the types of costs involved and the elements that need to be included when preparing a development proforma, not about the costs themselves. The following provides a general description of the categories that are typically included as well as a copy of the applicable section from the example development proforma to show how the information can be organized. All sizes on this example proforma are in square feet.

The **Property Description** section provides information about the property location, size, buildable area, maximum site coverage, zoning, etc.—whatever is pertinent to the property that defines what is possible in terms of development.

The **Proposed Development** section provides information about the proposed development such as total home area, size of common house, total built area (which includes the circulation space comprised of common hallways and stairwells), saleable area (which is the combined square footage of all the homes), total number of homes, and average home size. Assumptions need to be made about these features when preparing preliminary cost information.

The common house is generally identified as an amenity for the private use of the residents. Although groups use the common areas for occasional public events, they are not typically designated as commercial use spaces and the finishing can be residential quality. If the common house needs to be commercial quality, this adds substantial costs. When the home prices are established, the cost of the common house is included in the home purchase price, similar to conventional developments that have common amenity areas.

Experience has shown that the ideal number of homes in a community that supports ongoing connection among the residents is around twenty to forty. Much less than twenty is not enough to maintain the energy for common activities, but much more than forty is too many to develop the close connection that is desired in this type of neighbourhood. The site cost and constraints will dictate what is required to make the project financially feasible. Average home size is calculated by adding the square footage of all the homes, then dividing by total number of homes. In CDC's experience, the average home size can range from around 800 to 1,400 square feet or more and can include home types ranging from very small bachelor suites to five-bedroom homes. Urban projects tend to have a smaller average size with fewer bedrooms than suburban or rural projects. The size of the common house depends on the group's desires, their ability to absorb the cost, and their interest in staying within a certain range of market value.

Property Description

Property Address (not included in this example)	
Site Size (in square feet)	25,504 SF
Floor Space Ratio (FSR)	1.5

Proposed Development	Area SF	Total Number of Units	Average Area Per Unit
Total Saleable Area	32,900	35	940
Circulation	5,356		
Total Area Units and Circulation	38,256		
Common Amenities (FSR exclusion up to 10% of the Gross Floor Area)	2,800		
Total Built Area	41,056		

The proforma shows the estimated total costs for each category (land acquisition, soft costs, construction costs, financing, contingency). To prepare a feasibility study for a specific site, the development consultant will identify applicable categories and research local conditions and municipal development requirements to identify potential costs; in other words, a **Development Analysis**. In CDC's experience, financial institutions are willing to lend 75 percent of the estimated cost or appraised value (whichever is lower), by way of a construction loan. The financing bonus fees and lending rates will vary depending on the lender and perceived risk. If the project is sold out prior to construction start with 30 percent or more development equity in place, it is likely that the bonus fees and interest rates will be at the lower end of the scale.

The recommended contingency at the commencement of the project, once a site has been secured, is calculated at 12 percent of the total project value not including land or closing costs. At the start of construction, a 5 percent contingency on construction costs is typically required by financial institutions if the construction delivery method is some form of fixed price contract, and at least 10 percent is recommended if it is a construction management contract.

Development Analysis	Per Unit	Per Square Foot	Total
Phase 1: Acquisition (Land)			
Purchase Price	$120,000	$127.66	$4,200,000
Property Transfer Tax	$2,320	$2.47	$81,200
Total Acquisition Costs	$122,320	$130	$4,281,200
Phase 2: Pre-Construction (Soft Costs)			
Legal, Accounting, Appraisal	$2,857	$3.04	$100,000
Design Professionals, Project Management,	$31,257	$33.25	$1,094,000
Outreach	$143	$0.15	$5,000
Municipals, CACs, DCCs	$7,954	$8.46	$278,375
HPO Insurance	$3,290	$3.50	$115,150
Survey	$857	$0.91	$30,000
Municipal and Property Tax	$343	$0.36	$12,000
Insurance	$3,959	$4.21	$138,564
Disbursements and Travel	$400	$0.43	$14,000
Total Pre-Construction Costs	$51,060	$54	$1,787,089
Phase 3: Construction (Hard Costs)			
Site Servicing and Landscape	$9,007	$9.58	$315,260
Common House	$21,600	$22.98	$756,000
Building Construction	$295,118	$313.95	$10,329,120
Total Construction Costs	$325,725	$347	$11,400,380

Development Analysis	Per Unit	Per Square Foot	Total
Phase 4: Financing (Primary)			
Required Loan		$14,960,000	75%
Financing Bonus		$104,720	0.70%
Interest Rate		4.70%	
Development Permit		13	
Construction		18	
Sales Period		0	
Carrying Costs on Land	$1,248	$1.33	$43,690
Financing Bonus	$2,992	$3.18	$104,720
Quantity Surveyor	$858	$0.91	$30,000
Construction Loan Interest	$18,080	$19.23	$632,808
Total Financing	$23,178	$25	$811,218
Contingency Reserve (12% of Phases 2, 3, and 4)	$47,995	$51	$1,679,842
Grand Total	$570,278	$607	$19,959,728

The section below provides information about the member discounts (cost savings) and how this is included in the project's **Closing Costs**. Members who have contributed equity at the beginning of the project often have a substantial cost savings in their home price. The proforma figures are based on assumptions about the amounts of non-interest bearing required shareholder loans, carrying costs for additional shareholder loans to finance rezoning and construction, and estimates on the number of shareholders in place at commencement of construction.

In Canada, the GST is a "flow-through" tax during development. All the costs included in the proforma are net of the GST. At completion, each member will pay GST based on the purchase price of their home, so the proforma calculates that into the final cost.

The proforma provides a calculation of the average cost per square foot and average home price required to generate the revenue to cover the costs. This is only an average. The final price per square foot for each home will vary depending on the desirability, which is discussed further in the section on home pricing.

Closing Costs	Per Unit	Per Square Foot	Total
Member Discounts	$13,035	$13.87	$456,217
GST	$28,514	$30.33	$997,986
Average Home Cost (Includes GST)	$611,827	$651	$21,413,933

Home Pricing

Unless there are price restrictions registered on title, when a member decides to sell, the value of the home is based on the market: whatever a buyer is ready and willing to pay, and whatever the seller is willing to accept. Therefore, in order to ensure fairness in pricing during the development phase, CDC recommends working with a professional appraiser to support the group to agree to a pricing structure that considers market values. Home pricing is not an exact science; however, a qualified appraiser can provide an impartial perspective that is grounded in knowledge and experience.

For a project where the homes are sold at cost, it is not possible to know the final cost until project completion. Therefore, it is important to determine what happens in the event total project costs increase or decrease. Members agreed to use the percentage of value that was established when the units were appraised to determine change in cost. In most cases there was contingency remaining, but in two cases the final cost at completion was higher than expected. The following provides an example of the wording for a decision regarding this:

In the event that the cost of the development is greater or less than the amount determined at construction start, the difference in the unit purchase price for each shareholder will be based on the percentage of value their unit represents to the total project cost, and an addendum will be prepared for each purchaser identifying the cost increase or decrease prior to the completion date. In the event that there are excess funds available at construction completion, the shareholders may agree to retain funds for future improvements, and such funds would be considered a cost of the development.

Chapter 12 includes more detailed information about managing excess contingency or shortfall.

Most of the projects were approximately market value at the start of construction when members signed the purchase agreements, but they were somewhat less than local market value at completion. If the members make decisions that keep the costs in alignment with market values, and if the project is well managed, then the final cost at the time of completion can end up being somewhat less than what someone would pay for a comparable home in the neighbourhood.

CDC has also helped facilitate decisions to include some higher quality materials or methods than all members could afford where members with more means absorbed the added cost while the benefit was seen by everyone.

One group wanted to include a mechanical system for heating and cooling that was substantially more expensive than what the budget allowed. Most members wanted this upgrade and could afford to pay for it, but some members could not afford the added cost. It was more cost effective for the members who wanted it to pay for the whole building to be upgraded, buying at a bulk rate, rather than include it as an optional upgrade to be selected and paid for by each household. Therefore, the decision was made to divide the total upgrade cost (the difference between the standard system and the upgraded system) among the members who could afford it and add the cost to their home purchase prices.

Non-Market Housing Financial Implications

Chapter 8 provides information on the municipal requirements and legal agreements that supported the development of non-market housing. The information below describes how this was supported to make it financially viable. The local conditions need to be taken into consideration when looking at financial viability. When land costs are high, increasing density can have a big impact on reducing the cost per unit. What follows is a look at how this worked out among the Belterra, Quayside Village, Harbourside, and Driftwood Village Cohousing projects.

Belterra Cohousing (Bowen Island, BC): The allowable number of homes on the property was increased from one to thirty, which reduced the land cost per unit enough, even in this rural location where land costs were low compared with urban centres, to make it possible to include five homes at approximately 25 percent below market while keeping the other homes within market value for the area.

Quayside Village Cohousing (North Vancouver, BC): The floor area ratio was increased from 1.2 to 1.68, which allowed for an additional 5,040 square feet of saleable area. This made it possible to include four homes at 20 percent below market (because the increase in floor area ratio basically eliminated the land cost for these four homes) while keeping the other homes within market value for the area.

Harbourside Cohousing (Sooke, BC): The allowable number of homes on the property was increased from one to thirty-one, which reduced the land cost per unit enough to make it possible to include one home at 20 percent below market while keeping the other homes within market value for the area. The land cost was low compared with urban centres, and the increase in density did not add a lot of value, but enough to include the one non-market home without impacting the cost of the market priced homes.

Driftwood Village Cohousing (North Vancouver, BC): The property was located in an area that supported increased density but required a community amenity contribution based on the density requested.

The city agreed to allow the approximately $1.4 million that would normally have been payable in cash to the city to be used to reduce the home costs on the eight homes at 25 percent below market.

Home Selection Process

Members had priority for home selection based on the timing of their commitment as equity members. Homes were selected once the design had been completed, the disclosure statement filed, the construction costs identified, and the home desirability and the pricing established with a professional appraisal. Prior to selection, the members identified the type of home they wanted (e.g., one-, two- or three-bedroom), but they did not select the home until pricing had been established. We ensured that new members were aware of what home types were available before they committed to equity membership. If there were non-market homes in the development, only the households that qualified could choose from among them, but selection was still based on timing of commitment. This process has worked very well on all the projects—everyone has been able to purchase the home of their choice, perhaps not their first choice but one they have been happy with.

Reselection Prior to Completion

The development process typically takes several years to complete. During that time, circumstances can change for a household. Sometimes, the change in circumstances can be accommodated by making a switch from one home type to another. If there are still homes available of the type the household needs, then it is just a matter of revising the purchase and sale agreement. However, if there are no homes available of the type needed, then it is a matter of determining whether an existing member is willing to make a switch. This has happened a number of times, and the members have always found ways to accommodate the needs. Goodwill and caring were the ground on which the creative solutions were conceived.

Pricing and Paying for Optional Upgrades

As noted in the chapter on design, including some optional upgrades (features that members can choose to select or not) contributes to owner satisfaction when there is a diversity of needs in the group. It is important to ensure that the pricing fully covers all costs associated with the upgrades. In addition to the construction cost, the pricing should include design fees, course of construction insurance, and contingency. The full amount of the upgrade cost was due and collected at the time when the members entered into the agreement to purchase the home they had selected. This ensured there were no financing costs associated with the upgrades because the equity collected was used to pay for the upgrades during the construction process.

Homeowner Financing

CDC recommends working with a mortgage broker knowledgeable about community led housing to support members needing financing to secure the mortgage they require to make the home purchase at completion. There is a lot of confusion about the concept that can impact a purchaser's ability to secure financing. The broker needs to be able to answer the questions that financial institutions ask in a way that supports them to see that financing this type of housing is no riskier than financing a conventional home purchase.

Financial institutions have become more risk averse over the years. If something is hard to understand or out of the ordinary, they are less willing to finance it. Groups often contribute to the confusion by including information on their websites that is inaccurate, misleading, or at the very worst illegal (such as breaching the BC Strata Property Act by stating that potential purchasers need to meet certain participation requirements). Unfortunately, there are currently fewer financial institutions willing to provide homeowner financing than there were in the past due to the misinformation and confusion. Therefore, it is extremely important for the success of the project, and community led housing in general, that members understand what they need to consider in all their outreach efforts. The information needs to not only comply with applicable legislation but it should also consider how financial institutions assess risk when it comes to approving homeowner mortgages.

Furnishing the Common House

Many groups have found that it is feasible to furnish the common house almost entirely with items donated by members who are downsizing. In Canada, there are also many "buy nothing" groups—another great resource when looking to furnish common spaces. Many groups find it easier to visualize what is needed once they can see the physical space.

The items included in the development proforma for common amenity furnishings were things members thought essential to purchase new, such as appliances for the common house and common laundry, and perhaps the dining room tables to ensure a certain consistency in size and flexibility of use. If there was contingency remaining at project completion, most groups that CDC worked with chose to use it to purchase items that were desired but not included in the budget, rather than to reduce home prices.

Financial Management

The development will require someone to manage and monitor the budget, prepare cheques for invoice payments, keep financial records, ensure there are adequate funds in the account to pay the bills, and prepare monthly financial statements. The development company needs to be registered for goods and services tax (GST) with the Canada Revenue Agency (CRA), GST returns need to be filed either quarterly or annually (depending on how the registration has been set up), and someone needs to be able to respond to questions from the CRA as required. A certified professional accountant should be engaged to prepare the corporate tax returns. At the completion of the project, the financial management of the development account is much less complex and can be managed by the members.

CDC believes it is important for the project finances to be transparent and understandable to members since they are the directors and shareholders of the development company in the self-development model. Copies of current bank statements, invoices from professionals, monthly cash flow projections, and detailed account lists showing the current budget, costs to date, budget changes, and cost to complete should be prepared and provided on a monthly basis.

On the CDC-managed projects, funds contributed for associate and monthly membership fees did not count towards the home purchase. During the development phase, this was a petty cash account and was not accounted for as part of the development finance (not included in corporate tax returns or GST filing). The community account was managed by members according to protocols agreed to by members. If there were excess community account funds remaining when the development was completed, they were typically spent on common amenities, such as furnishings for the common house.

Managing Cash Flow

Whoever is managing the project finance needs to keep an eye on the monthly expenditures to ensure there are always adequate funds available to cover expenses. One of the roles of the financial manager is to determine the investment timeline, ensure there is sufficient commitment from members to cover costs, and communicate with members as required to manage the investments.

As noted in the section on financial management, CDC prepared cash flow projections every month. This ensures that the members were always aware of how much money was needed to keep the project moving forward.

Dealing With Unsold Homes

In a project where the developer is the resident group, the members are responsible for the costs of unsold homes at completion. Prior to the commencement of construction, it is important to look at the risk of having unsold homes and to determine how unsold homes would be financed in the event there are any. Two of the projects CDC managed had unsold homes at completion. In both cases, the members were able to secure interim financing and found buyers within a short period of time. The members who lent money for the equity portion received a return on their investment, and the financial institution that provided the construction loan lent the balance by way of a mortgage against the title on the unsold properties. It is very costly to deal with unsold homes, so members need to consider marketability at every stage of the development.

10

Establishing Feasibility, Finding and Securing a Site

A S NOTED IN CHAPTER 2, the development process for community led housing is not linear—many things need to occur concurrently. Likewise, our chapter structure is not intended to represent a sequential timeline. For most projects, site selection will occur fairly early in the process. The placement of this chapter is intended to emphasize the relationship between the site and construction, as well as the importance of the other dimensions of a community led housing development. Site selection is unlikely to be successful unless good professionals are in place. They support the group to have agreed to preliminary decision-making, organizational, legal, and financial structures before attempting to find and secure a site.

Once the members have agreed to the project objective, which describes the form and character of the community the group wants to create, the next step involves determining whether the dream is achievable. This chapter outlines the steps that have successfully supported groups to secure an appropriate and developable site.

Having a grasp on the information in this chapter at the getting started stage will help the group focus on what is required to make a project happen. The following provides an overview of the information that is contained in each section:

- **Initiation:** This section describes the steps a group can take to get clarity about the housing forms that are likely feasible in the neighbourhoods of choice as well as a general sense of the potential cost.

- **Site Selection Criteria:** Examples of site selection criteria are provided and some of the questions that need to be addressed before proceeding to site search are identified.

- **Elements of a Preliminary Feasibility Study:** The overview of what needs to be considered when preparing a preliminary feasibility study supports an understanding of what is required to make the project happen.

- **Review Project Objective:** Decisions will need to be made before proceeding to site search, and this section discusses what should be considered.

- **Finding and Securing a Site:** The steps that have supported groups to successfully find and secure an appropriate site are outlined in detail.

- **Site Feasibility:** This section provides information about what investigations are needed to generate an understanding of the opportunities and challenges of proceeding.

Initiation

The development requirements in the municipality where the group would like to locate have a big impact on what will be required to make a project happen. Each local government has a set of official community plans, zoning bylaws, and other regulations that govern residential development.

It is also important to identify the market values for similar types of homes in the neighbourhoods of choice. If the final cost of the homes exceeds local market values, then it will be more difficult to find members and finance the project.

After defining the project objective and identifying preliminary site criteria, the following questions should be considered:

- What does it cost for a new home in the preferred neighbourhoods?

- Are there developments in the neighbourhoods of choice similar to the one defined in the project objective? What does the local official community plan say about the long-term goals for the neighbourhood? Is there support from the local municipality for the type of development contemplated? Is there infrastructure in place (water, sewer, power) to support the type of development contemplated?

- Are there any particular requirements for new developments (for example, providing a certain level of green building, universal accessibility, or affordability) that need to be considered?

- Are there potential development sites available in the preferred neighbourhoods with zoning that matches the desired development type and density? If so, what is the asking price?

- If there are no available development sites with the zoning in place, what is the likelihood of being able to achieve a rezoning and how long is it likely to take?

- What are the requirements and how long is it likely to take to get all the municipal approvals needed to construct the development?

- Do the members have the time and capacity needed to participate in a development process?

As noted in Chapter 2 under the getting started section, the best way to determine the cost for a new home in the preferred neighbourhood is to visit recently constructed developments that are similar to the type of development being contemplated. For example, if a new thousand-square-foot townhouse is selling for $500,000, then you can calculate that the cost for land and building is in the $500 per square foot range. Although this price will include the developer's profit, completed homes in a community led development tend to cost about the same as conventional developments even if the group is the developer. So, although this will not be a completely accurate number because the final cost is dependent on the choices the group makes about design, it gives a good enough sense at the beginning of the project to start to establish feasibility. Documenting the information (home sizes, features, asking prices, date of visit, sales representative, etc.) will be valuable for anyone engaged to conduct a feasibility study that includes a market analysis. If there aren't any developments similar to what is being desired in the neighbourhood of choice, then it may not be possible to construct that type of project in the preferred neighbourhood, and it would be important to check with the local government authority on this.

If the members are not aware of any potential sites available for sale, a municipal planner can point out locations where the land use designation would support the type of development contemplated and can provide information about how long the approval process will likely take. A local realtor can identify potential sites and provide an estimate of what a site with the development potential needed would be worth. Having an idea of the time and money required to make a project happen will help a group to be realistic about whether this is something they have the capacity and interest to take on.

Site Selection Criteria

After determining that the neighbourhoods of choice can support the type of development contemplated, and at a cost that members are generally willing to accept, the next step will be to confirm the site selection criteria. The list below, from the Driftwood Village Cohousing community in North Vancouver, BC, gives a good example of criteria that can support a site search process:

- North Vancouver: between the bridges and below the highway

- walkable to transit, elementary school, grocery store, park or trail

- bikeable to secondary school, community centre, library, other services

- reasonable transit commute to downtown Vancouver

- set back from highways, transit terminals, port (to avoid noise, coal dust, diesel exhaust particulates)

- zoning in place or zoning potential to support a mix of townhouses and apartment-style units that can accommodate 20,000 to 25,000 square feet of buildable area, approximately twenty to thirty units

- assuming underground parking and storage (i.e., not individual garages)

Prior to starting the process of a finding a site, the members will need to know the following:

- What is the financial capacity of the group as a whole as well as the members individually?

- Are there professionals or other resources available to provide support?

- What will it take to develop a community in the neighbourhood of choice?

It is generally difficult to assess financial capacity without the help of a professional because many people are reluctant to reveal personal net worth to a fellow member. Establishing financial feasibility involves not only determining what individual members can afford to pay for a home but also needs to identify the potential equity that could be available to finance the development. The feasibility study should identify any financial issues and provide recommendations for potential solutions.

Finding professionals or other resources to provide support with the development process can be challenging, but as noted in Chapter 2, there are very few groups who achieve success without working with an experienced development consultant. Our hope is that this book can provide the support that a professional, who has knowledge and experience managing conventional developments, will need to guide a community led housing project to success. We recommend providing a copy of this book to local development professionals in the hopes it will help members find someone who is inspired to want to work with them.

Elements of a Preliminary Feasibility Study

The preliminary feasibility study should identify potential challenges and opportunities as well as the associated costs. It should also identify what it will take to keep costs in line with local market values and recommend a development strategy. It will ideally include a development proforma with an estimate of all the costs associated with developing the project, estimated average home costs based on the proposed density, possible alternatives to pursue if the original objective does not look feasible, financial analysis, a preliminary cash flow projection, potential risks, and the recommended steps to achieve success. The study should help ground the project in reality and support the group to focus on what they need to do to make a project happen.

There are two major factors that need to be determined early on and should be discussed as part of the preliminary feasibility study:

- character and form
- development strategy

Character and Form

Character and form refers to all aspects of the design, including building type, height, style, how the building relates to the site, choice of exterior materials, landscaping—essentially, everything related to physical appearance. The character and form of the development will impact the timeline, the financial plan, and the overall "shape" of the community, both physical and social. When preparing the proforma, the development consultant will make certain assumptions about the project and will estimate costs based on their best understanding of current conditions. Each project is different, and identifying what needs to be considered when evaluating the opportunity is a key part of the process. The final costs may vary considerably from the initial estimates if the scope of the project changes and will depend on the decisions the group makes over the course of the development. One of the responsibilities of the development consultant is to update the proforma throughout the life of the project and help keep members informed about the potential cost implications of the decisions they make.

Homes in a community led housing project can take many forms: single-family, duplexes, triplexes, fourplexes, townhouses, apartments, or a combination of these! Appendix A includes images of completed cohousing communities with these different housing types. The site location will impact the type of homes that are possible. For example, it is not practical to want to develop single-family homes in a dense urban context. The single-family housing form is more appropriate in rural or suburban locations.

The following general questions need to be answered to determine character and form:

- What home sizes are desired?

- What type of homes (townhouse, apartment, single-family) are desired?

- How many homes will there be in the community?

- How large will the common house be?

- What outdoor amenities will be included?

- Is it possible to include parking at grade, or will it need to be below ground?

- How much in the way of green building features will the group want to include?

- How much in the way of universal accessibility will the group want to include?

- What level of quality will the group want in the finished product?

- Is affordability a priority? If so, what concessions need to be made in relation to green building, universal accessibility, and quality?

Development Strategy

The development strategy essentially identifies how the project will be structured from a legal and financial perspective. Will the group self-develop, or will they need a developer partner? A conventional developer partner will expect to receive some financial benefit for taking the risk and may have other requirements as well. The more equity the members invest in the project, the more control they will have over decisions regarding the development. However, if the group does not have access to the equity that is required, then self-development may not be an option, and this will have an impact on both the legal and financial structure.

The following general questions need to be answered to determine the development strategy:

- Do the members have the financial capacity to generate the equity required to develop the project, or will a developer partner be required?

- What return will members expect to receive to attract the equity required to finance the development?

- If there is a developer partner involved, what payment and/or profit will they expect to receive?

- What are the steps required and how long is it likely to take to secure the approvals required to construct the project?

- What are the development servicing requirements and costs?

- What are the likely construction costs per square foot for the type of finishing the group desires?

- What are the local permit fees and development costs?

If the zoning is in place, then it is possible to calculate land cost per unit, but if it is not yet in place, assumptions will need to be made about the final density that will be approved based on discussions with local regulatory authorities.

The following provides descriptions of three types of strata development strategies that are possible in British Columbia. The model that is selected will impact the project financing requirements as well as the legal agreements for ownership.

Full build-out: All roads, servicing, infrastructure, common house, and all homes are constructed and the strata plan is registered upon completion of the development. Purchasers move in to a fully completed development at the end of the construction period. There may be additional common buildings that are constructed later, but for the most part, the community is complete. Most cohousing developments in Canada are based on this model.

Phased strata: The same type of model that is noted above, except that the project is completed in phases—meaning that a segment of the development is built out so that members can move in and another phase may be constructed at a later date. This approach may be practical for larger scale projects (for example, suburban projects with sixty-plus units) but is not generally practical for a development of twenty to forty units.

Bare land strata: Refers to a development where the lots are owned individually and the roads, common buildings, and remainder of the land are owned in common. Once the lots have been developed with roads and servicing in place, the remainder of the project can be built out completely, it can be built out in defined stages, or it can be built out over a long period, one house at a time. In this model, members could purchase a lot and build their own home. This approach may be practical in rural or suburban settings but is typically not possible in urban settings.

The following chart provides some comparisons of the three development models described above.

Full Build-Out	Phased Strata	Bare Land Strata
Development model requires all homes and common areas be completed to a level that allows for registration of the strata plan.	Built in phases.	Could be built out all at once or in stages. Once lots have been developed and the servicing is in place, the homes and common amenities can be constructed at any time.
Any home type is possible.	Any home type other than a single apartment building is possible.	Only certain home types are possible (single-family and duplex) and dependent on development strategy.
Community layout restricted mainly by fire safety, density, and topography.	Community layout restricted mainly by fire safety, density, and topography.	Community layout is much more structured to account for individual lots, and it is more challenging to ensure the common house is located where it will support spontaneous connection.
Equity and loan required to cover entire cost of development. If all homes are not sold at completion, debt financing is required to carry unsold homes.	Equity and loan required to cover full servicing costs but only construction costs for building homes and common amenities.	Equity and loan required to cover full servicing costs, but a number of different financing strategies are possible, such as owner financed/constructed homes.

Potential Risks

Chapter 2 provides an overview of the risks associated with a community led housing development in the section titled "Impediments to Success." The following is a list of the questions that should be addressed in the preliminary feasibility study to help identify the potential risks for the specific development.

- Are there local professionals willing and able to provide services to support the development? If not, what are other possible options?

- What are the current conditions and likelihood of experiencing rapidly escalating costs?

- What organizational structure will support a collaborative process?

- What is the recommended legal structure that will support a collaborative process while also meeting the requirements of government legislation?

- What happens if there is conflict between group members or with professionals? Are there ways to keep the project on track when there are disagreements?

- What is the likelihood of finding a site in the neighbourhood of choice that has the infrastructure and zoning potential to meet the desired goals?

- Are there qualified local construction contractors willing and able to provide services? If not, what are the other possible options?

- What is the likelihood of being able to attract the members needed to sell out the project prior to completion? Are there local demographics that need to be considered?

- What happens if costs are higher than anticipated and the price of a home becomes unaffordable for some members?

- What are some of the likely challenges associated with any of the innovative approaches that the group is contemplating?

- How does the legal and financial structure deal with the death of a member or other major life changes?

- How do you ensure that potential members are capable of contributing positively to a collaborative culture?

Review Project Objective

The preliminary feasibility study will determine whether it is necessary to revise the original project objective and should also clarify what other decisions need to be made to proceed. The members will need to decide whether they want to proceed based on the information and recommendations provided and, if so, where the money will come from and how it will be accounted for. Any money spent at this stage is not refundable, but if a project proceeds, it can be counted towards the equity contribution or down payment at completion.

Depending on current market conditions, the time available for making a decision once a potential site has been identified may be very short, possibly only hours in a hot real estate market. The members need to not only have the financial capacity to move forward with the site purchase, they also need to be nimble—ready to decide quickly and commit to taking the next step. To secure a site using conventional financing, the group will need to have the capacity to generate equity equaling 40 to 50 percent of the land cost plus around $500,000 to cover initial development costs (architect and other consultants, development or rezoning applications, etc.). If the feasibility study identified a shortfall of financial capacity to proceed with land purchase, then there will be a need to focus on building a membership with the financial resources required to purchase a site or on finding a partner that can provide financial assistance.

Working with a design professional to facilitate some preliminary design work will give a better sense of what might be possible and will help the members to clarify and refine the vision—particularly in locations that have complex land use regulations. The section on preliminary programming in Chapter 7 discusses this in more detail. In CDC's experience, membership can grow rapidly at this stage because potential members are attracted to a clear vision that is grounded in reality and a project that appears to be moving forward. It is also exciting to participate in design workshops and discussions.

Finding and Securing a Site

Obviously, without a site, there is no project. So, it is important to get started on the site search as soon as the group feels confident to proceed, even if there is just a small group of members at the time. Development sites are generally difficult to find. Many groups spend years looking for a site without success. The larger the group is, the more challenging it can be to find and agree on a site that is good enough; yet with high land costs, it is also necessary to have enough members with the financial capacity to move forward. This is a tricky phase. There are many reasons why a particular site may not be right for some people. However, if the group waits to find the "perfect" site, then the project may never happen. Finding ways to make the "imperfect" site that does come available work for the group is essential.

The steps for securing a site will vary depending on the situation, but the least risky and most successful approach is to look for sites that have the infrastructure needed to support the type of development being contemplated as well as the desired zoning in place or zoning potential based on what the local planner has identified as areas of greatest opportunity. Some groups are able to find an appropriate site through association, or word of mouth; in other cases, a member of the group owns property that has the desirability and development potential needed. If none of these options are available, then our recommended approach is to secure the services of a qualified real estate professional.

Selecting a Real Estate Professional

Armed with information provided by the local jurisdiction about what potential locations could support the proposed development, a group can approach a real estate professional to get assistance in finding and securing a site. It is important to be able to provide concise and specific site criteria so the real estate professional does not waste time looking for sites that are not appropriate. Once the site criteria have been confirmed by the members, a next step could be to ask a real estate professional's opinion about the likelihood of finding such a site and then refining the criteria as required to ensure they are grounded in reality.

In an urban context, it is very likely that a land assembly will be required to secure a property that is large enough to support a multi-family development. Land assemblies are complex, and the success thereof depends on being able to secure agreements with multiple parties. Much care needs to be taken to ensure nothing is said or done that negatively impacts the negotiations!

In the course of selecting a real estate professional, consider whether they meet the following criteria:

- has experience dealing with development sites and land assemblies

- has local area knowledge

- has the interest, time, and availability to work on the project

- is a good communicator, willing to provide regular updates

- has a good reputation and can provide references from past clients

During the course of interviewing potential candidates, consider asking the following questions:

- Do you work in a team? If so, what are the roles? Who is the primary contact person for communications? What experience do the other team members bring?

- Do you have the time and availability to work on a land assembly for the group?

- Describe what approach you would use to find a site.

- How long do you think this process might take?

- In the last one to two years, what development sites or land assemblies have you been involved with? How many? For what kind of projects?

- What locations, within the defined area of choice, would you recommend focusing on for the site search? Are there other areas that the group should consider? What is the current selling price per square foot for development sites in these areas?

- What would be our communication sequence or protocols if we engage your services?

- What is the payment structure, and how does it work?

- What are your expectations in terms of working relationship and contract for services? What happens if we find that our relationship is not working out?

- Can you share three references for similar projects?

Site Selection

Once a real estate agent has been selected, the site search can begin in earnest. Any potential sites identified will need to be reviewed to confirm they meet the criteria and have the potential for development at the desired density. In CDC's experience, there will be an opportunity to complete a site feasibility study before committing to the purchase, but the decision about whether to spend the time and money that it takes to do the study, which can be quite considerable depending on the situation, will need to be made prior to making the purchase offer.

As noted above, it is likely that members will need to make a decision quickly, so it is very important that an agreement on how they will make this decision is already in place. We believe if you find a site that is "good enough" and there are households who have the financial capacity to commit to purchasing the site, it is worth taking the leap to create community even if some members are not willing to continue because that site does not meet their needs or desires. Some members may not be willing to invest and choose to leave the group once a site has been selected. It is difficult to leave people behind, but if it takes too long to find a suitable site, it is likely some people will leave in frustration anyway. No matter what you do, at this stage the group tends to be somewhat unstable. The faster you can secure a site, the sooner you can get a project happening, which in itself will help to solidify and stabilize the group.

Making the Offer to Purchase

Actual purchase terms have varied based on market conditions and circumstances (length of time for feasibility condition, timing for completion, purchase price, etc.). The development consultant and realtor can provide recommendations on how to structure the offer to purchase to address the interests of the buyer and the seller in a win-win arrangement.

When the landowner is also a member of the group, there can be opportunities to structure the offer differently than when dealing with an uninvolved seller. For example, on one project that CDC managed, the seller, who was a member of the group, was willing to carry the property with a small non-refundable deposit until the rezoning had been approved. In this case, the group not only saved thousands of dollars on interest, but because they did not have to come up with the funds to purchase the land until after the rezoning was in place, they were able to move forward with a smaller group and work on building the membership needed to develop the project. The owner was able to continue to occupy and maintain control of the property, which saved the owner money as well as the inconvenience of having to move.

Assignment Clause

Typically, the development company is not set up until the subjects have been removed, which is why an assignment clause would be desired. This makes it possible for a member of the group to act as the authorized signing authority to secure the property, without having to spend the money to set up the company. If the seller is unwilling to accept an assignment clause, then it is important to set up a company right away in order to ensure no individuals assume the responsibility and liability associated with purchasing a development site. However, setting up the company prior to securing a site adds a layer of complexity and can be time consuming. In CDC's experience, none of the sellers had any problem accepting the assignment clause, particularly once they understood the rationale for including it.

Site Feasibility

If the offer is accepted, the project moves into the final feasibility phase. Essentially, the purpose of the site feasibility is to identify the challenges, opportunities, and likely costs of developing the project. Depending on the market conditions, the seller may be willing to allow more time to confirm site feasibility, but in CDC's experience thirty days has been typical. The following provides an overview of the information that is required for a typical investigation:

- conduct a title search

- meet with the local jurisdictional authorities to identify site development potential and requirements, municipal development costs and charges, documentation requirements, and timelines for approvals

- obtain a commercial appraisal for the site

- secure approval from a financial institution for a land purchase loan and discuss the possibilities for eventually securing construction financing

- confirm equity commitment from members to cover the difference between the land loan amount and the purchase price, plus enough to cover estimated soft costs for the design and rezoning process

- prepare a preliminary design concept plan to confirm the site will accommodate the project objective

- complete whatever studies are required to confirm feasibility, which typically involve, at least, geotechnical and environmental assessments

- research local market conditions

Ideally, the feasibility report will include the following:

- description of the property and proposed development

- consultant reports that were required to confirm feasibility

- overview of the development potential, including regulatory context and requirements, registrations on title, development servicing considerations, and financial analysis including member equity capacity and commitment

- project timeline with milestones and estimated completion date

- assumptions that were made when preparing the development proforma

- development proforma with estimated costs for a completed home in the community (updated from the preliminary budget prepared in the financial feasibility phase)

- market analysis

- cash flow projection

- potential risks

- recommendations for next steps

The feasibility study will identify the steps that need to be taken and the decisions that need to be made and enable the members to make an informed decision about whether to remove the conditions and proceed with the site purchase or to continue their search for a site that better meets their needs. If proper due diligence was done before securing the site, there should be no big surprises. If the decision is to proceed with the site purchase, then the project moves into the development phase, and efficient decision-making becomes essential to keep the project on time and on budget.

11

Construction

T HE CONSTRUCTION PHASE is where the rubber meets the road! The following provides a summary of what is included in this chapter and recommendations on when each section should be given greater consideration:

- **Overview of Construction Delivery Methods and Construction Contracts:** Understanding the different options for delivery methods and types of construction contracts will be important when discussing the strategy for selection of the professional team. The relationship between the construction contractor, the professionals, and the owner (group members) varies with the different construction delivery methods, which impacts the scope of professional services and fees.

- **CDC's Recommended Approach:** The decision about how to approach the construction contract is best made early in the process. The delivery method that CDC recommends involves the construction contractor early in the design phase.

- **Finding and Selecting the Construction Contractor:** This section describes the process that has been used successfully to select a qualified construction contractor.

- **Preparing for Construction:** This section provides an overview of the typical documentation required to apply for the building permit, new home warranty requirements for homes constructed in BC, recommended protocols for the construction phase, how to deal with changes, and typical construction terminology, all of which will be important to understand prior to construction start.

Overview of Construction Delivery Methods

How to approach the construction of the project is one of the major decisions the group will need to make. As noted in Chapter 3, for any given project, there are a number of construction delivery methods available. The information below provides an overview of the main options.

Design-Build

Design-build is a method of project delivery in which the owner enters into a single contract with a design-build contractor who engages all the consultants and subcontractors and performs the design services and the work under one agreement for a single pre-determined stipulated or fixed price. The owner is responsible for providing a statement of requirements and for reviewing and approving the construction documents.

Pros:
- design-build contractor has full control over design and construction schedule, which contributes to efficiency and potentially a faster timeline
- provides good framework for streamlined communication and rapid decision-making
- particularly suitable for standard or repetitive buildings
- client deals with a unified administrative entity

Cons:
- may not be suitable for complex or unique buildings
- when the contractor is selected upfront, a high level of trust is required
- projects are not awarded based on the lowest bid, so the owner may not get the most competitive pricing

Design-Bid-Build

The prevailing method of project delivery is design-bid-build, in which the owner engages an architect to prepare the design, drawings, and specifications. The design team produces a set of construction documents that are used as the basis of a competitive bidding process known as tender that may also inform design. Once the design is complete, the general contractor, selected by tender, is engaged. The form of contract is fixed-price, which is administered, reviewed, and certified by the architect. The contractor is responsible for cost overruns, unless the contract amount has been increased via formal change orders (only as a result of additional scope from the client or missing information on the drawings, not price overruns, errors, or omissions).

Pros:
- competitive lump-sum pricing
- user sign-off on complete documents before tendering

Cons:
- longer schedule
- major cost-saving potential often underutilized because there is minimal opportunity for the contractor to make recommendations about constructability
- promotes adversarial relationship between the contractor and the owner
- construction cannot commence until tenders are called
- lack of flexibility in accommodating new requirements or changes
- if the selection of the contractor is based on price alone, this could have an impact on quality
- lack of access to sub-trade and supplier information

Construction Management

A method of project delivery in which the owner engages an architect and construction manager at the start of the project, who work as a team during the design phase. Upon completion of the design, the project is tendered to trade contractors who enter into contracts with the construction manager or owner (depending on the form of contract). The final contract is typically cost-plus, which covers the project costs plus some amount of profit for managing the contracts.

Pros:
- teamwork and effective communication
- flexibility during design and construction
- effective use of joint expertise
- construction may begin before completion of drawings, resulting in shorter schedule
- disclosure of all subcontract prices to the client
- sensitivity to market conditions

Cons:
- requires careful selection of team members to ensure commitment to the team and process
- requires trust in team building and the selection process
- client's active involvement in decision-making process can cause delays
- flexibility and potential for changes during construction make budget management more difficult
- construction costs are estimated only, and final costs are not established until the end, which makes it very challenging to establish accurate home costs for closing

Construction Management at Risk

This method of project delivery is similar to construction management, where the construction manager acts as consultant to the owner in the development and design phases (often referred to as *preconstruction services*) but as the equivalent of a general contractor during the construction phase. This method entails a commitment by the construction manager to deliver the project at a guaranteed maximum price. The construction manager is responsible for cost overruns, unless the contract has been increased via formal change orders (only as a result of additional scope from the client, not price overruns, errors, or omissions).

Pros:

- teamwork and effective communication

- flexibility during design (construction manager is involved with estimating the cost of constructing a project based on the goals of the owner; decisions can be made to modify the design concept instead of having to spend a considerable amount of time, effort, and money redesigning and/or modifying completed construction documents)
- effective use of joint expertise
- construction may begin before completion of drawings, resulting in shorter schedule
- disclosure of subcontract prices to the client
- sensitivity to market conditions
- total cost commitment known in advance

Cons:

- requires careful selection of team members to ensure commitment to the team and process
- requires trust in team building and the selection process

Construction Contracts

In Canada, all construction contract documents are standardized and created by the Canadian Construction Documents Committee (CCDC), a committee that includes contractors, developers, engineers, architects, public and private sector owners, and a construction lawyer from the Canadian Bar Association. CCDC documents are relied on as industry standards for their fairness and balance for all parties involved in a construction project, and they have developed and kept current a series of standard construction contracts for use across the country. Each CCDC contract document has an identifying number. The CCDC website includes information about the different contract documents, their purpose, and how to purchase them.[1]

The delivery method impacts the type of construction contract that is appropriate, and there may be several contract options possible. The construction company typically has a preferred form of contract that they will feel comfortable working with. The type of contract, and any supplementary conditions that will form part of the contract documents, is determined in the negotiation process when making the contractor selection.

CDC's Recommended Approach

We recommend selecting the construction contractor early and involving them in the design phase. Before the project design is complete, the construction contractor is involved in estimating project costs. The design can then be changed to balance the costs, schedule, quality of materials, and scope of the project. Time, effort, and money are saved in this approach as opposed to having to modify or redesign any completed construction documents. The drawback is that this requires careful selection and trust in the team building and selection, but a robust selection process can address this. Working closely with a pre-selected local general contractor during the design phase helps ensure the design decisions stay on budget. The general contractor becomes part of the professional team and can help the group develop a project that is within their budget requirements.

A fixed-price contract provides the greatest certainty for the members in terms of identifying the cost for the completed development. Although construction management has its advantages, the uncertainty of the final cost makes it more challenging to determine the home purchase price when developing a project that has no profit. The approach that we have found works best is where the contractor acts as a construction manager during the design phase; then once the design has been completed, the project tendered, and the trades selected, the general contractor enters into a CCDC2 stipulated price contract for construction. The CCDC2 is a contract that establishes a pre-determined fixed price for the work. It is one of the CCDC contract types that is available. For several of the projects CDC managed, the selected contractor did not charge a fee during the design phase, even though they were providing skilled construction management services. The contractor appreciated the opportunity to be part of the process of helping to design a project and develop a budget that met the owners' needs and desires.

One of the key benefits of this approach is the development of a collaborative relationship between key project members. Who the key project members are will depend on the nature of the project, but they would typically include the development consultant, architect, engineers, and selected representatives of the owner (i.e., the construction focus members). Other delivery models can result in the architect and general contractor developing disparate priorities, which could lead to an adversarial relationship. But when the architect and construction manager are brought together at the earliest stage, as in this model, they are positioned to work collaboratively at solving mutual challenges and to maximize leveraging of individual experience and expertise, often resulting in faster delivery, better value, and a higher quality end product.

This approach offers unparalleled potential for reducing timelines by preventing bottlenecks in the design and tender processes. Having the construction manager and architect working collaboratively from the start of the project allows for a clearer view of the complete picture. Increased awareness and collaboration assist with early identification of project elements that can be started concurrently, and add flexibility for accommodating changes and revisions with the least impact on budgets and timelines.

As noted in the introduction, collaboration characterizes CDC's approach to the entire development process. Bringing in the construction contractor in the early stages of design develops relationships where everyone is working together to achieve a common goal. As well, the contractors' risk is reduced considerably over the conventional design-bid-build method because they are intimately familiar with the building and have been involved in the decisions about constructability. The fees, overhead, and profit tend to be more comparable to a conventional construction management approach where the contractor does not take the risk for cost overruns. The process of finalizing the construction budget is transparent, and the client has the opportunity to participate in the decision-making. This sets up a very different relationship from start to finish. Contractors with whom CDC has worked have expressed how much they enjoyed working in this kind of a collaborative environment where goodwill and caring contribute to everyone's efficiency and effectiveness.

Finding and Selecting the Construction Contractor

The image below, adapted by CDC from a Driftwood Village presentation, provides an overview of the different stages in which the construction manager or general contractor is typically involved.

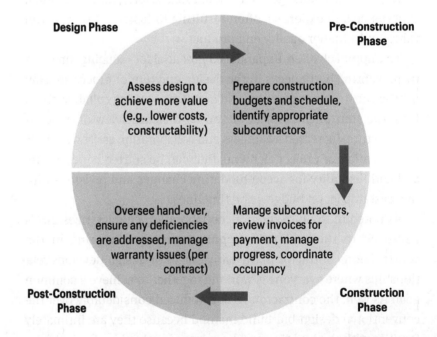

Design Phase

Assess design to achieve more value (e.g., lower costs, constructability)

Pre-Construction Phase

Prepare construction budgets and schedule, identify appropriate subcontractors

Oversee hand-over, ensure any deficiencies are addressed, manage warranty issues (per contract)

Manage subcontractors, review invoices for payment, manage progress, coordinate occupancy

Post-Construction Phase

Construction Phase

CDC believes the best time to get a general contractor involved is once the site has been secured, rezoning completed (if required), and preliminary concept drawings have been prepared by the architect. In some cases, CDC was able to recommend a particular general contractor based on experience. The architect may also have recommendations. However, if there is no known general contractor in the local area, then the following approach can be taken to identify and select a general contractor for the project.

The first step would be to confirm the criteria for selection (example provided below). The next step would be to identify potential companies that meet the criteria and make initial contact to determine whether they would be interested in providing services for the project. A request for proposal could then be sent out to the four or five companies who appear to best meet the criteria and who have an interest in providing services.

The context and situation can vary, so the following is meant only as an example of what information should be provided and what to ask for when preparing a request for proposal.

A project description should be provided to potential candidates and include information such as:

- how the project was conceived (not essential, but helps to give context)
- information about any professionals that have been engaged to date
- some very succinct information about the project (a couple of paragraphs)
- the location
- geotechnical and environmental assessments, current zoning, and any other relevant information about the site
- an overview of the project with preliminary concept plans
- information about the developer or owner group
- project budget and assumption about costs
- proposed and/or anticipated timeline

Make it clear that the following services will be required:

1 The fee proposed must include provision of the services required for all components of the work.

2 The successful firm will be responsible for providing expertise and advice for the following pre-construction services:

- refine the design and specifications as required to meet the owner's budget requirements

- help identify best green building options

- provide feedback and interim costing analysis at the following stages: initial massing or concept design; completion of schematic design; completion of design development; 25 percent construction documents; 75 percent construction documents

3 The successful firm will be responsible for managing the construction of all buildings; all site services, including storm water management systems, sanitary drainage systems, electrical duct banks and cables, data and communications duct banks and cables, water and fire lines, and any other services or utilities that may be required; the construction of all onsite and offsite civil works and hard and soft landscaping; and to apply and pay for any permits required by the local jurisdiction other than the building permit, which will be applied for and paid for by the client.

Applicants should meet the following submission criteria:
- awareness of green technology (Built Green, Passive House, or other green certification may be required)
- experience working with "non-profits" and unsophisticated developers
- local knowledge, proven track record, can oversee each step
- knows good subcontractors
- good communicator
- good team player, collaborative, adaptable
- organized, structured

- ability to work well with an architect
- ability to build on time, has availability for this project
- financial capacity to take on a project of this size
- experience with projects of this size and complexity
- references

The following is an example of language used in a fee proposal:

> The proponent shall provide a fee for the provision of the services relating to the work as described above. The fee proposal shall contain a fixed price fee for all staff anticipated to be involved in the pre-construction phase of the project and an estimate of reimbursable expenses. The proposal shall also include the proposed form of contract, supplementary conditions, and proposed fee for the construction phase.

Instructions to applicants should identify who to contact if there are any questions, the deadline for submission, the format for submission, and who to send the submission to.

It is important for the professional team that has been engaged prior to selection of the general contractor to be in alignment with the selection decision. As noted in Chapter 2, good development requires successful teamwork, and the general contractor is an important and impactful member of the team.

Preparing for Construction

It is essential to be well prepared and organized to ensure the construction phase is as efficient as possible. At this stage in the development, interest costs are high, so any delays will have a big impact on the budget.

New Home Warranty

In the province of BC, the Homeowner Protection Act (the Act) requires all residential builders who build and sell new homes to provide home warranty insurance for ten years to the owner who buys the new home. *Owner* is defined in the Act to mean a person who purchases a new home and includes a subsequent purchaser of a new home. Home warranty insurance protects new homes in BC against construction defects in materials and labour, building envelope and structural defects.[2] Other provinces may have similar legislation. It is important to know the requirements in your local area before embarking on a residential development.

The home warranty insurance is provided by a third party that has been approved by the BC Financial Services Authority and meets the requirements of the Homeowner Protection Act. Although the home warranty insurance does not come into effect until the completion of the project, the developer must show proof that insurance has been secured when they make the application for a building permit.

The following is an overview of what is required to make an application to secure new home warranty insurance in BC:

- copy of certificate of incorporation (if applicable)

- corporate organizational chart indicating all shareholders and percentage interest held by the individuals and/or companies; or a copy of partnership agreement or joint venture agreement (if applicable)

- commitment letter from all sources of financing for the project

- most current year-end accountant-prepared financial statements for applicant and for any parent company, holding company, or other entities with an ownership interest in the applicant company

- proforma budget for the project or opening statement from the quantity surveyor or cost consultant

- personal net worth statements for all individual owners of the company

- detailed resumés for all principals and key staff (work experience, education, qualifications, etc.)

- copy of construction contract with the general contractor or construction manager if the construction of the building is contracted out to a third party

- disclosure statement if building or project is multi-unit

- homeowner maintenance manual (the Homeowner Protection Act regulations require a maintenance manual be provided to owners of new homes)

- preliminary project information for multi-unit buildings

- builder application fee and home warranty registration fees at construction start

In the self-developed model that CDC has managed, the company that has been set up to develop the project is considered to be a residential builder and must be licensed under the Act. The BC Housing Licensing & Consumer Services department has a website that identifies the qualification requirements and process for applying to become a licensed residential builder. Since the company hired a licensed general contractor to construct the homes in CDC-managed projects, they were exempt from having to meet the strict qualification requirements for licensing as a residential builder; the company was required to be licensed as a developer, but this was a much simpler process.[3]

The Act's regulations set out the minimum standards of home warranty insurance coverage. Except for extended warranties, as described in the construction contract, the warranty period is two years from the date at which the occupancy permit has been issued for the specified home for materials and labour, five years for building envelope, and ten years for structural defects (a 2-5-10 warranty):

Two-Year Material and Labour Warranty

- first twelve months: coverage for any defect in materials and labour

- first fifteen months: coverage for any defect in materials and labour in the common property of a multi-unit building

- first twenty-four months: coverage for any defects in materials and labour supplied for the electrical, plumbing, heating, ventilation, and air conditioning delivery and distribution systems; in addition, coverage for any defect in materials and labour supplied for the exterior cladding, caulking, windows, and doors that may lead to detachment or material damage to the new home

Five-Year Building Envelope Warranty
Ten-Year Structural Defects Warranty

The developer is responsible for rectifying any construction defects. The Homeowner Protection Act Regulation defines *defects* as "any design or construction, that is contrary to the building code or that requires repair or replacement due to the negligence of a residential builder or person for whom the residential builder is responsible at law" and defines defects in the building envelope as "defects that result in failure of the building envelope to perform its intended function." For the CDC-managed projects, the construction general contractor, through the CCDC2 construction contract, took on the responsibilities associated with the home warranty and managed corrections associated with any construction defects.

Building Permit Application
During the site feasibility study stage, it is important to confirm the documentation requirements for the construction permit application. Every jurisdiction will have somewhat different requirements, but the following provides an overview of the documentation that in our experience has typically been required:

- architectural plans
- code consultant review
- site survey
- landscape plans and onsite/offsite cost estimates
- civil engineering plans and onsite/offsite cost estimates (as required)
- mechanical, electrical, geotechnical, and structural drawings
- archeological reports (as required)
- environmental impact assessments (as required)
- traffic management plan
- construction fire safety plan
- construction management plan
- liability insurance certificates
- professional schedules or letters of assurance
- new home warranty registration confirmation (province of BC)
- title certification for the property under development

Course of Construction Insurance

Prior to the commencement of construction, insurance needs to be in place to cover builder's risk and wrap-up liability. Typically the construction contractor and the commercial lender will want to review the insurance to ensure that it meets their needs.

Construction Communication and Protocols

Prior to the start of construction, it is important to clarify expectations and ensure that everyone is in agreement about the protocols that support an efficient construction process. Suggested protocols, which have proven to be effective, are identified below.

Identify a small group of equity members (shareholders of the development company) comprised of three to five individuals maximum, with the following qualities to act as member representatives during the construction phase:

- has good communication skills and the ability to respond to emails within the same day when required

- has the ability to read construction drawings (or has a willingness to learn)

- is available to attend committee meetings and monthly construction meetings

- has an accurate and thorough knowledge about the progress and decisions made to date

- is able to see things from the larger perspective and consider the best interest of the group as a whole

- has the ability to work effectively with other members of the team

- has the time and capacity to participate for the entire construction period

The recommended role of the construction focus is:

- to represent the community in making construction-related decisions that require immediate attention because of financial consequences associated with delay

- to communicate with the general membership regarding the progress of construction, keeping members informed and responding to questions as required

- to work with the development consultant and other professionals as needed

- to manage tours of the building as it progresses

There are a number of possible ways the group could choose to select the construction focus members. Role selection is discussed in more detail in Chapter 5.

Site visits and tours for members and potential members are generally possible once the building is at a stage where it is safe enough to walk around. The recommended approach is to have a construction focus member take on the responsibility of checking with the site superintendent prior to a proposed site visit to identify potential hazards and determine whether the site is safe for visitors. To meet workers compensation board (WCB) requirements, all visitors are required to wear hardhats, steel toed boots, and safety vests at all times when on site. Often groups will choose to purchase a quantity of this safety gear for use by members and guests and then donate it to Habitat for Humanity at completion. Construction sites can be full of hazards, and anyone who enters one must be vigilant. It is important to have all visitors sign a waiver prior to visiting the site, which should be kept on file.

Any issues that members may see during a site visit should be reported to the construction focus members only, who would then report back to the development consultant to ensure that messaging is clear, simple, and appropriate.

Site meetings are typically scheduled by the professional or general contractor as required. The purpose is to review construction progress, to make inspections, and to discuss any issues. At minimum, a monthly site meeting should be scheduled with the general contractor, architect, development consultant, construction focus members, and any consultants or trades that are required to discuss issues that need to be dealt with, make inspections, and/or to review the progress to date.

The development consultant should prepare a progress update report for the general membership, for presentation at the monthly general meetings. Any construction-related issues that had not been identified as time sensitive can be dealt with at that meeting. Regular field reviews completed by the project professionals should be made available to the members.

Changes to Construction Scope and Budget

It is important for the members to agree there will be no changes to the plans or specifications once construction commences, unless the changes are required for cost savings or constructability and have been identified by the professionals or construction team. Often members will want to add things or make changes that they didn't think of previously, but it is impossible to manage the budget when this opportunity is available during construction. If the group wants to ensure the project stays on time and on budget, then this is an important boundary to have in place.

Construction Terminology and Managing Changes

There are a number of terms that are typically used when managing a construction contract, which are identified below. Prior to construction start, it is important to establish the protocol for making changes and dealing with issues that may arise. The owner in this case is referring to the development company.

Request for information (RFI): The primary method for the general contractor to ask questions of the professional team. The RFI is typically sent to the architect, who coordinates the responses from the professionals. The RFI typically only comes to the owner's representative if it is a question that requires owner input.

Supplementary instruction (SI): The primary method for the professionals to issue instructions to the general contractor. SIs can be the result of either an RFI or a site visit and can often involve additional work and details that had not previously been included on the drawings. Often there is no cost associated with an SI, but sometimes there is an additional cost if the scope of work changes from what had been included in the construction documents.

Potential change order (PCO): If the general contractor identifies that there will be a cost involved when an SI has been issued, a PCO will be prepared with a quotation for the work. The architect will review for scope and may redirect the PCO to the appropriate professionals to review and provide their input. If there are issues, the PCO can be sent back to the general contractor for a requote.

Contemplated change notice (CCN): A notice prepared by the architect when there is a change in the original specifications due to unforeseen conditions. CCNs are issued to the general contractor who provides a quotation as a PCO (see above). It is important to deal efficiently with changes during construction because they can impact the budget as well as the schedule. If there are choices about direction, a PCO should go to the owner for approval. If it is time sensitive, the PCO should go to the construction focus members for review and decision. If it is not time sensitive, it should be brought to a general meeting of the members. If the work is something that is required and there are no real alternatives, the development consultant or other owner representative should have authority to approve the change based on recommendations from the professional team. The members should be informed of the change as part of the monthly project report.

Change order (co): Once accepted, the PCO can be carried forward to a CO, which authorizes the general contractor to proceed with the work. Once the CO is issued, it is sent to the general contractor to acknowledge, and the development consultant (or other representative that has been given authority) will need to sign it on behalf of the owner.

Certificate for payment: The general contractor will issue an application for payment for the work completed to date. The CCDC contracts require payments to be made within a stipulated time period. For a CCDC2 contract, the architect reviews the submission and also sends it to the applicable professionals for their review. If there are any questions or concerns, these are discussed with the general contractor prior to submitting to the owner. Once the application for payment has been reviewed and approved, the architect prepares a certificate for payment. For the projects CDC managed, the development consultant prepared the draw request if a draw was required, which was dependent on whether the owners' equity was sufficient to pay for the construction costs (see reference to additional shareholder loans in Chapter 9 under "Member Investments"). The draw request would go to the quantity surveyor, a professional engaged by the owner and approved by the financial institution that funded the construction loan. The quantity surveyor reviews the request and prepares a report for the financial institution recommending payment if there is agreement about the value of the work completed to date. The financial institution will then deposit funds into the owner's account based on the recommendations of the quantity surveyor, and this will be used to make payment to the general contractor.

Builders lien holdback: Every Canadian province and territory has its own builders lien act meant to ensure that contractors and workers who contribute to improvements on land are paid for their services

and materials. It is important at the outset of the project for anyone who is contracting services for construction to understand and
adhere to the requirements. On a construction project, an owner
could pay the contractor in full, only to see the contractor default
on its payment to a subcontractor. Or a subcontractor might fail to
pay its workers or suppliers. If all the unpaid parties filed liens, the
owner would potentially have to pay twice—once to the contractor and again to the lien holders. To avoid this unfairness, the BC
Builders Lien Act requires an owner to hold back 10 percent of each
payment to the contractor in a special account so there is money
available for payment of liens. In a builders lien holdback, the owner
must withhold 10 percent of the contract price until fifty-five days
after the general contract is substantially completed, abandoned,
or otherwise ended. If, after the fifty-five days are up, no liens have
been filed within the forty-five-day limit (and no lawsuit making a
lien claim has been filed), the owner can pay out the 10 percent to
the contractor. But if any liens have been filed, the holdback may be
used to help pay these liens. Often, the total of all liens filed by all
claimants is greater than the holdback, but the owner does not have
to pay lien claimants more than the holdback amount. The Act sets
out how claimants share the holdback.

Certificate of substantial completion: On completion of the project that
has been constructed under a CCDC2 contract, the architect issues a
certificate of substantial completion. This is what triggers the timing
for the lien holdback release. The certificate for payment identifies
the amount of the lien holdback that has accumulated to date.

12

Completion

T THE COMPLETION of construction and once the occupancy permit has been issued, the members can move into their new homes. As noted in Chapter 8, once the development is completed, the legal structure needs to accommodate individual tenure of the homes and shared ownership of the common property. The terminology used here to describe this change from development company to individual owners is *closing*.

Managing Shortfalls or Excess Contingency

Prior to preparing the legal and financial documents for closing, a decision needs to be made about how to deal with any shortfall or excess in contingency. As noted in Chapter 9, for the CDC-managed projects, the members agreed to use the percentage of value that was established when the homes were appraised and pricing was finalized to determine any increase or decrease in cost. Until the project is complete and all costs have been confirmed, the exact amount of the contingency cannot be determined; it can, however, be fairly accurately estimated approximately two months prior to completion. If there is an expected shortfall, it is a matter of identifying how much needs to be added to home purchase prices to cover the project costs. If there is an excess, then it is a matter of deciding if there will be any reduction in the home purchase price and/or if the excess will be used to cover unbudgeted items that are desirable for the group.

The following table provides an example of how to revise purchase prices in the event there is a shortfall of $100,000, calculating the increase based on the percentage of value that the home being purchased represents in relation to the cost of the completed project.

Home Purchase Price (not including GST)	Percentage of Value	Percentage of Value Multiplied by $100,000 Shortfall	Revised Purchase Price (not including GST)
$500,000.00	3%	$3,000.00	$503,000.00
$900,000.00	5%	$5,000.00	$905,000.00

This same formula would apply in the event that the decision is made to reduce the final costs by $100,000, except in that scenario the home prices would be reduced by $3,000 and $5,000, respectively, resulting in revised purchase prices of $497,000 and $895,000.

If the decision is made to use any excess to cover unbudgeted items, we have found that it is in the best interest of maintaining community harmony to create a priority list prior to completion. Deciding how to spend excess funds can be a very challenging discussion, and having professional facilitation supports equal participation by all members.

Insurance for Completed Building

Insurance for the completed building needs to be put in place with the issuance of the occupancy permit. This typically includes property coverage, commercial liability, equipment breakdown coverage, directors' and officers' liability, and volunteer accident insurance. To secure a quote, an estimated cost to rebuild is required as well as an estimate for any common furnishings and fixtures that are to be covered under the policy. In our experience, the insurance company will want to secure an appraisal after completion to confirm values, but to get the insurance in place it is typically acceptable to provide estimated replacement values based on the actual construction costs. The insurance underwriters will also typically ask for information about the building construction and whether there are any occupant restrictions that could impact fire safety, for example whether or not propane barbeques will be allowed. It will be important for the members to have agreements in place that clarify expectations about occupant behaviour. Living in community agreements are discussed in more detail in Chapter 13.

In BC, a description about the insurance is included in the disclosure statement. The following is one option for clearly identifying how the cost for insurance will be handled at closing:

> The developer will replace the course of construction insurance coverage on completion of the construction of the development with property damage and bodily injury liability insurance for the strata corporation in an amount not less than $2,000,000.00 and full "major perils" replacement insurance on:

(i)	common property;
(ii)	common assets;
(iii)	common buildings shown on the Strata Plan; and
(iv)	fixtures included in the common buildings.

> The estimated costs of the premiums are included in the proposed strata budget attached to this disclosure statement. The first year's premiums will be paid by the developer, but each purchaser will credit the developer on closing with an appropriate proportionate share (determined by the developer) of those premiums. The purchaser is responsible for insuring the contents of such purchaser's applicable strata lot.

The estimated cost for insurance at completion should follow the same formula as the allocation of strata fees since the building insurance will be included in the operating budget going forward.

Municipal Property Taxes

Properties are assessed each year to determine the market value, which is used to calculate the amount of municipal property taxes payable. When the building is under construction, the assessment is based on the value of the land plus the value of the construction that has been completed to the date of the assessment. Once the building has been completed, the assessment is based on market value. When the building has separate titles (strata title or condominium), each home will have an individual assessed value.

During construction, the development company is responsible for paying the municipal property taxes. Once the occupancy permit has been issued for the completed homes and the title for the home has been transferred, the new owner takes responsibility for paying the municipal property taxes. In some cases, the timing will be such that the municipality has assessed the value before the title is transferred; but in most cases, the amount of taxes applicable to each home needs to be calculated by the developer and applied to the cost at closing. A practical way to approach this is for the cost to the homeowners for their share of the municipal taxes to be based on the percentage of value if the municipality has not yet completed the individual assessments.

Occupancy Permit

Securing the occupancy permit at the completion of construction often feels more challenging than it should be because of all of the bureaucratic requirements that need to be satisfied before this final permit can be issued. It is a *huge* milestone that must be met before the closing on the sale of the homes can occur. In addition to the requirement for documentation from the professionals that the construction has been completed satisfactorily, the local jurisdictional agency will also typically require documentation confirming that all life safety equipment has been tested (such as elevator operation, fire alarm monitoring, sprinkler test confirmation, etc.), a fire safety plan has been prepared, and schedules from all of the professionals as well as some of the important trade contractors have been provided. These schedules include assurances of compliance with local building codes.

Paying Off the Construction Loan

At the completion of the development, the interest payments on the construction loan are typically very high because a large amount (if not the full amount) of the construction loan has been funded. Interest rates on commercial loans are higher than interest rates on residential financing. It is in the best interest of the project to pay off the construction loan as soon as possible.

The most cost effective approach is for members to close on the purchase of their homes as soon as the occupancy permit has been issued, regardless of when they plan to move in. Once the date has been confirmed for the issuance of the occupancy permit, the financial institution will provide a payout statement, which defines the amount of loan and any outstanding interest as of the date of completion. We ensured the closings were coordinated so that the commercial loan payout could be in a single payment, which resulted in reduced financial charges. The loan payout process needs to be negotiated with the involvement of the company's legal counsel as well as the financial institution providing the construction loan because there are many aspects that need to be considered in this undertaking.

Closing Documents

For BC strata title projects, the following is a list of the closing documents that are typical, which gives a sense of what would likely be required in other provinces or states. It is important to consult with the company lawyer to confirm the requirements well before closing so nothing holds up this final stage. If the completed project is registered as a cooperative or other type of legal ownership structure, then the documents will likely vary considerably.

- vendor's (or seller's) statement of adjustments
- freehold transfer
- certificate of residency
- goods and services tax certificate
- order to pay
- Form B: Information Certificate
- Form F: Certificate of Payment
- Form V: Schedule of Unit Entitlement
- Form X: Strata Corporation Mailing Address
- Form Y: Strata Bylaws
- purchaser's statement of adjustments

The developer prepares the vendor's statement of adjustments, the information certificate, and the certificate of payment and provides the lawyer with the strata corporation mailing address and strata bylaws for filing. The surveyor prepares the schedule of unit entitlement. The vendor's and the purchaser's lawyers prepare the remaining documents.

Vendor's Statement of Adjustments

The company's statement of adjustments gives a breakdown of the money that is to be paid to the development company at completion. It includes the following information:

- name of the developer

- names of the purchasers

- address and legal description of the home being purchased

- mailing address if different from the above

- completion date when the funds need to be transferred to the developer from the purchaser

- all the payments previously made to the company (shareholder loans, optional upgrade payments) as well as any member discount resulting from the contribution of additional shareholder loans

- all the payments still owing (insurance; municipal taxes; GST payable, including purchaser rebate if applicable; cost overruns if applicable)

- purchase price based on market value for calculation of GST and property transfer tax

- actual purchase price if different from the above

- the balance owing to the developer, not including legal fees or property transfer tax (or anything else to be paid to government authorities that is not the responsibility of the developer to collect and pay)

Freehold Transfer

The freehold transfer document is prepared by the lawyers and transfers the title from the development company to the purchaser. It is signed by an authorized signatory of the developer and includes the following information:

- legal description
- market value
- transferor
- freehold estate transferred
- transferees

Certificate of Residency

The certificate of residency is prepared by the lawyers and confirms the legal address of the developer.

Goods and Services Tax Certificate

This tax certificate is prepared by the lawyers and identifies the GST that is applicable to the home purchase. The sale is subject to GST when it is a new home. See Chapter 9 for more about the GST in relation to pricing the homes. The vendor (developer) is registered for GST and collects and submits the GST to the government of Canada.

Order to Pay

The order to pay is prepared by the lawyers and identifies the total sales proceeds, the amount required to pay out any financial charges, the amount owing to pay the vendor's legal fees, and the balance payable to the developer.

Form B: Information Certificate

The information certificate is prepared by the developer and is typically only needed for homes requiring mortgages at closing. It is a standard form that can be downloaded from the province of BC website. It provides information about the monthly strata fees, parking stall allocation, storage unit allocation, current budget, developer's rental disclosure, etc.

Form F: Certificate of Payment

The certificate of payment is prepared by the developer and is required to confirm there are no strata fees owing.

Form V: Schedule of Unit Entitlement

This document is prepared by the property surveyor and is the legal document that confirms the unit entitlement value for each of the homes. Identifying the values for unit entitlement is described in more detail in Chapter 8.

Form X: Strata Corporation Mailing Address

A mailing address needs to be identified for the strata corporation; this form is prepared by the vendor's lawyer and requires information from the developer to complete. Whenever possible, a separate postal box should be set aside among the project's post boxes for strata business to avoid having to change addresses when there is a change in treasurer for managing strata corporation finances.

Form Y: Strata Bylaws

The strata bylaws document is prepared by the vendor's lawyer and requires information from the developer to complete. This is the last opportunity to make any revisions to the bylaws before they are registered on title. Any subsequent changes will require approval from the owners based on the requirements of the Strata Property Act and will cost money to file.

Purchaser's Statement of Adjustments

The purchaser's statement of adjustments is prepared by the purchaser's lawyer and provides information about the final payment that needs to be made to the lawyer at closing. It includes the purchaser's legal fees, property transfer tax, and any fees or taxes payable to government authorities that are not the responsibility of the developer to collect and pay.

Homeowner Financing

If the purchasers require a mortgage to pay for their home at completion, they will need to have made arrangements to secure homeowner financing well before the completion date. The recommendations regarding this are discussed in Chapter 9.

Completion Coordination and Warranty Period Protocol

Once the construction has been completed, it is important to identify protocols for managing any deficiencies or construction-related issues. The following is an overview of how CDC has managed this on past projects.

Protocol before Move-In

1 At a construction progress meeting sixty days before the expected occupancy date, the general contractor will identify the proposed completion date for the building.

2 The company will then give formal notice to the purchasers for occupancy and the date for completion (when funds are due, to close on the purchase of their homes).

3 Once a home is close to completion, the architect will go through and identify any issues. The issues will be recorded, and the general contractor will coordinate the trades to rectify them.

4 A schedule is set up for the owners to walk through the home with a representative of the general contractor before the scheduled completion dates and once the above noted issues have been rectified. At that time, the general contractor will do a review of the operating systems with the homeowner. A homeowner manual will be prepared and provided to the purchasers at completion. This is discussed in more detail below.

5 If required, a dollar amount, determined by the architect, will be held back from the final payment to the general contractor (a deficiency holdback) to cover the cost for dealing with any outstanding deficiencies that have not been dealt with at completion. The holdback will not be released until there is confirmation that all deficiencies have been rectified. Anything that does not operate properly or for which installation is incomplete is a deficiency and is dealt with as a priority by the contractor so as not to delay occupancy of the building. These are items that should be completed before the owners move in. Anything that does not affect the use and operation of the home or is more cosmetic in nature (e.g., paint touch-ups) is dealt with by the contractor as time permits, and the building can be occupied during this time period.

Protocol after Move-In

- Members will need to form a warranty task group to act as communication liaison with the general contractor, the individual homeowners, and the home warranty insurance company.

- During the period following occupancy, homeowners can continue to identify anything that may be a deficiency or that ceases to operate properly. Homeowners who have warranty issues provide written communication that fully details the issue to the warranty task group. The notice must be provided on or before the expiry date of the applicable coverage of the new home as defined in the home warranty certificate provided at completion. The warranty task group is responsible for reminding homeowners about deadlines.

- The warranty task group reviews the written information to confirm whether it is a deficiency as defined in the maintenance manual and warranty coverage. Once it has been confirmed as a deficiency, the written information will be submitted to the general contractor, and a copy will be provided to the home warranty insurance provider.

- Anything of an urgent nature is dealt with quickly, and anything less urgent can be scheduled for completion at some point prior to the expiry of the warranty period. The general contractor will prefer to address similar items from several homes at one time, rather than making multiple trips.

The following provides an example of the scope of the work for the member warranty task group:

- coordinate the collection of deficiency or warranty items from homeowners

- visit homes to review items or issues that homeowners have identified

- confirm whether the item is a deficiency that belongs on the list

- help members understand how things function in their homes if the issue is a case of not knowing how something is supposed to work

- provide the construction contractor with organized information, ideally according to the trade associated with the work—including images can be helpful

- work with homeowners to coordinate access for the trades once dates have been identified to deal with the issues and provide updates as required

Homeowner Warranty and Maintenance Manual

Once construction has been completed, the general contractor or construction manager needs to provide information that will support the homeowners to maintain their homes and common areas over time. Ideally, this information should be made available in soft copy format and posted to allow all homeowners easy access. Appendix G includes an example of a table of contents for a completed multi-family cohousing development's common property and unit manual. The contents will vary somewhat for every project, but this gives an idea of the type of information that should be made available.

Sometimes the warranty period for a particular product goes beyond the requirements of the Homeowner Protection Act that is discussed in Chapter 11, in which case the group would be responsible for managing the warranty with the manufacturer or installer that has provided the extended warranty. Similar to the management of the warranty period, CDC recommends having an agreed-to streamlined, coordinated process for dealing with any issues that may arise. All communication should flow through a group of authorized owners (the warranty team) who would manage communication between the homeowner and the manufacturer or installer.

Monthly Maintenance Fees

In BC, the Strata Property Act (SPA) defines how the payment of monthly maintenance fees will apply at completion: The owner developer must pay the actual expenses of the strata corporation that accrue in the period up to the last day of the month in which the first conveyance of a strata lot to a purchaser occurs. After that, the owners are responsible for all other costs.

As noted in Chapter 13, the members will need to finalize the operating budget to establish the fees for the first year. The revised budget will need to be approved at the first annual general meeting (AGM), which must be held within six weeks of occupancy (assuming at least 50 percent of the homes have been sold by that time—requirements for holding the first AGM are provided in the SPA). In BC, prior to the approval of the revised budget at the first AGM, the monthly maintenance fees must be based on the budget that was filed with the disclosure statement.

Company Requirements after Move-In

As noted in Chapter 11, in the province of BC developers are required to secure home warranty insurance prior to the issuance of a building permit. The warranty insurance providers have certain requirements, and typically the development company must be active for a minimum of five years after project completion. The following provides an overview of what is required to manage and maintain the development company:

- manage corporate records: file annual company report, manage any changes in directors and shareholders, file transparency register as required

- pay invoices and record any development company expenses

- file GST returns

- file corporate tax returns

- collect any outstanding bond refunds

- coordinate communication with the general contractor as required to manage deficiencies and warranty items

- coordinate communication as required with the home warranty insurance provider

CDC recommends retaining directors and officers liability insurance for the five-year period if it is possible to secure it at a reasonable cost. In Canada, directors are responsible and personally liable for ensuring the goods and services tax (GST) filing is completed and that any GST owing to the Canada Revenue Agency is paid.

So, what happens if someone who was a director and a shareholder of the development company sells their home prior to the end of the five-year period? Should they be allowed to resign, or should they be required to remain as a director and shareholder until the company has been dissolved? Some of the groups with whom CDC worked required homeowners who sold after completion to resign as directors, sell their share back to the company for a dollar, and sign an indemnification agreement. Other groups required everyone who had been directors and shareholders during development to remain in that position until the company was dissolved. There are pros and cons to either option that need to be carefully considered. CDC recommends securing advice from the company's legal counsel before making the decision.

How to Prepare for Living in Community

"It is helpful to have a picture of a destination rather than focusing on what you don't want—would you tell a taxi driver 'I don't want to go to the Empire State Building'?"

LINDA NICHOLLS, senior faculty at the Haven Institute, Gabriola Island, BC

B Y THE time a project is under construction, the destination is clearly in sight—as is the destination for this book as we begin this final chapter about preparing groups for living in their completed communities. In the iterative process we have described, it takes a community to complete a community. As should be evident by now, collaborative relationships are the key to just about everything in creating each project. The process of creating the housing itself builds community as members work with peers and professionals to design the project and ground it in its own unique realities. As the project moves from dream to reality, members gradually assume more responsibility, and eventually the project transitions to full member control when the professionals are no longer involved. This is a continuation of the community-building process that combines the unique energy of a group's members with professional support to channel that energy towards success.

Adjusting Expectations

Grounding the project in "what is" reminds members that this is not a utopian process, nor will living together after project completion be paradise. While groups welcome this transition from the development phase to the residential phase, the transition can also be challenging. The completed community will no longer have development consultants to support their process in community meetings or to respond to many of their concerns. There will inevitably be construction deficiencies that need to be corrected, and a member team will need to manage these with the contractor. As in all other ways of living, life in the completed community will not be perfect. This will be disappointing for some members.

Clarifying and adjusting members' expectations is an ongoing process for the development consultants and the founding members. From the beginning of each project that CDC managed, it was important that new members knew what they were getting into. Before someone became a shareholder of the development company, as described in Chapter 8, fellow members oriented newcomers and a CDC team person always reviewed the responsibilities and obligations of becoming an equity member. Spending social time together, while virtual during the pandemic, was an important community-building activity that helped adjust expectations. Groups' websites highlighted their shared values, the primary one being a belief that living in community will be preferable to other ways of living. However, what makes it preferable for one household may be different for another, so consideration and respect for differences is a part of community living.

Members face additional challenges as a project completes. Not least, they must move—often downsizing their space and their stuff—and moving is known to be one of life's most stressful events. Moving into community living can amplify doubts that normally surface during a move, such as whether this is the right decision. Some may be challenged to afford a unit as their first home while others may be conflicted about moving from a spacious home on an acreage to a small apartment in a dense, multi-family community. Whatever their housing history, people must get used to interacting with each other more frequently and in different circumstances than in monthly meetings. Understandably, people are often not at their best at project completion! With all these stressors and adjustments, members benefit from having their living in community agreements and governance structure in place well before they move in.

Good planning, clear communication, and attention to community-building are important at all stages of project development. Not surprisingly, they also support the transition to living in community at project completion. As we wrote in Chapter 5, building community connection is one of the main reasons for using consensus decision-making.

During construction, building that community connection takes on additional importance as decision-making literally becomes concrete, and the idea becomes physically real. Cohousing pioneer Kathryn McCamant has said that during construction is when the community members should get out of the way of the building process except for a few members whom the group selects to liaise with the professionals. Members need to "focus on selling all the units, raising the money, and building relationships with your future neighbours. You are really deciding the kind of culture you want to live in... You can hire a bookkeeper. You can hire an architect. What you cannot hire out is the work of building community." McCamant says one of the pleasures of her work is to watch people shift their focus from "I" to "we": "They walk into the room to join the project as individuals but they end up being a real community by the time the project is done."[1] Much of the community-building work during construction consists of crafting the governance structure and community agreements that will guide life in the completed community.

Community Agreements: An Overview

From the early days of a project, clarity about a pet policy, rentals, parking, any special focus, children, or any age restriction can be important for building the member group, obtaining permits, and meeting other requirements. During construction, members have time to focus on refining these agreements, developing others, and finalizing the organizational structure they want to have at move-in. The following are some of the recommended "living in community" topics for discussion before move-in. Some of the agreements or processes may be the same as during the development phase and some may change after completion, but working through this list becomes a priority for a group's meeting time during construction.

- agenda coordination
- email communication
- business activities on site
- children

- committee tasks, mandates, and authority (who does what)
- common house furnishing
- common spaces booking systems
- conflict resolution
- decision-making (who participates, how are decisions made, is there a voting alternative process)
- document management
- facilitation
- garbage and recycling systems
- gardens and grounds
- community meals
- neatness levels
- noise
- parking
- participation in management and maintenance of common areas
- pets
- rental
- sales of homes—management
- smoking, barbeques, bonfires
- storage
- zones of special privilege in common areas

In brief, the work of preparing agreements for these topics begins with the group identifying the tasks that the community will be responsible for after move-in, then deciding who will do them— what member volunteers will do and what will be contracted out. The next step is to allocate these tasks among a committee structure that members develop and agree upon to replace the organizational structure that applied during development. After agreeing on the aims and tasks of each committee, the group decides on committee mandates. The group also reviews the decision-making process it used during development and makes any desired changes for living in community. The rest of this chapter offers details about each of these steps that new cohousing groups can follow.

Governance: Transition from Development Phase to Strata

In the larger world, governance refers to a process whereby elements (or members) in society wield power, authority, and influence and enact policies and decisions concerning public life and social well-being. In community led housing, governance refers to organizational and decision-making structures and processes. These are framed by the community for:

- managing the buildings and finances
- making decisions
- shaping and responding to community needs and desires

As described in earlier chapters, CDC has recommended that groups accept particular governance processes for the development phase. These agreements fundamental to living in a community should be reviewed as the project nears completion, but they may not need to change depending on what the members want. For example, if guidelines for email communication and behaviour in meetings served a group well during development, there may be no need to change them at project completion.

During the development phase, each community also must make legal agreements about what kind of ownership structure to use on completion, that is, whether to form a condominium. Strata or condominium title was the chosen path for all the groups that worked with CDC. During development, CDC managed the preparation of a disclosure statement for each group as described in Chapter 8. This statement included preliminary versions of the proposed strata bylaws and an estimated budget with strata fees for the first year after move-in. Groups generally agreed to allow rentals, partly so that any shareholder unable to sell their home would still likely get financing and be able to close on the purchase if they had a tenant. Usually, the communities also allowed some pets. All the groups that CDC worked with followed the recommendation for every owner to be on strata council as a way of supporting the consensus decision-making process after move-in.

As completion neared, a decision was required about who could attend community meetings, which would effectively be strata council meetings when all owners are members of council. In CDC's experience, owners generally welcomed tenant attendance and participation in strata meetings and consensus decision-making. Groups generally adopted the consensus decision-making process as the normal decision process for their strata. By the time each project was complete, groups had a lot of experience with consensus decision-making. They had seen how it could encourage people to open their minds. People with open minds can and do change them, so a group can arrive at a decision everyone can support, even those who like it the least.

More challenging than the decision to retain consensus decision-making was the decision about whether the strata, like the development company, would have a voting alternative process. A few groups chose to require a consensus for every community decision, but most groups agreed to have a majority vote for (1) anything that the owners agree does not require consensus or (2) when a decision has not been reached at three consecutive meetings. CDC recommended that groups opt for a simple majority in their voting alternative process, but some groups preferred a super majority or no voting alternative process at all.

One task awaiting members as they prepared for living in community was to review, and revise as required, the strata operating budget for the first year that had been prepared during the development phase for the disclosure statement. They also needed to be aware that soon after move-in they would need to begin planning for their first depreciation report, which is a requirement under the Strata Property Act in the province of BC.

The other part of governance to revisit was the organizational structure that each group used during development (with communication and email protocols, and meeting management recommendations). At the beginning of the final year in each project's development, CDC presented groups with examples of the organizational structures in a conventional strata and in several completed projects (see Appendix H). Reviewing these examples initiated the transition process from the development phase to living in community as groups began to imagine how they wanted to organize themselves after completion.

As a next step, CDC created a document for each project to guide members through the transition. Members were asked to identify from the following list (1) what they wanted to continue to do in the same way as during development and (2) what they wanted to do differently or add to:

- what the community organizational structure is
- who can participate in meetings
- who exercises power
- how power is exercised
- who provides expertise or knowledge
- how communication is structured
- who provides financial management
- who prepares agendas and plans meetings
- who facilitates meetings

For each consideration on the list in the transition document, CDC included a summary of the situation "now"—i.e., during development, and specific questions about what members wanted after completion. In a regular monthly meeting near the start of construction, CDC would create nine small groups or breakout rooms and assign one of the questions for each group to discuss and take notes on, including why it would be a good idea to know this information before moving in and when each group thought their question should be decided (e.g., soon or later). As each of the groups worked through these questions, they discovered why it might be important to establish an organizational structure for living in community, and they recognized what decisions were required to start the process. This supported each group to care about and get involved in each element of the transition to self-governance.

In addition to the transition document about what kind of structure was wanted, CDC provided groups with a general overview of the process for determining the organizational structure for living in community. The order of the discussions varied somewhat depending on the group process, but this document gave an idea of what needed to happen. How long the transition process took was influenced by the monthly cycle of meetings, the pace and efficiency of members' participation, and the extent of any delays to construction completion.

Typically, each of the steps listed in the overview of the process might take at least a month, so it was important to start the process of developing organizational structure early enough that it was completed by move-in without having to rush. To encourage members and support them to stay focused, CDC varied facilitation formats—including a visioning exercise, for example, or a soap box. The time was also used to further train members as facilitators and agenda planners.

In our experience, during the final months members tended to focus on organizing their personal moves, and it could be challenging for people to envision their lives after they had settled into their new homes. It is typically somewhat chaotic around move-in, but the response to that chaos makes all the difference. Communities, and each member, have the opportunity to turn the corner on fear and find joy in the transition to living together in community. A separate planning exercise about move-in can partly address this. CDC also made every effort to leave the last couple of months in each project free of meetings so members could focus on moving.

Living in Community Tasks and Participation

CDC created a living in community tasks and participation list and invited each group to decide what members would do themselves, what they would hire others to do, what did not need doing, and what should be added. A participatory technique CDC often used to begin this consideration was a "card storm." On Post-it Notes, or in the Zoom chat function, participants wrote down each task they thought would need to be done once they were living in their new community and who would do it.

When members agreed that the task list was complete (enough for now), the tasks were sorted into categories, which in turn generated possible committees. Members named these committees, often creatively (e.g., hearts and spades for a garden team), and identified members who were willing to focus the initial discussions for each committee. Fine-tuning then occurred as members reviewed the task lists for completeness and found places to accommodate "orphan" tasks within the proposed committees. The community would then approve its list of tasks in a general meeting. For example, one community approved thirty-eight tasks distributed among seven committees nine months before move-in. With a list of tasks in hand, each committee identified its aims in one or two sentences.

Agenda Planning and Facilitation

Answering the question of who prepares agendas and plans meetings was challenging for some of the groups with whom CDC worked. Until they had some experience with agenda planning in this context, it could be difficult for a group to know what it would want. CDC provided all groups with some training and practice in agenda planning to support them to answer this question, but our experience suggests that the answers may continue to change along with the community. For example, an established community might shift from a team of agenda-planning volunteers to an elected steering committee.

A steering committee typically does more than just draft agendas. It can support the community in organizing how it spends its time, energy, and resources. It can handle strategic planning as well as tracking and prioritizing particular community concerns as they arise, keeping the whole community on track using the community's values to set the priorities and develop a strategic long-term plan. The steering committee can also ensure that the community's agreements are up to date and that they are easy for members to find. Because of the power a steering committee may hold and the responsibility it carries, using some sort of election process is preferable to inviting people to volunteer.

Only a few of the groups with whom we worked had created steering committees by the time we wrote this book. The relative power of a steering committee and the challenge of finding qualified members are two obstacles that groups encountered. Although interested members simply volunteer for most teams and committees, experienced community facilitator Laird Schaub recommends that members should be elected to a steering committee. CDC used Schaub's secret ballot election process with some groups and a sociocratic election process with others. Both yielded results that worked well enough for those groups at move-in.

Would the members planning the agendas be different from those running the meetings? CDC encouraged groups to separate agenda planning from facilitation and minute-taking, following the recommendation of Laird Schaub. This effectively shares power as well as the workload within a group.

Plenary Worthy and Plenary Ready

Part of the process of creating either a steering or agenda-planning committee was to define what "plenary worthy" and "plenary ready" would mean when planning a group's meetings. A *plenary* simply means a meeting of the whole, including people who would ordinarily meet in smaller teams or committees. *Plenary worthy* refers to those topics that should (or must) be placed on the agenda for a community or strata meeting rather than being considered and decided at a committee level, or not at all. These plenary worthy criteria continued to guide agenda preparation after move-in.

Groups sometimes were unsure of what plenary worthiness meant in practice, so CDC developed a mixture of light and serious plenary worthy scenarios for members to practice during development. These are included as Appendix I. A group's criteria for plenary worthy can make the difference between short, engaging, important meetings and long, tedious, inconsequential ones, so we encouraged groups to pay attention to their decisions about what should, and shouldn't, come to a community meeting.

Being *plenary ready* is another dimension: Is the topic sufficiently prepared to come to a plenary meeting? Answering this question usually falls to the agenda or facilitation team. As they prepare the monthly meeting's agenda, they check with the person presenting an agenda item to be sure there is sufficient information and that it is clear enough. Is the item coming for information or for a discussion or for a decision? Can the supporting information be linked or added in a note on the bottom of the agenda?

Part of CDC's contract was to work with steering or agenda-planning and facilitation committees or teams to plan general meetings collaboratively during the last year or so of the development process. This provided valuable training for those who would be handling the meetings after move-in. A typical protocol was for the agenda planners to receive agenda requests by a set date, then draft a rough agenda for review with CDC. Once the agenda was ready to circulate to the members, CDC met with the facilitation team to identify who would lead which parts of the meeting and how they would facilitate it. After the plenary meeting, CDC usually attended a debrief meeting to discuss how well the agenda and facilitation planning had worked.

Organizational Structure after Move-In

The organizational structure we described in Chapter 4 transitioned to a "living in community" structure in the final phase of each project. With CDC's guidance, each group adopted the full organizational structure that would apply after move-in. With the organizational structure in place, the members who had volunteered to serve on the committees got to work developing the committees' mandates and completing the tasks that needed to be done by move-in or soon thereafter. The variety of organizational structures in CDC's completed communities indicate how one size does not necessarily fit all!

With clearly defined aims and distribution of authority, sociocracy offers a structure that could potentially work well for the ongoing management of a completed community. We believe the living in community phase is a time when members could more easily transition to a sociocratic organizational structure because the likelihood is that they will have developed the trust in each other that comes from having worked closely together for many years in a respectful, collaborative environment. However, it may be difficult for groups used to working in a particular way to make the change—we have not attempted to facilitate that kind of transition. Sociocracy for All includes detailed resources on how to introduce sociocracy into an established organization.[2]

Our belief is that whatever organizational structure a group chooses, what is most important is that it be effective for managing the community and that it supports good relations among neighbours. If that is not happening, then something needs to be adjusted.

Committee Mandates

Each group developed their committee mandates for after move-in using the questions noted earlier in this chapter. First, CDC encouraged members to identify what aspects of their mandates would be common to all committees. Next, the committees completed drafting their mandates, which were brought to a regular meeting of the whole group for approval. The transition document was then reviewed again to identify and make whatever other decisions were required. The goal was to ensure the members were ready to take over management of the completed community.

Timelines and Task Lists

CDC created and updated a living in community tasks timeline that supported the member groups and project management team to manage the detailed tasks of preparing for living in community. The timelines provided a synopsis of items on the more detailed task lists allocated amongst the committees. This was a helpful tool for the committees to complete their tasks within the timeline, and it supported the agenda-planning process.

CDC's practice was to update the living in community tasks timeline after each monthly general meeting and to forward the updated version to the agenda-planning committee. CDC would then review the timeline with members at the agenda-planning meeting and determine together whether the tasks were ready and at which meetings they would be discussed.

During this phase of the project, even more than before, the focus of community-building meetings was on holding the discussions members needed in preparation for coming to consensus on motions in the general meetings. The timeline showed each committee how much time it had to finalize motions for decision-making.

The Destination

So as one journey ends, at the completion of the new community, another begins for the members: the journey of living well together in community. While the destination—creating a successful project—is so important that it has been the focus of this entire book, the jour-ney also matters, not just to those living in community but to anyone wanting to live more collaboratively with others on this planet. We invite readers to use what they have learned in this book to create their own community led housing projects. We hope the path we have outlined here will be walked by many new communities, and CDC is ready to provide support along the way with workshops and advice tailored to individual projects.

Overview of Completed Projects Managed by CDC

CDC Cohousing Development Consulting Inc. provided full-service development management services for these communities:

Quayside Village Cohousing, North Vancouver, BC, completed 1998
Cranberry Commons Cohousing, Burnaby, BC, completed 2001
Roberts Creek Cohousing, Sunshine Coast, BC, completed 2005
Creekside Commons Cohousing, Courtenay, BC, completed 2007
Wolf Willow Cohousing, Saskatoon, SK, completed 2012
Belterra Cohousing, Bowen Island, BC, completed 2015
Harbourside Cohousing, Sooke, BC, completed 2016
Little Mountain Cohousing, Vancouver, BC, completed 2021
West Wind Harbour Cohousing, Sooke, BC, completed 2021
Driftwood Village Cohousing, North Vancouver, BC, completed 2021
Ravens Crossing Cohousing, Sidney, BC, completed 2021

The following information has been included for each project:

- images with site plan
- project statistics, zoning, density bonuses, relaxations, exclusions
- any reductions in municipal fees
- grants or preferred loans
- number of founding members
- how the site was secured
- length of time to get development approvals and complete construction
- length of time to build the group and find purchasers for all the homes

Measurements are indicated in acres, hectares (ha), or feet (ft), and square feet (SF); floor space ratio (FSR) and floor area ratio (FAR) have also been included.

Quayside Village Cohousing

North Vancouver, BC (completed 1998)

Site size: 75 ft × 140 ft (10,500 SF)—three lots consolidated

Gross floor area: 20,475 SF (not including underground parking)

Indoor common amenity areas: 2,526 SF within the building structure, includes a common kitchen and dining area, entrance lounge, guest room, washroom, office, laundry, children's playroom, and third-floor meeting room with spectacular views of the Burrard Inlet and city of Vancouver

Building height: four stories on Chesterfield, three stories on 5th

Number, types, and average home size: Intergenerational community with one commercial strata lot and nineteen residential strata lots: one-, two-, and three-level homes with bachelor, one, two, and three bedrooms, average size of 772 SF. Townhomes have direct access to ground level. Constructed on a slab over parking with elevator access to the courtyard and apartments.

Zoning: Original zoning allowed a single-family dwelling on each lot. City policy supported increased density in this location. Final zoning is Comprehensive Development 338 Zone. Conditions of the rezoning required the development of five non-market homes at 20 percent below market value, as well as a two-bedroom universally accessible below market rental unit. Charges were registered on title to ensure the homes remain affordable in perpetuity.

Floor space ratio: Density increased from 1.2 to 1.68 FSR (not including exclusions). This increase made it possible for the inclusion of the non-market homes for purchase to be cost neutral. Over time, the revenue from the rental unit generated enough income for the community that it covered the cost of developing the unit.

Gross floor area exclusions: 3,226 SF exclusions: 2,526 for indoor amenity area, 700 for common storage

Setbacks: front 10 ft (reduced from 20); rear 4.5 ft (reduced from 20); side 7 ft (reduced from 15)

Parking: The parking was reduced from 24 to 22 vehicle parking stalls.

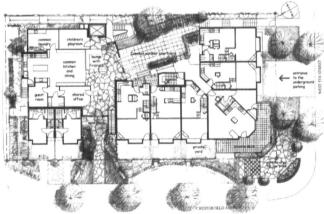

(top left) Quayside Village street view, **(top right)** Quayside Village inner courtyard, **(bottom)** Quayside Village site plan

Reductions in municipal fees, grants or preferred loans: Grant from CMHC Environmental Research to support the installation of a pioneer grey water recycling system. CMHC had tested a grey water recycling system in their "Toronto Healthy House Project" and wanted to further the research on a larger scale. Quayside Village installed the system in order to further the efforts of water conservation and to take part in ongoing research to advance the technology for grey water recycling.

Number of founding members: five

How the site was secured: The city of North Vancouver introduced the group to a small local developer who was willing to enter into a fee for services contract. The developer had connections with local real estate agents and was able to identify a suitable site within a month of entering into an agreement with the group. The five founding members purchased the site, hoping they would be successful at attracting others. (A giant leap of faith, especially considering this was in 1996 when cohousing in Canada was virtually unknown!)

Municipal approvals and construction completion: Once the site had been purchased, it took less than two years to secure municipal approvals and complete construction.

Occupancy: Sixteen of the homes were sold prior to completion, as well as the commercial strata lot. The rental unit had a tenant in place as soon as the occupancy permit had been issued for the completed building. The other two homes were sold within two months of completion.

Cranberry Commons Cohousing

Burnaby, BC (completed 2001)

Site size: 121.97 ft × 164.94 ft (20,117.73 SF)—five lots consolidated

Gross floor area: 26,662 SF (not including underground parking)

Indoor common amenity areas: 2,491 SF, includes common kitchen and dining, lounge, children's playroom, laundry, two washrooms, guest room, office, meeting or auxiliary guest room, and third floor reading room, as well as a 600 SF workshop and approximately 300 SF storage room in the underground parking area

Building height: 3.5 stories, 43 ft

Number, types, and average home size: Intergenerational community with twenty-two residential strata lots: one-, two-, and three-level homes with bachelor, one, two, and three bedrooms, average size of 972 SF. Four buildings with townhouse style units, stacked townhouses, and single-level apartments. The buildings are centred around a common courtyard constructed on a slab with parking below and elevator access to the courtyard and apartments.

Zoning: Original zoning allowed a single-family dwelling on each lot. City policy supported increased density. Final zoning is CD Comprehensive Development District (based on RM4 Multiple Family Residential District).

Floor space ratio: Density increased from 1.1 to 1.3 FSR to support the development of an intergenerational community with extensive common areas. RM4 at that time supported a stacked townhouse design with a maximum 3.5 stories. Exemptions allowed for an elevator and exterior walkways to more readily accommodate families at ground level and elders on upper floors. Typical stacked townhouses had one-level units at grade with two-level units above, which is not supportive of families who benefit from easy access to ground level for children's play.

Gross floor area exclusions: 4,533 SF added density: 2,491 SF for amenity space, 2,042 SF for circulation

Setbacks: front 16 ft (reduced from 25 ft); rear 16 ft (reduced from 30 ft); side 14 ft (reduced from 20 ft) in order to create a more spacious common courtyard

Parking: The vehicle parking required for development approval was far in excess of the amount needed by the residents. An application was made for a relaxation at the time (trade for environmental upgrades) but was unsuccessful. However, in 2022 a successful application was made for a zoning amendment to reduce the parking from 31 to 27 vehicle parking stalls in order to convert four spaces to enclosed bicycle parking. There is still more vehicle parking than required, but at least now there is a large secure place for all the bicycles!

Reductions in municipal fees, grants or preferred loans: With the support of grants from the BC provincial government's Renewable Energy Technology Program and the Canadian federal government's Renewable Energy Deployment Initiative, solar hot-water panels were installed to offset the domestic hot-water load.

Number of founding members: seven

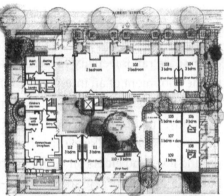

(left) Cranberry Commons inner courtyard,
(top right) Cranberry Commons site plan,
(bottom right) Cranberry Commons street view

How the site was secured: The city of Burnaby had acquired land to construct a fire hall but did not need all the property. Cranberry Commons members had been working with a real estate agent for over a year to try to find an appropriate site. The realtor supported the group to secure the anchor property at the end of the block that was not owned by the city, which gave the group priority to negotiate with the city to purchase adjacent properties. The final consolidation included five lots: the anchor property plus four purchased from the city.

Municipal approvals and construction completion: Once the site had been purchased, it took less than two years to secure municipal approvals and complete construction.

Occupancy: All the homes were sold prior to project completion. The average home price was about 20 percent above market when compared with the cost of a conventional strata home in the neighbourhood at that time. The purchasers, as well as the mortgage lenders, were able to see the added value of the common areas.

Roberts Creek Cohousing

Sunshine Coast, BC (completed 2005)

Site size: ~5.8 ha (original site was 8.06 ha; 1.66 ha became park dedication, 0.56 ha sewage treatment facility)

Gross floor area: 33,673 SF for residential units at construction completion; zoning allows for additions

Common amenity buildings: 2,840 SF stand-alone common house with a kitchen, dining area, lounge, children's playroom, laundry, guest room, office, and three washrooms; two refurbished school portables approximately 1,200 SF each were converted into common space, one of which became a woodworking shop; the combined floor area of all buildings located on common property cannot exceed 21,528 SF, and the floor area of a single building on common property cannot exceed 3,500 SF

Building height: cannot exceed 26 ft (two stories)

Number, types, and average home size: Intergenerational community with 31 bare land strata lots: combination of single-family homes and duplexes, one- and two-level homes with one, two, three, and four bedrooms and an average home size of 1,086 SF. All homes face onto a pedestrian street and have private outdoor areas that back onto green space. The total floor area in a dwelling cannot exceed 2,100 SF, allowing for the possibility of additions. Parcel coverage cannot exceed 40 percent. The combined floor area of all auxiliary buildings located on a strata lot cannot exceed 215 SF.

Zoning: The unconsolidated property consisted of two different county residential zones with minimum lot sizes. Based on the property size, 33 homes would have been allowed. The density was reduced slightly to 31, and the homes are clustered with a zoning designation of Comprehensive Development One (CD1). Of the original site area, 1.66 ha was dedicated as park; 1.93 ha of the 5.8 ha remaining has a restrictive covenant (habitat protection area) prohibiting the placement of any structure or building. The Sunshine Coast Regional District required the dedication and construction of a paved road to access the development as well as a community septic system, the ownership of both were transferred to the district at completion of construction.

Setbacks: The setbacks are defined in the CD1 bylaw to allow for clustering of the homes on small lots.

Parking: The parking is clustered behind the common house so the residents must pass the common house to get to their individual homes. The zoning required 1.5 parking stalls per dwelling for a total of 47.

Number of founding members: eight

How the site was secured: The members identified a number of possible site options, none of which were listed. CDC was engaged to prepare a feasibility study. The decision was made to purchase two properties, one of which was required to provide access to the development site. The portion not required for the development was subdivided off and sold. The purchase and sale of the two properties were coordinated through the lawyers, and it took close to 18 months to finalize negotiations.

Municipal approvals and construction completion: Once the site had been purchased, it took approximately two and a half years to secure municipal approvals and complete construction.

Occupancy: All homes were sold prior to project completion. At initiation of the project, the value was estimated at approximately 20 percent above market, but on completion the home prices were approximately 20 percent below market due to the rise in land values during that period.

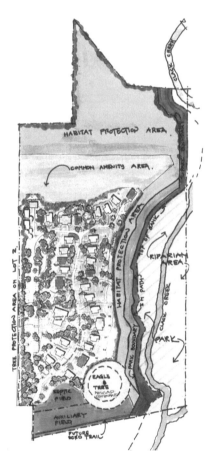

(left) Roberts Creek site plan, **(top right)** Roberts Creek street view, **(bottom right)** Roberts Creek common house

Creekside Commons Cohousing

Courtenay, BC (completed 2007)

Site size: 8.9 acres (original site was 9.8 acres, six lots were subdivided off and sold to non-cohousing purchasers)

Gross floor area: 52,579 SF at construction completion

Common amenity buildings: 3,500 SF stand-alone common house with kitchen, dining area, lounge, office, common storage, children's playroom, meeting room, laundry, three washrooms, and two guest rooms; a separate workshop and storage building were constructed immediately after completion; accessory buildings for common use (workshop, storage, carports, greenhouses, recycling, composting) are limited to total floor area of 16,000 SF

Building height: cannot exceed two stories with a maximum height of 31 ft

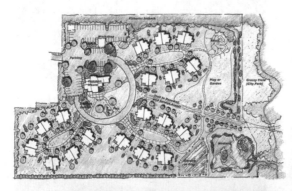

(top left) Creekside Commons site plan, **(bottom left)** Creekside Commons duplex dwelling, **(right)** Creekside Commons community path

Number, types, and average home size: Intergenerational community with 18 duplex dwellings (36 homes): one- and two-level homes with two, three, four, and five bedrooms, average home size of 1,363 SF. Maximum total site coverage 30 percent. Each dwelling is permitted a private accessory building with a total floor area of 161.5 SF.

Zoning: The main parcel was rezoned from Mobile Home Park Residential to Comprehensive Development Fourteen (CD-14). The overall density was reduced from 63 to 35 dwellings. Upgrades to the trail and bridge in the adjacent Piercy Creek Park were provided in lieu of the park acquisition Development Cost Charge payment. Group made financial and volunteer contributions to streamside enhancement that inspired support for the development from local environmental stewardship organizations.

Setbacks: front 23 ft, rear 23 ft, side 14.75 ft (this only applies to the setback from the property boundary; there are no internal setbacks other than those defined under the building code)

Parking: The parking is at the edge of the site and is clustered close to the common house so the residents must pass by to get to their individual homes. The zoning required 1.5 parking stalls per dwelling with 10 percent retained for visitors. A total of 64 surface parking spaces were constructed.

Number of founding members: five

How the site was secured: The first group meeting was held in December 2004 to generate interest in the project. Members moved into their homes less than three years later! The founders who organized the first meeting had identified a potential site on the multiple listing service (MLS). Less than one month later, CDC was engaged to prepare a feasibility study. Even though the study indicated that the completed homes would be about 40 percent above market in that area at that time, five households took the leap to purchase the land.

Municipal approvals and construction completion: Once the site had been purchased, it took just a little over two years to secure municipal approvals and complete construction.

Occupancy: All homes were sold prior to project completion. During the development and construction phase, the market had caught up; at completion, the cost was close to market value for a comparable home in the city of Courtenay.

Wolf Willow Cohousing

Saskatoon, SK (completed 2012)

Site size: 131.5 ft × 137.9 ft (18,134 SF)

Gross floor area: 29,067 SF (not including parking)

Indoor common amenity areas: 4,434 SF within the building structure includes common kitchen and dining, lounge, laundry, two washrooms, two guest rooms, two multi-purpose rooms, exercise room, sauna, and workshop; extensive enclosed walkways on the upper levels function as additional communal spaces that support spontaneous connection among neighbours. None of the previously completed projects that CDC had managed required a commercial kitchen; however, prior to issuance of the occupancy permit, the city of Saskatoon required a sign be posted in the common kitchen by the cooking range stating, "This appliance is to be used for the reheating of previously prepared food only. Surface or deep frying is not permitted." The requirement for a commercial kitchen was not made clear at the building permit stage. So, no fried food for common meals at Wolf Willow!

Building height: four stories

Number, types, and average home size: Senior-focused community with 21 residential strata lots: single-level homes with one bedroom plus den, two, and three bedrooms, average size of 994 SF. Constructed on a slab with parking and main common amenity area at grade. Units, enclosed walkways, and open courtyard are on the upper floors with elevator access.

Zoning: The zoning designation in place when the site was secured was mixed use district 1 (MX1), which included multiple unit dwellings as a discretionary use. The project was required to pave the rear lane and construct public sidewalks along the two sides of the property that were adjacent to a street as a condition of approval for discretionary use.

Parking: The zoning required one space per dwelling unit plus 0.125 visitor spaces per dwelling unit; 24 parking stalls were developed.

Reductions in municipal fees, grants, or preferred loans: The city of Saskatoon's Vacant Lot and Adaptive Re-Use Incentive Program encouraged infill development to intensify land use within established neighbourhoods downtown. An application was made, and an incentive amount of $90,000 was approved and paid at the completion of the development.

(top left) Wolf Willow street view,
(bottom left) Wolf Willow common garden,
(right) Wolf Willow site plan

Number of founding members: four

How the site was secured: The site was listed for sale and was identified by the members as property they wanted to consider for their project. CDC was engaged to prepare a feasibility study, and the decision was made to purchase the property.

Municipal approvals and construction completion: Once the site had been purchased, it took two and a half years to secure municipal approvals and complete construction.

Occupancy: Two of the homes were unsold at project completion; however, purchasers interested in being a part of a community were ultimately found. The building is located in a neighbourhood that was undergoing transition at the time. It was challenging to overcome the stigma associated with the location even though it was within easy access of the downtown core of Saskatoon, connected to the network of paths extending along the west side of the river and only a few minutes' walk from the farmers' market, library, shops, parks, and other services.

Belterra Cohousing

Bowen Island, BC (completed 2015)

Site size: 5.5 acres (original site was 10 acres, 4.5 acres was land dedicated as Terminal Creek park)

Gross floor area: 28,600 SF

Indoor common amenity areas: 3,500 SF stand-alone common house with kitchen, dining area, lounge, office, children's playroom, multi-purpose room, laundry, three washrooms, two guest rooms, and a workshop; the combined floor area of all buildings located on common property for common use cannot exceed 19,900 SF

Building height: maximum three stories

(top) Belterra rendering, **(bottom left)** Belterra site plan,
(bottom right) Belterra street view

Number, types, and average home size: Intergenerational community
with 30 stacked townhomes clustered in five buildings: one- and two-
level homes with studio, one, two, and three bedrooms, average size
of 952 SF; 25 of the homes are market and five are non-market or
price-restricted units.

Zoning: The official community plan was amended to accommodate an increased density from one dwelling unit to a maximum of
30. Zoning was revised from Rural Residential 1 to Comprehensive

Development 16. Conditions of the rezoning included: park dedication and riparian land conservation (4.5 acres), trail construction within the park, five price-restricted units sold to qualified local buyers at approximately 20 percent below market with housing agreements registered on title ensuring a maximum increase in value over time based on the consumer price index, Built Green Gold certification, rainwater collection, and protection of sensitive landscape zones. Belterra was also required to repair, upgrade, and install chip seal on the Mount Gardener access road (Carter Road West)—approximately 900 linear feet of road.

Setbacks: The setbacks are defined in the CD16 bylaw to support the development of clustered housing.

Parking: Parking is located at the edges of the site, at the upper section within close proximity of the homes to support aging in place. The zoning required 1.5 parking stalls per dwelling.

Reductions in municipal fees, grants or preferred loans: Canada Mortgage and Housing Corporation (CMHC) approved a $20,000 seed funding grant and a $60,000 interest free loan to support the development of the five price-restricted housing units at 20 percent below market value with charges on title to ensure the homes remain below market in perpetuity.

Number of founding members: nine (when the site was purchased by the cohousing company)

How the site was secured: The first founding member household owned a property they wanted to develop as a cohousing community for themselves and others who were willing to join with them. They engaged CDC to provide cohousing development services. The official community plan (OCP) needed to be amended before any outreach for membership could commence. A group formed around the site, and once the zoning had been approved, the cohousing development company purchased the site from the founding members.

Municipal approvals and construction completion: It took two and a half years to get the amendment to the OCP. It was not possible to do the amendment and rezoning at the same time. In order to meet the requirements for a multi-family sewage treatment system that was cost effective, the property needed to be subdivided into two parcels. The rezoning and subdivision took another two years. Construction was completed approximately two and a half years later.

Occupancy: All homes were sold prior to project completion.

Harbourside Cohousing

Sooke, BC (completed 2016)

Site size: 0.762 ha (original site was 0.808 ha; a 0.046 ha strip along the waterfront was subdivided off and transferred to District of Sooke to allow for the future construction of a waterfront boardwalk)

Gross floor area: 30,599 SF

Indoor common amenity areas: An existing 3,900 SF building constructed in 2008 was converted into the common house. It includes a main floor kitchen and dining area, a full kitchen on the lower level, a caregiver suite, three common washrooms, reading room, two guest rooms, common storage, and a large multi-purpose room. There was also a 310 SF workshop on the waterfront and enclosed gazebo on the dock. An additional 669 SF was constructed in building three that includes an exercise room and art studio. A 200 SF recycling room, spacious bicycle and kayak storage areas, and a 600 SF personal storage room was constructed in the apartment building.

Building height: principal dwellings maximum 49 ft (four stories); accessory buildings maximum 20 ft

Number, types, and average home size: senior focused community with 31 strata lots and a secondary suite (caregiver suite) for a total of 32 dwellings: apartment building (13 units) with elevator and direct connection to the common house, three fourplexes and three duplexes on the hillside to the waterfront; all are single level comprised of one-, two-, and two bedrooms plus den units; average home size of 840 SF

Zoning: Original R1 zoning allowed one single-family dwelling with accessory uses. The official community plan supported the increase in density in this location. The final zoning is Comprehensive Development (CD13) allowing 40 units per hectare. There is no limit to the number of accessory buildings or structures that can be constructed as long as lot coverage does not exceed 40 percent. The lot coverage was 17.4 percent at construction completion. A minimum 5 percent of the lot area was required as common amenities for the residents. Harbourside was required to mill and pave Horne Road and provide a concrete sidewalk along the full length of the newly paved road (approximately 150 ft in length) as well as provide a dedication to allow for the future construction of a waterfront boardwalk.

(left) Harbourside aerial view,
(top right) Harbourside dwelling interior,
(bottom right) Harbourside site plan

Parking: There is covered parking under the apartment building with all other parking uncovered in various locations on the site. The zoning required one parking stall per dwelling; 39 parking stalls were constructed.

Reductions in municipal fees, grants, or preferred loans: A refund of 50 percent of the building permit fee was given because the project achieved Built Green Gold. The Community Amenity Contribution (CAC) of $25,000 was waived because the entire development was considered affordable compared with senior care facilities. The Canada Mortgage and Housing Corporation (CMHC) $20,000 seed funding grant and $60,000 interest free loan supported the development of the one affordable housing unit at 20 percent below market with charges on title to ensure the home remains below market when it is sold. This was not a requirement of the rezoning but a voluntary decision by the cohousing group to support a long-time member in purchasing a home in the community.

Number of founding members: eight

How the site was secured: During the early exploration phase when the group was considering different site possibilities, a member of the local community who wanted to be part of the cohousing development proposed selling their property to the group. CDC was engaged to prepare a feasibility study, and the decision was made to purchase the property. CDC helped negotiate the purchase and sale.

Municipal approvals and construction completion: Once the site had been secured, it took approximately three years to secure municipal approvals and complete construction.

Occupancy: All homes were sold prior to the start of construction.

Little Mountain Cohousing

Vancouver, BC (completed 2021)

Site size: 99.12 ft × 110.63 ft (10,966 SF)—three lots consolidated

Gross floor area: 31,297 SF (not including vehicle parking, bicycle storage, workshop, and music room in underground parkade)

Indoor common amenity areas: 2,699 SF within the building structure includes common kitchen and dining, lounge, children's play room, laundry, three washrooms, guest room, co-work room, multi-purpose room, recycling room, and informal lounges on each level to support spontaneous connection among neighbours; underground parkade has ~300 SF music room, ~500 SF workshop/bicycle repair room, and enclosed bicycle storage room designed to accommodate 41 bicycles

Building height: six stories with roof deck that includes raised planters for gardening

Number, types, and average home size: Intergenerational community with 25 strata lots: two-story homes with direct access to the street and single-level units on the floors above; one, two, three, and four bedrooms; average size of 893 SF. Constructed on a slab over parking with elevator access.

Zoning: Original zoning allowed a single-family dwelling on each lot. City policy supported increased density in this location. Final zoning is Comprehensive Development (CD-1). Construction of a pedestrian walkway between Little Mountain and the adjacent building to the south was a condition of development approval.

Floor space ratio: not to exceed 2.3 for all uses (other than those specifically excluded)

Gross floor area exclusions: 2,699 SF exclusions for amenity floor area (20 percent allowed / 12 percent proposed); 3,394 SF excluded for unit storage, Passive House wall thickness, service space for heat recovery ventilators

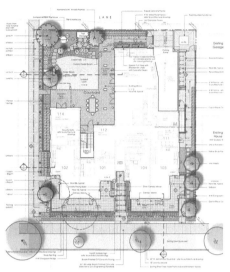

(top left) Little Mountain street view,
(bottom left) Little Mountain common roof deck,
(right) Little Mountain site plan

Setbacks: 3 inch side yard encroachment to accommodate Passive House walls.

Parking: Parking was reduced from 25 to 20 based on a traffic engineering report supporting reduced vehicle use in cohousing and the group's private car share program. A condition of the rezoning was a requirement to document shared vehicle use and report back to the City of Vancouver.

Reductions in municipal fees, grants or preferred loans: The project was not required to connect to the neighbourhood energy system, which would have been very costly, because it met green house gas reduction requirements for heating and domestic hot water. The Passive House design required minimal space heating demand, and domestic hot water was supplied with a central heat pump system.

Number of founding members: Two people took the leap to get the project started and engaged CDC to help build the group and make the project happen. By the time the site was secured approximately 16 months later, there were 18 committed households.

How the site was secured: The group entered into a contract with a local developer to help them find and secure an appropriate site. A lump sum payment was made to the developer once the site had been purchased, and no further services were rendered by the developer after that point.

Municipal approvals and construction completion: Once the site was purchased, it took two years to secure municipal approvals and almost two and a half years to complete construction, which was severely impacted by closures and restrictions imposed by the Covid-19 pandemic. The group dealt with the delays, challenges, and cost overruns with grace.

Occupancy: All homes were sold prior to the completion of construction.

West Wind Harbour Cohousing

Sooke, BC (completed 2021)

Site size: 0.452 ha (original site was 0.637 ha; a 0.01675 ha strip on the waterfront was transferred to District of Sooke, 0.1 ha was subdivided off and sold, and 0.0683 was dedicated to District of Sooke for the road)

Gross floor area: 42,858 SF (not including underground parking)

Indoor common amenity areas: An existing approximately 4,500 SF single-family home originally constructed in 1960 and renovated in the '90s was refurbished and retained for common use. It includes a kitchen and dining area for guests or future caregiver, art room, den, reading room, three guest rooms, sewing room, three full and one half bathrooms, and a workshop. The newly constructed 2,955 SF common area includes a large common kitchen and dining area, washroom, lounge, office, community storage, exercise room, and maker space plus additional areas for recycling, personal storage lockers, and secure bicycle storage.

Building height: six stories (not more than 82 ft) with roof deck for common enjoyment of spectacular views

Number, types, and average home size: Senior-focused community with 34 strata lots: single-level one- and two-bedroom homes with dens; average size of 880 SF. Constructed on a slab over parking with elevator access.

Zoning: Original R1 zoning allowed one single-family dwelling with accessory uses. The official community plan supported an increase in density in this location. Final zoning was RM4, allowing 90 dwellings per hectare (40 units) with no limit to the number of accessory buildings as long as lot coverage does not exceed 70 percent (lot coverage was 34.4 percent at construction completion) and 10 percent of the lot area developed as an amenity for residents. In lieu of cash payment for the increased density, a three-metre-wide strip of land on the waterfront was dedicated to the District of Sooke to allow it to construct a boardwalk in the future. There was also a requirement to construct and dedicate an extension to Goodmere Road with street lighting, concrete sidewalks, and street trees.

Parking: There are 22 vehicle parking stalls in an enclosed underground parkade, 13 stalls of uncovered parking on the slab by the main building entrance, and 14 stalls at the entrance to the development. The zoning required 1.5 parking stalls per dwelling with standards reduced to 50 percent for properties located in the town centre (total of 26 required); 49 stalls were constructed, most will allow for future installation of electric charging stations.

Reductions in municipal fees, grants or preferred loans: Of the building permit fee, 50 percent was refunded because the project achieved Built Green Gold. A CMHC grant of $25,000 was used to reduce the cost of two homes by providing interest-free loans that are repayable upon the sale of the strata lot to another purchaser.

Number of founding members: ten

How the site was secured: The property owners let it be known in the local community that they wanted to live in cohousing and develop it on their waterfront property. A group of interested people came together in response but also wanted to explore other options. CDC was engaged to review the feasibility of the different options, and the decision was made to purchase this property. CDC helped negotiate the purchase and sale.

Municipal approvals and construction completion: Once the site was secured, it took two years to secure municipal approvals and just over two years to complete construction. Excellent management on the part of the construction company ensured minimal impact of Covid-19 restrictions on the project timeline and little cost increase.

Occupancy: All homes were sold prior to completion of construction.

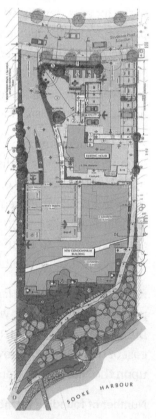

(top left) West Wind Harbour aerial view, **(bottom left)** West Wind Harbour street view, **(right)** West Wind Harbour site plan

Driftwood Village Cohousing

North Vancouver, BC (completed 2021)

Site size: 119.99 ft × 119.93 ft (14,391 SF)—three lots consolidated

Gross floor area: 39,327 SF (not including underground parking)

Indoor common amenity areas: 2,707 SF of amenity area, including common kitchen and dining, lounge, children's play, laundry, three washrooms, guest room, office, and multi-purpose room; 575 SF workshop, recycling room, 29 storage lockers, and storage for 55 bicycles in the parkade

Building height: five stories with roof deck that includes raised planters for gardening

Number, types, and average home size: Intergenerational community with 27 strata lots: two- and three-story homes with direct access to the street and single-level homes on the floors above, two, three, and four bedrooms; average size of 994 SF. Constructed on a slab over parking with elevator access; 19 homes are market and eight are non-market. The development attracted families with children because the non-market homes made it possible to purchase size-appropriate accommodation in an inner-city neighbourhood.

Zoning: Original zoning allowed a single-family dwelling on each lot. City policy supported increased density in this location. Final classification is Comprehensive Development 707 Zone (CD-707). The project was required to repave a section of Chesterfield Avenue, install street lighting, sidewalk and bicycle lane, upgrade and pave the rear lane, remove invasive plant species from the adjacent Wagg Creek riparian area, replant the area with native species, and construct a fence to separate the riparian area from the laneway.

Floor space ratio: increased from 0.35 to 2.13

Gross floor area exclusions: Total common amenity is 2,707 SF, and 5 percent GFA exclusion (1,966 SF) was supported. Exclusions totalling 2,794 SF were also supported for storage, open corridors, eight universally adaptable units, garbage and recycling, and inclusion of the heat recovery ventilators.

Parking: Parking was reduced from 28 to 27 based on the group's private car share program. A condition of the rezoning was a requirement to document shared vehicle use and report back to the City of North Vancouver.

Reductions in municipal fees, grants or preferred loans: The City of North Vancouver had a policy that clearly outlined expectations when a developer applied for an increase in density, which involved the payment of a cash Community Amenity Contribution (CAC). The city approved the provision of eight non-market or price-restricted homes in lieu of a CAC payment, which supported the development of eight homes at 25 percent below market. Housing agreements are registered on title to ensure the home prices remain at 25 percent below market in perpetuity.

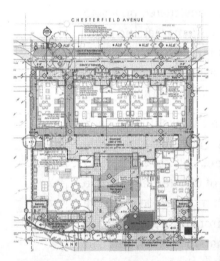

(left) Driftwood Village site plan,
(top right) Driftwood Village street view,
(bottom right) Driftwood Village inner courtyard

Number of founding members: There were three households when CDC was engaged to provide development management services. When the site was secured nine months later, there were 19 committed households.

How the site was secured: CDC supported the group to develop clear site criteria and engage a land use planner and real estate agent to advance the process of finding and securing an appropriate site. The realtor identified several options that were explored with the City of North Vancouver. The properties that were ultimately selected had not been listed for sale but were identified as a result of the realtor's local connections and understanding of the requirements.

Municipal approvals and construction completion: Once the site had been purchased, it took two years to secure municipal approvals and just over two years to complete construction.

Occupancy: All homes were sold prior to completion of construction.

Ravens Crossing Cohousing

Sidney, BC (completed 2021)

Site Size: 26,307 SF (irregular shape)—three lots consolidated

Gross floor area: 47,039 SF (not including underground parking)

Indoor common amenity areas: 3,294 SF of amenity area includes common kitchen and dining, office, lounge, games room, art room, laundry, common storage, three washrooms, and two guest rooms; there are 36 storage lockers and 49 bicycle parking stalls in the parkade

Building height: four stories with roof deck

Number, types, and average home size: Intergenerational community with 35 single-level strata lots: one, two, and three bedrooms, many with dens; average size of 905 SF. Constructed on a slab over parking with elevator access.

Zoning: Multi-family Residential RM7 zoning was in place when the site was purchased. The project was required to apply for a development permit, the approval of which included construction of 2,700 SF of concrete sidewalks, installing boulevard topsoil, sod and street trees, relocating the town water main, and upgrading the storm water connection.

Floor space ratio: The RM7 zoning allowed for a density of 1.3 FAR, which could be increased to a maximum of 2.0 FAR with a payment to the town of $150/square metre for anything over 1.3. The final density was 1.52 FAR.

Gross floor area exclusions: All of the indoor common amenity area was excluded from the gross floor area calculations when determining the density, as well as 4,176 SF for balconies and sundecks.

Parking: One parking stall per dwelling unit was required; 35 vehicle parking stalls were constructed.

(left) Ravens Crossing common roof deck, (top right) Ravens Crossing rendering, (bottom right) Ravens Crossing site plan

Number of founding members: In May 2016, CDC was invited by a group of people to give a workshop on what it takes to develop a cohousing project. After the workshop, a few people continued to meet; by end of 2016 there were only two households remaining. A member of the CDC team supported these two households to create a clear statement of intention. With that in place, they did more outreach and were able to attract others to join them. By September 2017, there was a large enough group in place to enter into a contract with CDC. By the time the site was secured approximately seven months later, there were 11 committed households.

How the site was secured: CDC was engaged to provide development management services and supported the group to develop clear site criteria and engage a land use planner and real estate agent to advance the process of finding and securing an appropriate site. The realtor identified several options that were explored prior to finding the site that was selected and purchased seven months later, which had been listed for sale on the open market.

Municipal approvals and construction completion: Once the site had been secured, it took 10 months to get the development approval, approximately one year to complete the final design and secure the building permit, and 18 months to complete construction.

Occupancy: All homes were sold prior to completion of construction.

Image Credits

Unless otherwise noted here, the photographs in Appendix A have been taken by CDC; all images have been used with permission by CDC Cohousing Development Consulting Inc. Credits are listed next to image captions in the order in which they appear.

Quayside Village inner courtyard: Photo by Graham Meltzer

Quayside Village site plan: Drawing by Courtyard Group Architects

Cranberry Commons site plan: Drawing by CDC Cohousing Development Consulting Inc.

Roberts Creek site plan: Drawing by Judith Reeve Landscape Architecture

Creekside Commons site plan: Drawing by Tim O'Brien

Creekside Commons community path: Photo by Odete Pinho

Wolf Willow common garden: Photo by Wolf Willow Cohousing

Wolf Willow site plan: Drawing by Mobius Architecture

Belterra rendering and Belterra site plan: Drawings by Mobius Architecture

Harbourside aerial view: Photo by Stephen Hindrichs

Harbourside site plan: Drawing by Small & Rossell Landscape Architects Inc.

Little Mountain street view and Little Mountain common roof deck: Photos by Martin Knowles

Little Mountain site plan: Drawing by Durante Kreuk Ltd.

West Wind Harbour aerial view: Photo by Matthew Neumann of Matthew James Photo

West Wind Harbour street view: Photo by West Wind Harbour Cohousing

West Wind Harbour site plan: Drawing by Small & Rossell Landscape Architects Inc.

Driftwood Village site plan: Drawing by Durante Kreuk Ltd.

Driftwood Village street view and Driftwood Village inner courtyard: Photos by Driftwood Village Cohousing

Ravens Crossing common roof deck: Photo by Ravens Crossing Cohousing

Ravens Crossing rendering: Drawing by Mobius Architecture

Ravens Crossing ground level plan: Drawing by Small & Rossell Landscape Architects Inc.

Legal Structures and How Cohousing Fits

The legal structure is one of the decisions the group will make over the course of their development. Financial institutions often assume that cohousing is a legal structure such as a cooperative or some other form of shared equity, which is incorrect. Cohousing is not a legal structure but a form of neighbourhood designed to meet the needs of the residents that allows for the balance of privacy and community. Cohousing groups choose the legal structure that best meets their needs.

Ownership Structure

Conventional Strata Title/Condominium: Strata title/condominium allows for individual ownership of homes and common ownership of shared amenities. Each home has a separate title and can be mortgaged individually. This is a common ownership form in Canada, and, subject to the purchaser's qualifications, mortgages are generally readily available.

Cooperatives/Share Structures: The cooperative owns the home. Members purchase shares, which gives them the right to occupy the home. This is not a common ownership form in Canada, and it can be very difficult to get a mortgage because the shareholder does not hold title to the home.

Cohousing: Typically, cohousing groups in Canada choose strata title/ condominium, not cooperative, because of the wider availability of financing and the lower threshold required for a down payment.

Regardless of the legal structure chosen, the community is ultimately bound by the rules and laws set out by the provincial acts governing stratas/condominiums or co-ops/share structures.

Financing the Development

Conventional Strata Title/Condominium: An individual or corporation provides the equity to finance the development and construction with an expectation of selling the homes once development is completed. Non-market homes have covenants registered on title to ensure the homes remain affordable for perpetuity.

Cooperatives/Share Structures: Federal and provincial governments have funded various programs to help Canadians create non-profit housing co-ops, but that funding has not been available for many years. Without the government programs, there are no financial advantages and many challenges to setting up as a cooperative.

Cohousing: The future residents participate in the planning and development and often provide the equity to finance the construction. Once the development is completed, the construction loans are paid off and the purchasers take possession based on the ownership structure chosen. To date there has been some limited government funding to support the inclusion of non-market homes in cohousing.

Purpose

Conventional Strata Title/Condominium: In general, the purpose of a conventional strata title/condominium project is to develop housing that will generate a profit for the developer, but this structure can also be not-for-profit.

Cooperatives/Share Structures: The purpose of government-funded cooperatives was to create affordable housing.

Cohousing: In general, the purpose of cohousing is to create a neighbourhood that meets the needs of the residents and allows for the balance of privacy and community. Affordability and environmental sustainability are commonly held goals.

Resale

Conventional Strata Title/Condominium: The value of the home fluctuates with the market, unless there are covenants in place that restrict the resale in some way. Each homeowner is responsible for finding a buyer and can sell their home at whatever price the market will bear and to whomever they please. In BC, the Strata Property Act prohibits the strata corporation from restricting the owner to freely sell their strata lot.

Cooperatives/Share Structures: The board of directors of the housing cooperative determines who can purchase shares in the cooperative. In the government-funded cooperatives, the share value is fixed and does not fluctuate over time. When a shareholder leaves the cooperative, they sell their shares at the price they paid for them. In equity co-ops, the share is based on market value.

Cohousing: Resale of cohousing homes follow the rules of the legal structure it holds. Cohousing communities typically maintain waiting lists of people interested in being a part of the community.

Examples for the Use of Coloured Cards

CDC used the following system to help facilitate equal participation in discussion and decision-making. The cards have a different meaning for each context.

Discussion

In this context, the purpose of the cards is to provide a tool for managing the discussion. Participants hold up a card before speaking. The facilitator recognizes them in the following order: (1) red (or blue), (2) yellow, (3) green. In this context, the cards have the following meanings:

Green: A wish to contribute to the discussion.

Yellow: The desire to ask or answer clarification questions, not to offer opinion or comment—the purpose is to help move the discussion forward if it seems to be stuck.

Red (or blue): To indicate a problem with the process or the need for a break. Examples include discussing topics not on the agenda and going overtime. May be raised at any time during discussion and takes priority over green and yellow.

When more than one card of the same colour is raised, the facilitator attempts to ensure that individuals are heard in the order that the cards were raised.

Decision-Making

The effective use of the cards in decision-making is intimately tied to the process used *prior* to an issue coming to the group for a decision as well as the *responsibilities* associated with the use of the red (or blue) card. Within this context, the cards have the following meanings:

Green: Indicates consent, gives permission to proceed.

Yellow: Indicates reservation, expresses concern, is often call "standing aside."

Red (or blue): Indicates standing in the way. This card is used if you believe the proposal is not in the best interest of the group.

Note that a member who shows a red (or blue) card is expected to contribute to finding a solution that will work for everyone, so raising a red (or blue) card requires a commitment of time and energy. In some instances, the member(s) opposing the original solution may come up with an alternative proposal, which can be brought forward along with the original proposal. Sometimes a blending can occur. Sometimes both proposals are presented, and the one with the most support passes. At one established cohousing community, if the person standing in the way does not follow through on their obligation to help find a solution, their block is considered invalid.

Unlike many decision-making styles that allow for only a "yes" or "no" vote, *the consensus process allows for a continuum of responses to a proposal*. When making decisions on contentious issues, it is useful to remember the variety of responses that can still be accepted as consent:

- "I love it."

- "I like it."

- "I don't like it, but I can live with it, and I'm willing to support the group if we choose to go ahead with it."

- "I don't think it's necessary, but I'm willing to support the group if we choose to go ahead with it."

- "I need to stand aside. I have significant reservations, and I would like to have them recorded in the minutes. Then I will feel OK about allowing the group to go ahead with the decision and I will not hinder its implementation."

Examples of Optional Upgrades

Optional upgrades add to complexity and increase costs—the more variation from one unit to the next, the higher the likelihood of mistakes and increased costs to the development. Only upgrades that are very important for owner satisfaction should be considered. The following provides examples of upgrades that were selected on some of the projects CDC managed.

Item	Requirements	Level of Complexity
replace 60″ × 34″ tub-shower combo with low threshold shower complete with shower door	coordination required with architect, mechanical engineer, mechanical contractor, and construction team	medium/ high
add a 24″ wide × 36″ high × 8″ deep over-the-toilet cabinet with two doors and four shelves (per bathroom) in same material as vanity cabinet	coordination required with architect (to confirm location in all unit types), cabinet manufacturer, cabinet installer, and construction team	medium
add electric in-floor radiant heating in bathroom floor (under tile)—cost is per bathroom	coordination required with architect, electrical engineer, electrical contractor, flooring installer, and construction team	medium/ high
upgrade from standard Marmoleum click flooring to allow for laminate in any units and Marmoleum slate on first and second floor only	identifying upgrade cost is an issue because flooring cost is impacted by volume purchased; coordination required with architect, flooring contractor, and construction team	high

Item	Requirements	Level of Complexity
replace standard electric range with an induction range	coordination required with appliance supplier and construction team	low
add the installation of a washer and dryer	coordination required with appliance supplier and construction team	low
upgrade countertops in kitchens and bathrooms from laminate to quartz, retain standard sinks and faucets	another trade is required for the countertop installation; coordination required with construction team	low/medium
upgrade countertops in kitchens and bathrooms from laminate to quartz, revise sinks and faucets	another trade is required for the countertop installation; coordination required with architect, mechanical engineer, mechanical contractor, and construction team	high
add kitchen island with electrical outlet (outlet is required by code)	coordination required with architect, electrical engineer, electrical contractor, cabinet manufacturer, cabinet installer, and construction team	high

Municipal Policies Supportive of Cohousing

The following provides a few examples of ways that municipal policies can be structured so they are supportive of cohousing.

Common amenity spaces not included in density calculation: The extensive common facilities are designed to support connection. At minimum, the common facilities include a kitchen and dining room to accommodate at least 65 percent of the residents for a common meal and usually comprise at least 7 percent of the gross floor area not including parking. However, most cohousing projects include much more: children's play space, meeting room, guest rooms, lounge, workshop, etc. Therefore, if the common amenity spaces are excluded from the floor space ratio calculation, this allows for the construction of extensive common spaces without the land cost being factored into the cost of developing these spaces.

Additional circulation space not included in density calculation: The circulation space is designed to enhance and support spontaneous connection among residents. It is desirable to include wide hallways that will accommodate tables and chairs. Obviously there must be enough clearance for fire safety, but including wider hallways can add considerably to the opportunities for spontaneous connection. It is not affordable to do this if the land cost needs to be factored into the cost of developing these spaces.

Density calculated based on FSR/FAR rather than units per acre: Cohousing tends to include smaller units because access to the extensive common areas make it possible to live in a smaller home. When the density is based on floor space ratio (also known as floor area ratio), this allows for more units per acre when the units are small.

DCCs based on $ per square foot of saleable area: When development cost charges are based on number of units, rather than size, smaller units pay a higher proportion of DCCs than larger units, relative to the total cost. Calculating DCCs based on unit size is beneficial to keeping those charges lower for cohousing residents because the unit sizes tend to be smaller than most conventional developments. Common facilities do not add to infrastructure costs because when residents are using the common facilities, they are not using the facilities in their individual homes.

Reduce parking requirements: Cohousing has documented lower vehicle use than conventional developments. Residents share rides, share cars, and tend to walk, cycle, and use public transit more because there is a commonly held value of living more sustainably. Experience with past developments has shown that parking needs for the residents varies depending on access to local amenities, public transportation, bike trails, etc. However, typically no more than one parking stall per unit is required; in urban neighbourhoods that have easy access to shops and services, the need for resident parking is even less.

Allow residential grade kitchen equipment for common house: The common kitchen in cohousing is for the residents of the community to enjoy occasional shared meals together. Mostly it is used for heating food and baking. Deep frying and activities that have the potential of creating fire hazards typically do not occur in a cohousing common kitchen, therefore commercial grade equipment is not required.

Reduce building setbacks: In cohousing the focus is on creating common outdoor spaces that allow for community connection, with less focus on private yards. Private yards are also important, but they can be smaller because the residents feel comfortable using common spaces together. Reducing setback requirements from the street, lanes, and other properties can allow for a larger common courtyard or common outdoor space. For example, at Cranberry Commons in Burnaby, BC, the setbacks were reduced as follows: front by 16 ft (reduced from 25 ft); rear by 16 ft (reduced from 30 ft); side by 14 ft (reduced from 20 ft) in order to create a more spacious common courtyard.

Affordable housing: Cohousing attracts people whose primary goal is to live in a community where residents know and care about each other. This attracts people with different financial capacities. Cohousing groups strive to be inclusive, and diversity contributes to community health and well-being. However, it is very challenging to create affordable housing with high land, construction, and financing costs. In areas where land costs are high, density bonuses can contribute to affordability whereby homes can be developed without the land cost associated. As well, using community amenity contributions (CACS) to include an affordable housing component is another avenue that can contribute to creating some affordable housing. For example, Driftwood Village Cohousing in North Vancouver constructed 30 percent of the homes (total of eight) at 25 percent below market with covenants in place to keep the homes at that below-market rate for perpetuity. The affordable homes were provided as the CAC for the project.

———————

If the local government supports initiatives to include some permanent affordable housing in a development, then in our experience cohousing residents are more than willing to manage the process so that the homes remain affordable for perpetuity, eliminating the need for a housing authority to manage the resales over time. There are likely other strategies that could be used towards creating more affordable housing, such as reducing development costs charges, fast-tracking the approval process, or even delaying payment of the development cost charges. Financing is expensive, and reducing financing costs can have a big impact on reducing the costs of developing a project. In addition, if a project can demonstrate that the local government is involved in supporting affordable options, then other levels of governments may be inspired to contribute in some way.

Example of a Development Proforma

Property Description

Property Address (not included in this example)	
Site Size (in square feet)	25,504 SF
Floor Space Ratio (FSR)	1.5

Proposed Development	Area SF	Total Number of Units	Average Area Per Unit
Total Saleable Area	32,900	35	940
Circulation	5,356		
Total Area Units and Circulation	38,256		
Common Amenities (FSR exclusion up to 10% of the Gross Floor Area)	2,800		
Total Built Area	41,056		

Development Analysis	Per Unit	Per Square Foot	Total
Phase 1: Acquisition (Land)			
Purchase Price	$120,000	$127.66	$4,200,000
Property Transfer Tax	$2,320	$2.47	$81,200
Total Acquisition Costs	$122,320	$130	$4,281,200
Phase 2: Pre-Construction (Soft Cost)			
Legal, Accounting, Appraisal	$2,857	$3.04	$100,000
Design Professionals, Project Management,	$31,257	$33.25	$1,094,000
Outreach	$143	$0.15	$5,000
Municipals, CACs, DCCs	$7,954	$8.46	$278,375
HPO Insurance	$3,290	$3.50	$115,150
Survey	$857	$0.91	$30,000
Municipal and Property Tax	$343	$0.36	$12,000
Insurance	$3,959	$4.21	$138,564
Disbursements and Travel	$400	$0.43	$14,000
Total Pre-Construction Costs	$51,060	$54	$1,787,089
Phase 3: Construction (Hard Costs)			
Site Servicing and Landscape	$9,007	$9.58	$315,260
Common House	$21,600	$22.98	$756,000
Building Construction	$295,118	$313.95	$10,329,120
Total Construction Costs	$325,725	$347	$11,400,380

Development Analysis	Per Unit	Per Square Foot	Total
Phase 4: Financing (Primary)			
Required Loan		$14,960,000	75%
Financing Bonus		$104,720	0.70%
Interest Rate		4.70%	
Development Permit		13	
Construction		18	
Sales Period		0	
Carrying Costs on Land	$1,248	$1.33	$43,690
Financing Bonus	$2,992	$3.18	$104,720
Quantity Surveyor	$858	$0.91	$30,000
Construction Loan Interest	$18,080	$19.23	$632,808
Total Financing	$23,178	$25	$811,218
Contingency Reserve (12% of Phases 2, 3, and 4)	$47,995	$51	$1,679,842
Grand Total	$570,278	$607	$19,959,728

Closing Costs	Per Unit	Per Square Foot	Total
Member Discounts	$13,035	$13.87	$456,217
GST	$28,514	$30.33	$997,986
Average Home Cost (Includes GST)	$611,827	$651	$21,413,933

Example of a Maintenance Manual's Table of Contents

Members are requested to follow the agreed-to communication protocol prior to contacting any trades or the new home warranty insurance provider. (Underlined items link to documents on the members private website.)

Completion Coordination and Warranty Period Protocol
New Home Warranty Registration Numbers
Residential Construction Performance Guide
Travelers New Home Maintenance Manual and Warranty Coverage
Division Categories

Record and As Built Drawings
Record and As Built Drawings

Division 1: General Requirements
Consultant and Trade Contact List
General Contractor Warranty Management

Division 2: Site Work
Detention Tank Warranty and Maintenance
Civil Works Warranty and Maintenance
Irrigation Zones
Irrigation System Operations Manual
Landscape Warranty and Maintenance

Division 3: Concrete
There are typically no warranties associated with the concrete work.

Division 4: Masonry
Masonry Warranty

Division 5: Metals
Guardrails, Handrails, and Privacy Screens Warranty

Division 6: Wood and Plastics
Finish Carpentry Warranty and Maintenance

Division 7: Thermal and Moisture Protection
Cladding Workmanship Warranty
Fibre Cement Siding Warranty
Gutters Warranty and Maintenance
Insulation Warranty and Cut Sheets
Roofing, Slab Waterproofing, Vinyl Decking Warranty
Silicone-Modified Polyester Paint Warranty

Division 8: Doors and Windows
Doors and Hardware Warranty and Maintenance
Mirrors and Shower Doors Warranty and Maintenance
Overhead Parkade Gate Warranty and Maintenance
Windows and Patio Doors Warranty and Maintenance

Division 9: Finishes
Drywall Warranty
Flooring Warranty and Maintenance
Paint Colours and Formulas
Paint Warranty and Maintenance
Tile Warranty and Maintenance

Division 10: Specialties
Bike Racks and Storage Lockers Warranty
Mailbox Warranty
Wire Shelving Warranty

Division 11: Equipment
Appliances Warranty and Maintenance

Division 12: Furnishings
Cabinets Warranty and Maintenance
Countertops Warranty and Maintenance
Window Coverings Warranty and Maintenance

Division 13: Special Construction

This section includes things such swimming pools and hot tubs. These are typically not included in community led housing developments, but if they are, then warranties would need to be added.

Division 14: Conveying Systems

Elevator Final Acceptance

Elevator Repair Parts Manual

Elevator Operating Manual

Elevator Warranty

Division 15: Mechanical

Mechanical Systems Warranty

Mechanical Systems Operating and Maintenance Manual

Division 16: Electrical

Electrical Installation Warranty

Electrical Operations and Maintenance Manual

Entry Phone Operations Manual

In-Floor Heat Warranty

In-Floor Heat Thermostat Operation

Lighting Warranty

Thermostat Owners Guide

Comparisons of Some Different Organizational Structures

Conventional Strata

In this structure, the Strata Corporation (owners of the strata lots) elects a Strata Council at the annual general meeting to represent the interests of the Strata Corporation. Owners may attend the Council meetings, but they are only allowed to speak when invited by Council. The primary decision-making body is the Strata Council, except for decisions defined under the Strata Property Act that need to be made by all the owners at an annual or special general meeting.

Property
Management
Company

Annual
and Special General
Meetings of the
Strata Corporation

Strata Council

Resident
Work Bees
(optional)

Cohousing Strata Example One

In this structure, residents organize into six main committees. The committees determine when they will meet and have decision-making authority based on approved mandates. The steering committee prepares agendas, with input from residents, for community (strata council) meetings held once a month. Legally, all owners are members of the Strata Council and are encouraged to attend monthly community meetings. The primary decision-making occurs at the community meetings, except for decisions defined under the Strata Property Act that need to be made at an annual or special general meeting.

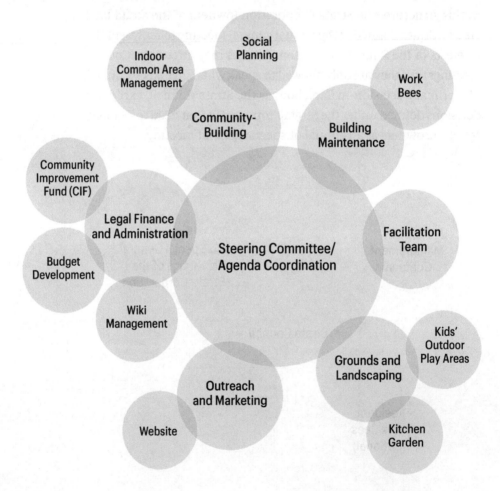

Cohousing Strata Example Two

In this structure, residents organize into four main committees to perform tasks. Additional temporary task groups are created as needed and are attached to a committee. The committees determine when they will meet and have decision-making authority based on approved mandates. The facilitation team prepares agendas, with input from residents, for community (Strata Council) meetings held once a month. Legally, all owners are members of the Strata Council and are encouraged to attend the monthly community meetings. The primary decision-making occurs at the community meetings, except for decisions defined under the Strata Property Act that need to be made at an annual or special general meeting.

Cohousing Strata Example Three

In this structure, residents organize into five main circles to perform tasks. Each circle has an approved mandate, an elected operations leader, and a representative to the general circle. The general circle is composed of representatives from each of the circles. The primary decision-making is in the circles, except for decisions, as defined by the Strata Property Act, that need to be made by all the owners at an annual (AGM) or special general meeting (SGM).

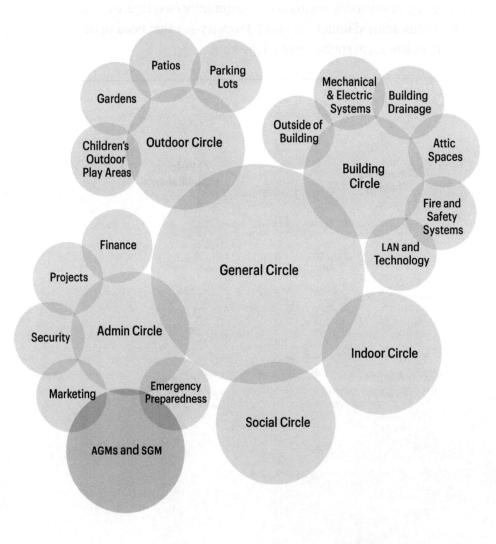

Examples of Plenary Worthy Scenarios

The following criteria were adopted by members as a community guideline to define what is considered plenary worthy for the community meetings:

- approval of changes to community governance (decision-making, organizational structure)

- any changes to policy (bylaws, community guidelines, rules, etc.)

- any changes or revisions to committee or team mandates

- yearly budget approval, including contingency reserve fund

- approval of any extraordinary expenditures that are not within the approved fiscal operating budget or committee mandates

- any decision that is not within the approved mandates of the committees

- approval of strategic plans

The exercise below was created to support members in thinking about how the criteria they had defined would apply to agenda topics. They met in small groups to consider and discuss and then presented their rationale in the large group. The possible responses were provided to the meeting facilitator to support the discussion.

Molly has two cats that are used to going in and out of her unit through a cat door whenever they want. Another member, Tom, believes Molly's cats are stalking birds. The community has a limit of two pets but no policy about cats' behaviour. Tom requests time on the agenda to discuss whether Molly should have to keep her cats indoors.

Possible response: Bring it to the committee that deals with pets to see if there is a solution that does not require a policy. If that committee determines that a policy is desired, then it would become a plenary worthy topic because it potentially involves a change to existing agreements.

———————————

The committee that manages the landscaping has the authority to select planting within a certain budget limit. The committee has decided to purchase some fruit trees; however, two landscape committee members have not been able to agree on what fruit trees to plant, and where. The committee keeps getting stuck in what seems like a power struggle between the two members. The committee wants to bring the item to a community meeting for resolution. If they can't get it worked out soon, they will miss the main seasonal window for planting.

Possible response: Whether this is deemed plenary worthy depends on which option the community prefers. One option is to bring this to the committee that is responsible for supporting community members to deal with conflict to see if a mutually agreeable solution can be identified. If the community uses a voting alternative process, then this decision could qualify as a required decision. Since the committee has the authority to make the decision, another option would be to use the voting alternative process to identify a solution that is supported by the majority of the committee members.

———————————

During development, members postponed deciding how decisions would be made after move-in. Now that they have all moved in, one of the committees wants a plenary discussion about whether to continue to make all decisions by consensus or to have a voting alternative process.

Possible Response: As noted in the plenary worthy criteria listed above, anything associated with community governance should be decided on by the whole group, therefore this is a plenary worth topic.

––––––––––––––

Amidst another pandemic, the committee that manages the common areas has changed the guidelines to limit access to groups of six and to require physical distancing. They believe they have the authority to do this based on their agreed-to mandate. They want to announce the change at a plenary.

Possible response: The plenary worthy criteria above does not include anything about announcements. So, according to the agreed-upon criteria, this is not considered to be plenary worthy if the authority to change the guidelines fits within the mandate of the committee. The committee will need to find another way to inform the community about the change. If, however, the committee believes announcements should be included in the plenary worthy criteria, then that topic (not the announcement) would be considered plenary worthy because it would involve a change in policy.

––––––––––––––

The committee that manages common area furnishings is considering what kind of furniture to buy for the common patio. The budget for this has been approved, and the committee has been given authority to make the purchase. However, the committee members have sample materials that they want members to dot vote on in preparation for deciding which furniture to purchase. Is the dot voting plenary worthy?

Possible response: The list of plenary worthy criteria above does not include anything about soliciting feedback from members when the committee has been given the authority to make the decision. So, according to the agreed-upon criteria, holding this vote is not considered to be plenary worthy, and the committee will need to find another way to get feedback from members.

———————

Winston wants to replace his tub-shower combination with a walk-in shower. He wants to ask permission from the strata in a plenary to do this.

Possible response: If one of the committees has authority to approve this change, then according to the criteria it would not be considered plenary worthy. However, if approval for this is not within the mandate of any of the committees, then, yes, this would be a plenary worthy topic.

Acknowledgements

I T TOOK MORE THAN ELEVEN VILLAGES to write this book—one for each of the projects that CDC completed plus every one of the forming groups that reached out for advice along their journey. We are grateful to them all for asking good questions and for giving us the broad range of experience with creating communities that we share in this book. And a very special thank-you goes to those courageous members who took the leap of faith with us to make their projects happen. Without them, there would be no projects and no book.

Kathryn McCamant and Charles Durrett's book *Cohousing: A Contemporary Approach to Housing Ourselves* introduced the concept to North America—the inspiration that led many of us to find a way to create cohousing in our local area. We thank them for their pioneering efforts and for their ongoing commitment to create a better world one neighbourhood at a time.

To Alan Carpenter for his enthusiasm and unending commitment to cohousing and for inviting Ronaye to participate in the development of Quayside Village, the project that started her career as a cohousing development consultant—a life with meaning and purpose.

To our families and especially our spouses, Brad Cassidy and John Boquist, we give our heartfelt thanks for anchoring us safely in the sea of challenges that accompany any book project and for nurturing and supporting us every step of the way.

We want to express special thanks to our first readers, Brad Cassidy, Lysa Dixon, Kathy McGrenera, Odete Pinho, and Mackenzie Stonehocker, for their careful and thoughtful feedback—invaluable in supporting us to make the information more accessible to readers.

We are grateful to experts Lysa Dixon (Mortgage Professional, Averbach Mortgages) and Richard Ledding (Founding Lawyer, Ledding & Company LLP), with whom we worked on cohousing projects and who provided advice or assistance related to our book, and to all the professionals with whom we have worked over the years—too many to name—who showed patience and understanding and confirmed how rewarding it can be to work intimately with the member group in a community led housing process.

Notes

1. Introduction

1   Models of community led housing in the UK are described in "Housing for People, Not for Profit," a collection of articles edited by Lisa K. Bates in *Planning Theory & Practice* 23, no. 2 (2022): 267–302, doi.org/10.1080/14649357.2022.2057784; Community Led Housing online lists these four types of housing, https://www.communityledhomes.org.uk.

2   Supplementing CDC's experience creating cohousing, Margaret Critchlow's anthropological experience with other forms of community led housing includes her research and books on housing cooperatives (*New Neighbours: A Case Study of Cooperative Housing in Toronto*, with Matthew Cooper [Toronto: University of Toronto Press, 1992]) and Pacific Islanders' self-help housing (*Home in the Islands: Housing and Social Change in the Pacific*, edited with Jan Rensel [Honolulu: University of Hawaii Press, 1997]).

3   See for example Charles Durrett and Kathryn McCamant, *Creating Cohousing: Building Sustainable Communities* (Gabriola Island, BC: New Society Publishers, 2011); Chris ScottHanson and Kelly ScottHanson, *The Cohousing Handbook: Building a Place for Community* (Gabriola Island, BC: New Society Publishers, revised edition, 2005); Diana Leafe Christian, *Creating a Life Together: Practical Tools to Grow Ecovillages and Intentional Communities* (Gabriola Island, BC: New Society Publishers, 2003).

4   "What Is Cohousing?" Canadian Cohousing Network, June 2, 2022, https://www.cohousing.ca/about-cohousing/what-is-cohousing/.

5   Lisa Prevost, "They Took a Chance on Collaborative Living. They Lost Everything," *New York Times*, February 11, 2022.

6   James Hoggan and Grania Litwin, *I'm Right and You're an Idiot: The Toxic State of Public Discourse and How to Clean It Up* (Gabriola Island: New Society Publishers, 2016).

7   "Those convinced against their will are of the same opinion still" is a family saying Ronaye recalls from her childhood, one alternately attributed online to Ben Franklin, Mary Wollstonecraft, Dale Carnegie, and others.

8   Richard Wagamese, *Embers: One Ojibway's Meditations* (Madeira Park, BC: Douglas & McIntyre, 2016), 76.

2. What It Takes to Develop a Community Led Housing Project

1   See Chapter 1 in Christian, *Creating a Life Together*.

2   Charles Durrett, "Your March News & Updates on Cohousing," The Cohousing Company newsletter, March 2022. More issues of the newsletter are available at https://www.cohousingco.com.

4. Organizational Structure

1   "PmWiki is a wiki-based content-management system (CMS) for collaborative creation and maintenance of websites. PmWiki pages look and act like normal web pages, except they have an 'Edit' link that makes it easy to modify existing pages and add new pages into the website, using basic editing rules. You do not need to know or use any HTML or CSS. Page editing can be left open to the public or restricted to small groups of authors." Information from https://www.pmwiki.org; more on the features of PmWiki can be found at https://www.pmwiki.org/wiki/PmWiki/Features.

2   Ravens Crossing members created a video of their impressive construction progress during the first pandemic year, 2020, which can be viewed at https://youtu.be/vCAmzHDzIA8.

3   Kavana Tree Bressen's website can be accessed at http://effectivecollective.net; Laird Schaub's *Community and Consensus* blog can be accessed at http://communityandconsensus.blogspot.com/.

5. Decision-Making

1   Readers can learn more about this approach created by the Group Pattern Language Project, buy a deck, or download a free PDF at the Group Works website, https://groupworksdeck.org.

2   C.T. Butler and Amy Rothstein, *On Conflict and Consensus: A Handbook on Formal Consensus Decisionmaking* (Burlington, VT: Food Not Bombs Publishing, 1987). Self-published and now in its sixth edition, the book can be purchased and downloaded at www.consensus.net. In the fourth edition, the authors adopted the label *secular consensus* to distinguish "this model of consensus from both the more traditional model found in faith-based communities and the rather informal consensus commonly found in progressive groups." In the sixth edition, they replaced *secular* with *formal* consensus: "We wanted to clearly indicate that the model of consensus we were proposing was distinct, but we did not want to exclude the valuable work of faith-based communities" (1991, page 4).

3   Ellis Carter, "Reconsidering Robert's Rules of Order," Caritas Law Group, Tucson, AZ, https://charitylawyerblog.com/2021/08/16/reconsidering-roberts-rules-of-order/.

4   Kavana Tree Bressen, "Consensus Decision-Making," Effective Collective, https://effectivecollective.net/library/consensus-handout.pdf.

5   M. Scott Peck, *A World Waiting to Be Born: Civility Rediscovered* (Toronto: Bantam, 1993), 311.

6   Tim Hartnett, *Consensus-Oriented Decision-Making: The CODM Model for Facilitating Groups to Widespread Agreement* (Gabriola Island, BC: New Society Publishers, 2011), 2; see also Hartnett's article "Consensus & Unanimity" on his website, http://www.groupfacilitation.net/Articles%20for%20Facilitators /Consensus%20&%20Unanimity.html.

7   M. Scott Peck, *The Different Drum: Community Making and Peace* (Toronto: Simon & Schuster, 1987), 72.

8   Tim Hartnett, "The Different Ideologies of Consensus," Group Facilitation, http://www.groupfacilitation.net/Articles%20for%20Facilitators/Different%20 Ideologies%20of%20Consensus.html.

9   Butler and Rothstein, *On Conflict and Consensus*, 12.

10 Sociocracy for All, https://www.sociocracyforall.org.

6. Building Community Membership

1   "Burning souls" is "a term for vision-driven founders who work zealously to manifest their dreams." Christian, *Creating a Life Together*, 15.

2   Yana Ludwig and Karen Gimnig, *The Cooperative Culture Handbook: A Social Change Manual to Dismantle Toxic Culture and Build Connection* (Rutledge, MO: Foundation for Intentional Communities, 2020), 112.

3   To see all posts labelled *power dynamics* on Laird Schaub's blog *Community and Consensus*, go to http://communityandconsensus.blogspot.com/search/label /power dynamics.

7. Design and Development

1   Clifford W. Schwinger, "Tips for Designing Constructable Steel-Framed Buildings," Modern Steel Construction (March 2011), https://www.aisc.org/globalassets /modern-steel/archives/2011/03/2011v03_tips_for_design.pdf.

2   Kathryn McCamant and Charles Durrett, *Cohousing: A Contemporary Approach to Housing Ourselves*, 2nd ed. (Berkeley, CA: Ten Speed Press, 1994).

8. Legal Structure and Agreements

1 "About," The BC Securities Commission, https://www.bcsc.bc.ca/about.

2 "Unit Entitlement," Government of British Columbia, https://www2.gov
.bc.ca/gov/content/housing-tenancy/strata-housing/operating-a-strata
/finances-and-insurance/unit-entitlement.

3 "Information Collection under the Condo and Strata Assignment Integrity
Register," Government of British Columbia, https://www2.gov.bc.ca/gov/content
/housing-tenancy/real-estate-bc/condo-strata-assignment-integrity-register
/information-collection.

9. Financial Structure

1 Canada Revenue Agency, "Fair Market Value: Definitions," in "Fair Market Value
for Purposes of Part IX of the Excise Tax Act (Revised)," Government of Canada,
October 16, 1997, https://www.canada.ca/en/revenue-agency/services/forms
-publications/publications/p-165r/fair-market-value-purposes-part-excise
-tax-act-revised.html.

11. Construction

1 The descriptions of different types of construction contracts and their purpose can
be found on the Canadian Construction Documents Committee website,
https://www.ccdc.org/documents/.

2 "Third-Party Home Warranty Insurance," BC Housing, https://www.bchousing.org
/licensing-consumer-services/builders-developers/third-party-insurance.

3 "Qualification Requirements for New Residential Builders," BC Housing,
https://www.bchousing.org/licensing-consumer-services/builder-licensing
/qualification-requirements.

13. How to Prepare for Living in Community

1 "Katie McCamant's webinar 'From Dream to Reality' with Q&A," Canadian
Cohousing Network, January 2022, https://www.cohousing.ca/resources/webinars/.

2 Ted J. Rau and Jerry Koch-Gonzalez, *Many Voices, One Song: Shared Power
with Sociocracy* (Amherst, MA: Sociocracy for All, 2018); see also https://
www.sociocracyforall.org.

Glossary of Terms

In this book, these terms have been used with the following definitions and interpretation best suited to the context.

additional shareholder loan An investment made to the cohousing development company that is in addition to the required shareholder loan.

affordability A cost low enough that an individual or household can afford to make the payment without financial hardship.

assignment A sales transaction where the original buyer of a property allows another buyer to take over the rights and obligations of the agreement of purchase and sale, before the original buyer has closed on the purchase of the property.

associate membership A membership whereby a household pays a small fee that provides them with access to the cohousing project's records for a period of time and the opportunity to get to know the group and determine whether they want to get involved in the project prior to making any legal or financial commitment.

cohousing Housing that includes the future residents in the design and development of fully self-contained homes along with extensive common spaces, including a kitchen and dining room for occasional shared meals, and amenities to support ongoing social connection among residents.

cohousing development company The legal entity that is set up to enable a group of individuals to generate the finances and enter into the contracts that are required to self-develop a cohousing project.

common property Everything that is not an individual strata lot in a condominium or strata title ownership structure.

community led housing Housing that includes the future residents in the design and development so that the final product is responsive to their needs. It can include a variety of housing forms, one of which is cohousing.

consensus People working together to reach as much agreement as possible in a collaborative, agreement-oriented process. Consensus decision-making generally has specific agreed-upon rules.

constructability The ease and efficiency within which structures can be built based on the assumption that the more constructable a structure is, the more economical it will be to construct.

construction loan The financing that is secured by the cohousing company to construct the development.

developer's architect An architect who is knowledgeable about what is required to design homes and buildings that are cost effective yet aesthetically pleasing and attractive to potential purchasers.

development consultant A person, or company, that has the knowledge, expertise, and experience to successfully manage a real estate development.

dot voting A simple way of identifying preferences using dot stickers or markers as indicators. Also known as "dotmocracy."

equity membership The next phase of membership in a project when someone who has been an associate member commits to take on the legal and financial responsibilities and obligations that are required to become a director and shareholder of the company that is developing a cohousing project.

founding member An individual, or household, who is a founding shareholder of the cohousing development company.

green building Construction methods and materials that contribute to environmental sustainability.

homeowner financing The loan that a purchaser secures if they need financing to pay for a home in the completed development.

limited common property Common property that is designated for the exclusive use of one or more strata lots in a condominium or strata title ownership structure.

non-market housing A home that sells at a price that is lower than what a similar home (size and type) in that particular location would sell for in an open market and that has covenants registered on title to ensure that the home remains at a price that is less than market value for perpetuity.

official community plan The document, created by a local government authority, that identifies the long-term vision and overarching goals for a specific geographical location.

priority sequence The order in which cohousing equity members agree to select their homes once the design has been completed.

proforma A financial overview that projects the potential costs for a particular development.

required shareholder loan The minimum investment that all shareholders make to the cohousing development company.

shareholder An individual, or jointly two or more individuals, identified as the legal registered owner of a share in the cohousing development company.

sociocracy The system of governance of society by society as a whole that was founded by Gerard Endenburg.[*]

---

[*] Hope Wilder, "Gerard Endenburg: Founder of Sociocratic Circle Method and Trailblazer of Self-Management," Sociocracy for All, https://www.sociocracyforall.org/gerard-endenburg-founder-of-sociocratic-circle-method-and-pioneer-of-self-management.

strata lot The individual home or lot in a multi-family development, the dimensions of which are defined on the strata plan that is registered with land titles at the completion of the development.

universal accessibility A design that supports individuals with mobility impairments to inhabit a space and live independently.

unsophisticated client Someone without much knowledge, expertise, or experience in real estate development.

wiki The PmWiki web-based content management system written by Patrick R. Michaud and used to create private password-protected websites to support the cohousing development phase.

zoning bylaw The document that implements the land use planning envisioned in the official community plan and regulates how land, buildings, and other structures may be used.

Index

About the Authors

RONAYE MATTHEW is the primary consultant at Cohousing Development Consulting (CDC), an expert development management firm, where she has guided eleven cohousing projects to completion. After earning a degree in environmental studies from the Faculty of Architecture at the University of Manitoba, Matthew spent her early career working with diverse residential developers in Alberta and British Columbia. In 1996, she shifted gears to cohousing development and never looked back. She has lived at Cranberry Commons in British Columbia since its completion in 2001.

MARGARET CRITCHLOW spent twenty-five years as a professor of social anthropology at York University in Ontario. She first discovered the importance of community led housing through her field research with Vanuatu villagers in the South Pacific. A leading voice in academic cohousing discourse, Critchlow has authored and edited books on housing cooperatives, customary land tenure, colonial history, and development issues. Critchlow is now a community-building facilitator at CDC and has lived at Harbourside Cohousing in British Columbia since 2016.

JOIN THE COMMUNITY LED HOUSING MOVEMENT!

Spread the Word

- Share the book with others who want to create a community led housing project, with those who work in the sector, and with anyone else who might be interested in sustainable housing and collaborative living.

- Invite us to speak at your event for inspiration or to address specific topics important to your group.

- Watch our webinars for a deeper dive into aspects of the book that most interest you.

- Engage us to lead workshops customized to your or your group's needs.

Connect with Us

Email: cdc@cohousingconsulting.ca

Book Website: communityledhousing.ca

Company Website: cohousingconsulting.ca

Help Build More Community Led Housing

If you enjoyed the book, please write a review on your preferred book retailer's site. Your review will not only contribute to the book's success but will help build more community led housing. Thank you!

Made in United States
Troutdale, OR
10/27/2024

24173416R00230